LIFE
IN THE
GLASS
HOUSE

LIFE IN THE GLASS HOUSE

Tales from the United Nations

MILES STOBY

UNICORN

Published in the UK by Unicorn
an imprint of the Unicorn Publishing Group LLP, 2021
5 Newburgh Street
London W1F 7RG

www.unicornpublishing.org

10 9 8 7 6 5 4 3 2 1

ISBN 978-1-913491-83-3

Typesetting by Vivian@Bookscribe

Printed in the UK by Short Run Press

———◄○►———

"Ah, when to the heart of man
   Was it ever less than a treason
To go with the drift of things,
   To yield with a grace to reason,
And bow and accept the end
   Of a love or a season?"

Reluctance
Robert Frost

———◄○►———

CONTENTS

Introduction **11**

PART ONE: LIVING IN THE GLASS HOUSE

1 **MATTERS OF PRINCIPLE**   18
Disaster in East Timor – Questioning national sovereignty – Australia will look after East Timor

2 **VARIOUS ENTERTAINMENTS**   25
The Wishing Star – A UN Day Concert – A Louise Fréchette soirée – The inexpedient Hans von Sponeck – Off with Africa's head

3 **A TERRIBLE BETRAYAL – AND UNRELATED DISTRACTIONS**   31
The monstrous tragedy of Srebrenica – A touch of Kerry – It costs twice as much

4 **DIPLOMATIC CONVERSATIONS**   35
A People's Assembly – Worrying about Burundi – The travelling Secretary-General

5 **BOWING TO ZEUS**   39
Jesse Jackson – Being overheard – Briefing the SG – Surviving Rwanda

6 **HAIL THE PRO-CONSUL**   46
Fun people – Richard Holbrooke – Red Alert

PART TWO: LOCKED IN THE GLASS HOUSE

7 **THE DAY OF FOLLIES**   50
The $10 billion man – An invitation to Waldheim – Saddam Hussein – The Mouth from the South

8 **AN AMERICAN FEAST**   56
Jesse Helms – Keeping our eyes on the larger goal – Weasel words – Africa Month

9 THE REST OF THEM 64
Ekéus lives – Hans von Sponeck defiant – The importunate Theo-Ben – A small demurral – The rest of them

10 SADDAM'S GRAVEYARD 70
Weighing the cost – Honour bound – The perils of Iraq

11 PREPARING FOR THE SUMMIT 73
Theo-Ben triumphant – Our Big Brother

12 GETTING IT RIGHT 78
Battling poverty at the Russian Tea Room – The Millennium Report – Placating the Namibians

13 SHOOING THEM AWAY 83
Earth Day – A large French mirror – On going along – Kurt Waldheim comes in through the window

14 KNOWLEDGEABLE, CRISP, WITTY AND SINCERE 88
Mismanaging Sierra Leone – Executive Outcomes – A long list of culprits – The Millennium Forum

15 REGRETTING THE RUFFIANS 98
Mugabe of Zimbabwe – Crown Princess Victoria of Sweden – An absence of dissent – Too long, too long – M. Henrie Konan BEDIE is no longer the head of state of Côte d'Ivoire – Untimely Arabs

16 TAKING WATER IN HIS WINE 105
Painful reminiscences – Richard the "Dark Prince" Butler – A North-centred agenda – The Shebaa Farms

---

PART THREE: A CROWNING SUMMIT

---

17 MILLENNIUM PRELIMINARIES 114
The Finnish-Namibian War – We know who is sleeping with whom – The Holy Men – A San Marino conundrum – The escape of Madeleine Albright – A gulf appears

18   A MILLENNIUM SUCCESS   125
Man without a Gun – Another triumph for Kuwaiti diplomacy – Bill Clinton – Fidel Castro – Jacques Chirac – Kofi's achievement – Could this be love?

PART FOUR: LOST IN THE GLASS HOUSE

---

19   A LUTA CONTINUA   132
The new blue helmets

20   MESSENGERS OF PEACE   136
A flock of celebrities – Not good, not good at all

21   FEARING FOR THE FUTURE   141
A Democratic redoubt – Waiting to see the SG

22   FA LA LA LA LA, LA LA LA LA   145
The irritating Third World – Does anyone know any Republicans? – Banquo's Ghost

23   A HISTORIC TURNING POINT   151
The UN surrenders – The Pro-Consul's farewell – Australia, looking after East Timor

---

PART FIVE: TURMOIL IN THE GLASS HOUSE

---

24   DEATH IN BAGHDAD   168
Sergio de Mello – An inevitable involvement – A foot in the door – Working well with the victors

25   A LONG DAY IN WASHINGTON   175
Secosotus – Gary Cooper – Colin Powell

26   TAKING A STAND   180
The Pro-Consul (Retired) redux – George W. Bush, Colin Powell and Condoleezza Rice – Terror and sex slaves

27   A FORK IN THE ROAD   185
Cri de coeur – Australia, still looking after East Timor – Why have the Arabs turned against us? – It's happening in all the Departments

28 APPOINTMENT IN SAMARRA 194

Lethal miscalculations – The elusive buck – A chat with Louise

29 ISSUES OF CONSCIENCE 202

The revolt of Kofi Annan – Supping with Sasakawa – The Panel to save the world – The Americans say no – Lunch with "The Boys"

30 SOME SORT OF ACHIEVEMENT 217

America alone again – A stab at reform – The Great Smoking War

31 RETURNING TO THE FOLD 223

Back to Baghdad – Dictating democracy

32 NEW ENTERTAINMENTS 226

The Big Leak – Returning to Iraq – Eavesdropping on Annan

33 MAKING IT WORK TO SERVE THEIR ENDS 235

Lakhdar Brahimi – Ayatollah Ali al-Sistani

34 COMING HOME TO ROOST 238

Oil-for-food – Rwanda persistent – A question of accountability

35 A CACOPHONY OF CATASTROPHES 247

The protest of the sixty – Reflecting on Rwanda – The Bees of Baghdad – Accusing headlines – Anticipatory genuflection – A Cyprus stumble – The Great Brahimi – Ultimate responsibility – Learning to vote right – A Hollywood production

36 CONTINUING CATASTROPHES 268

"Lewd" Lubbers – Emergency sex – Integrity in doubt – The attacks on Dileep Nair – The exoneration of Lubbers – My friend Benon – Containing a scandal

37 FASHIONING A LEGACY 280

Into opposition – Adjusting history on Iraq – Drawing a line – Saving Darfur

38   A KIND OF ACCEPTANCE   286
His Life – A suitable ending – The Little One – Watch your back, Mister, watch your back

---

PART SIX: **THE TRAVAILS OF THE SECRETARY-GENERAL**

---

39   DEALING WITH THE MESSES   296
An illegal war – The pardoning of Lubbers – The absolution of Nair – A Staff vote of No Confidence in the senior management of the UN – The inconvenient son – Exploiting the defenceless

40   A RARE AND VALUABLE HOMAGE   304
A standing ovation – Beating a retreat

41   AN AGENDA FOR RECOVERY   310
*The art of defenestration – **An autogolpe** – Attending to The Host Country – A beleaguered Secretary-General – Volcker reports – Getting the relationship with the US right – The fall of Lubbers – Successive triumphs*

42   CASUALTIES OF WAR   327
The internment of Benon – Vindication – The shaming of Nair – George Soros and a slight hiccup

43   THE LONG VALEDICTION   335
The admonitions of Mr. Volcker – At odds with the Third World – In Larger Freedom – A staff vote of No Confidence in the Secretary-General – The departure of Louise – The determined Mr. Bolton – The Fraudulent Eight

44   ENDING   351
Final flurries – Kumbaya

Postscript: Heathrow Airport   354

Index   356

INTRODUCTION

This is an accidental memoir. At some point some thirty years ago when I was still working for the United Nations, I had begun to make scribbles on stray bits of paper, more notes to myself than anything else, on what was occurring all around me and, from time to time, the role I was playing in the cavalcade.

Eventually I decided to organise the effort, which at first took the form of a diary and, thereafter, became a journal of events rather than a record of my own personal doings. It took me a while to identify the motivation behind this activity, which I came eventually to realise was spurred by a profound concern as to the direction in which the UN was proceeding in a post-cold war world. It was only later, much later, after I had left the Secretariat but was still occupied with the business of the UN, that I began to think that the accumulated material might contain the makings of a memoir.

I had come to the UN early. Born in Guyana then educated in England, I was re-acquired by my country when I joined our incipient diplomatic service upon our independence. By the end of 1967 I had experienced my first United Nations General Assembly Session. I was instantly entranced and empowered, a colonial in transition, caught up in the Third World's assertion of its UN presence, a bevy of nations freshly set free, vibrant and optimistic, curious and proud. Spoiled by my first contact I determined to dedicate my life to the Organisation. Subsequently I never left it for long until, in 1978, I returned for good to the promise of the United Nations.

By 1997 I had reached the rank of Director, the most senior in the professional international civil service. It was then, a few days after he had assumed office in January of that year as Secretary-General, that Kofi Annan called me at home (where I was recovering from the flu) and asked me to join his Executive Office to play a major role in the change and reform programme that he intended to launch. I was to have the title of Deputy Executive Director for

UN Reform. "Prepare yourself, young man!" he said ending the conversation with a chuckle.

I was delighted.

By this time I had known Kofi Annan for over twenty years. We had once both been mid-level officials, but then he had taken off. He had moved effortlessly upwards, mastering one difficult assignment after another, without leaving a ripple in his wake. I had followed his progress with affectionate admiration.

During the following years I held a number of posts. Following the 1997 Annan Reform (which was generally deemed to be a success), I was appointed to be in charge of a UN Fund to utilise the billion dollar donation that Ted Turner, the American media entrepreneur, had gifted to the UN. The position came with a promotion to Assistant Secretary-General, a political appointment and the equivalent of a Minister of State in a national government, and with the more weighty title of "Executive Director" of the Fund. I was unsure as to whether I was suited for the position but eventually accepted anyway. Who, after all, could refuse the most glamorous post around? My instincts, however, turned out to be correct. I did not last. I was of the view, on which I acted, that I was meant to run an operation based on UN principles of objectivity and independence. This contrasted with "Team" Turner's belief that the money was theirs and thus we were theirs too. Our job was to serve as a mere post office.

At his invitation, I returned in January 1999 to his Executive Office. My new function was to be the Coordinator of Preparations for the Millennium Summit, a planned gathering of some 150 world leaders due to take place at the UN in September 2000. Its purpose was to define the UN's role as we moved into the new century. It was likely to be the grandest event that the UN had ever staged and, potentially, the most significant. I welcomed the appointment and was grateful for his continued support.

Dwelling again on the 38th Floor, where the Secretary-General's personal staff was housed, I had a good sense of the key activities that were taking place at the United Nations. In an interview he gave to a German newspaper that first year, Shashi Tharoor, his spinmeister, remarked, "You have to be an idealist to join the UN and a realpolitiker to survive." But how far should one go in playing the realpolitiker's game? In what instances should one acquiesce? And when should one stand firm? As a Secretary-General, would steering an honourable course be possible in a dishonourable political environment? As an international civil servant, could one provide service while maintaining a principled stance? These concerns were, of course, not new as they had bedevilled the United Nations from its inception. But they had lost none of their relevance.

By the late summer of 1999 I decided that I would try to set it all down, more to get it straight in my own mind than anything else. The UN that was now evolving was not the one that I had pledged to serve. That UN had been my haven where I had gone for political, intellectual and moral comfort. These separate safenesses came together and were as one when I entered the building, contentedly enveloped in its embrace. I could find protection there amongst those who shared my views. I could find succour there as part of an enterprise where the range of issues covered all humankind's concern. And I could find satisfaction there from imagining that I was part of a noble calling.

Over the years these feelings waned but never dissipated. Time sapped some of the energy from my avowals but never exhausted it even as the Organisation changed substantially. When I arrived at the UN it was a place where, at least in the General Assembly, political action was determined by the countries of the South. The countries of the North were constantly on the defensive as their colonial past was repeatedly thrown at them and as they scuffled with the Soviet bloc for Third World approbation. These youthful years were also ones of expansion when new UN organisations were established in the fields of trade and development, industry, population, agricultural development, food, science and technology and transnational corporations, largely as a result of initiatives taken by the South. The future seemed unbounded.

Optimism eventually abated. The newly-independent countries

came to discover that the task of governance was difficult, onerous and resistant to easy accomplishment. The new UN bodies struggled to successfully promote the causes of their creators. And it was found that the West might have surrendered their colonies but not the worldwide levers of political and economic control. With the collapse of the Soviet Union the old political order began to be restored. The counterweight of the Soviet bloc no longer existed. The Third World groupings remained but were of diminished effectiveness as the countries of the South made necessary, individual arrangements with the Cold World victors in order to ensure a degree of security and economic progress for their nations. The West was able to revel in its political, military, economic and cultural supremacy and was not shy in doing so.

The United Nations did not escape the effects of this dominance. By the time Kofi Annan became Secretary-General, less than ten years after the fall of the Berlin Wall, recognition of the new realities had already set in.

The UN was now struggling to find its way within an international order of ill-designed signposts. For my part, I had begun to feel troubled about the decisions that were being made amidst the new uncertainty and the compromises gratefully grasped as the organisation sought to make accommodations with unanticipated realities.

I was also prompted by another impulse. It seemed to me that the behaviour of the people around me often bordered on the bizarre and the unintentionally hilarious. They were joined by another group, a well-intentioned band of celebrities and lesser lights, attracted to the new, image-conscious United Nations that was in the process of being fashioned. Overall, the pressures of events, and the urge of ego, were giving rise to gambol and cabaret. I also set myself the task of capturing this particular flavour.

Much of this memoir recounts my activities as I sought to navigate the corridors of the United Nations. But the period of this account coincides with Kofi Annan's tenure as Secretary-General during which time his presence had become such a force that the image of the UN had been fashioned by his performance. This was unusual. Hitherto, the actions of the Security Council, the General Assembly and other UN bodies contributed as much or more heavily to that assessment. U Thant and Perez de Cuellar made no impact on the global public save for the former's ill-judged decision to withdraw UN troops from the Sinai without first consulting the Security Council, an undoubted contributing factor to the 1967 Arab–Israeli war. Kurt Waldheim made a brief though unfortunate impact when his murky role in the massacres of Serbian civilians during the Second World War and suspicions of his having a Nazi past came to light. The only predecessor of Annan's to attract similar public attention and to make his image the UN's own was Dag Hammarskjöld. But Dag was not a figure immured from controversy as was, in the end, to be the case with Annan himself. During the latter part of this work Kofi Annan's actions came, perforce, to dominate the narrative but his presence pervades throughout.

In the course of this telling themes presented themselves, persistent and unforced, and demanded recognition. Events, meanwhile, unfolded at a relentless pace and of a nature that was beyond imagining. This was a boon to me in terms of providing material for the work. It would have been far preferable for the Organisation, however, if many of these happenings had passed us by.

This then is a memoir of a time in my life while serving the United Nations.

PART ONE:
LIVING IN THE GLASS HOUSE

"The sky was pastelled in spectacular shades of scarlet and gold; the palm trees and the salman trees were black against it...

We drove out of the dock area... We drove very slowly. At the gates we were stopped our passes checked.

A policeman said, 'Will you out your cigarette, please?'

I outed it."

The Middle Passage
V.S. Naipaul

1

MATTERS OF PRINCIPLE

*Disaster in East Timor – Questioning national sovereignty –
Australia will look after East Timor*

Disaster in East Timor

Friday, 10 September 1999

The independence referendum in East Timor, supervised by the United Nations, is ending horrifically. It had been held to determine the future of the country, which had been annexed illegally by Indonesia some twenty-five years ago. In spite of crude intimidation by paramilitary forces and the Indonesian Army itself, some 80% of the East Timorese electorate have voted for independence. Now CNN shows Indonesian gangs marauding through the streets burning and pillaging. Dili, the capital, is being destroyed. Thousands of East Timorese have been killed and some 500,000 driven from their homes into the surrounding hills.

The East Timorese have shown enormous courage in demanding independence in the face of Indonesian threats and harassment. But they must have done so in the expectation that the UN would protect them from their Indonesian oppressors if events took a nasty turn. Now we are in danger of betraying East Timor as we have betrayed Srebrenica and Rwanda. There is a deep sadness connected with these betrayals, the sadness of inattention, of lack of resolution, of overstatement. No one intended these betrayals but they are betrayals all the same.

The UN has begun to come under attack for the inadequacy of its security arrangements in East Timor. In reply we have contended that, in negotiating the agreement to hold the referendum, it was necessary to trust in the Indonesian government's ability to uphold its guarantees of security. The UN was not naïve about the history of violence in East Timor during the past twenty-four years. "Nobody in his wildest dreams thought what we are witnessing could have happened. We knew there were security problems but not the carnage and the chaos we have seen", we have asserted.

But was this outcome really beyond imagining? In fact, there had been intimations of it. The Indonesians proved in the military coup and slaughter in 1965, when a million perished in their country, that they were well acquainted with brutality, and repeated the lesson ten years later in East Timor when 100,000 died at the hands of the invading Indonesian army, the same army that was recently assigned by the UN to protect them. As the independence campaign progressed, paramilitary groups of East Timorese, in conjunction with Indonesian troops, initiated violence in various parts of the country resulting in scores of deaths. In February 1999, Ramos-Horta, the pro-independence leader, said: "Before [Indonesia] withdraws it wants to wreak major havoc and destabilisation, as it has always promised. We have consistently heard that over the years from the Indonesian military in Timor."

As militia leaders warned of a "bloodbath", Indonesian "roving ambassador" Francisco Lopes da Cruz declared: "If people reject autonomy there is the possibility blood will flow in East Timor". In July, the commander of the Indonesian armed forces in Dili told the Australian *Sunday* television programme: "I would like to convey the following: if the pro-independents do win [the referendum]... all will be destroyed. And East Timor won't be as we see it now. It will be worse than twenty-three years ago."

The UN had tried to shepherd East Timor to independence, but had relied on Indonesian's benign intentions against the reality of historical experience. We had done well to push the Indonesians to hold the referendum, but we have failed to anticipate this tragedy and provide international protection for the East Timorese. Shouldn't we be prepared to recognise this?

Questioning national sovereignty

Tuesday, 20 September

In his opening address in the annual General Debate of the General Assembly today, the Secretary-General has questioned the concept of national sovereignty as we know it.

"State sovereignty, in its most basic sense, is being redefined by the forces of globalisation and international cooperation," he says.

"The state is now widely understood to be the servant of the people and not vice versa."

The SG next raises the related question of humanitarian intervention, as in the case of the NATO involvement in Kosovo in contrast to the Security Council's inaction in the face of the genocide in Rwanda.

"This developing norm in favour of intervention to protect civilians from wholesale slaughter will no doubt continue to pose profound challenges to the international community. Any such evolution in our understanding of state sovereignty and individual sovereignty will, in some quarters, be met with distrust, scepticism, even hostility. *But it is an evolution we should welcome.*" The SG's own views have been evolving for some time. They are in direct response to the tragedies of Rwanda and Srebrenica and the experience of NATO's invasion of Kosovo to deter Milosevic's barbarities. I had taken part in conversations with him on the subject, in the context of the preparation of his report for the Millennium Summit, in company with Louise [Fréchette, Canadian, Deputy Secretary-General] and John [American, Assistant Secretary-General, charged with policy development].

Towards the end of one conversation the SG had turned to me.

"You've been very quiet," he'd said genially. "Haven't you been involved in these discussions?"

I had muttered something about having touched base with John from time to time, and then I plunged in. I told him that if we proceeded with this sort of approach it would be interpreted as an attack on the role of the state and on the concept of national sovereignty. I stressed instead that "democratisation" of the UN to lessen its domination by one superpower was bound to be the major concern of many states, including some of America's closest allies. As we leave I notice that the SG is looking quizzically at me.

The SG had looked tired. It was late in the afternoon, at the end of another of his impossibly long days. How in God's name does he keep it up, I had wondered?

The SG has made a most unconventional statement that challenges the basis on which the Charter and the architecture of international relations has rested since the end of the Second World War. He delivers it in professorial mien, almost as an academic discourse. And it will be noted for the absences as much as the propositions. For he does not condemn unilateral action by a state, or group of states, in cases of dire humanitarian or other crises brought about by political convulsions, and he does not say all such interventions require Security Council approval. As Secretary-General, pledged to uphold the provisions of the Charter, whose bulwark is state sovereignty and non-interference in the affairs of states, what he is saying is more than a little provocative.

Wednesday, 21 September

The SG's speech has provoked a sharp reaction from Third World countries. On the day of the speech itself, following Annan's presentation, the President of the General Assembly, Theo-Ben Gurirab, and the President of Algeria, Abdelaziz Bouteflika, speaking in his capacity as the Chairman of the Organisation of African Unity, openly criticised it. And, thereafter, Third World countries have been unanimous in their opposition.

Their concern is obvious. The concepts of the inviolable nature of national sovereignty and non-interference in the internal affairs of states have been the bulwarks that developing countries have had available to employ against the powerful. Indeed, these are often their only defences. Annan is now questioning the contemporary validity of these concepts. Coming after the Kosovo intervention by NATO he will be seen as subscribing to notions of self-justified Western intervention, unsanctioned by the United Nations. For me, stemming from Latin America, the experience of that continent, where intervention had been commonplace during the twentieth century on the basis of similar protestations, is instructive. Always the country had to be saved from itself in the interests of preserving democracy, opposing communism, preventing anarchy, curtailing human rights abuses, stemming the flow of drugs or protecting the citizenry.

For who would be the candidates for humanitarian intervention? Certainly not any developed countries in the Western camp. Turkey had been repressing Kurds for years without hindrance. Nor would the Chinese suppression in Tibet or the Russian one in Chechnya be stemmed as a result of humanitarian intervention from the West. No, it would be developing countries but which ones? Those that were large enough or were tied to the West were unlikely to have to face humanitarian intervention either. And even if you were small enough, and your sins profound enough to warrant intervention, it would not happen if you failed to possess the added lure of strategic positioning, as Rwanda had discovered. Countries like these would escape the benefits of humanitarian intervention.

Thursday, 7 October

I'm in a taxi returning from the airport and the SG's calling me on the phone. He has apparently been calling me since yesterday but have only just connected.

He tells me that he is struck by the point that I had made about democratisation. Chirac had recently stressed the same point in a letter to him, which he wanted me to see. He would send it to me.

I don't know what to make of this.

Australia will look after East Timor

Friday, 15 October

Agreement has now been reached to remove the Indonesian army and paramilitary forces from East Timor and replace them with international peacekeepers. Australia will take the lead in commanding these troops and will, in fact, supply most of them. The UN will then take over the administration of the country and guide it to independence. But there is a background to Australia's interest in accepting a role in East Timor's future.

In January 1978, Australia gained the distinction of becoming the first country to recognise Indonesia's annexation of East Timor as the twenty-seventh province of Indonesia. Australia has maintained that distinction, as it remains the only country to have done so. This formal recognition had been preceded by de facto recognition in 1976. The entire purpose of all these actions emerged clearly in 1989 when Indonesia and Australia signed an agreement for the exploitation of the multi-billion oil and gas reserves that had been discovered beneath the Timor Sea. This unconscionable recognition was followed by Australia's concluding a Defence Treaty with Indonesia in 1995.

[According to de-classified documents of the Australian Ministry of Foreign Affairs released in 2000, Gough Whitlam, the then Prime Minister of Australia, had defined his country's position as early as September 1974 when he told officials, "I am in favour of incorporation [into Indonesia], but obeisance has to be made to self-determination."]

So Australia, the only country in the world to recognise Indonesia's annexation, and whose coveting of East Timor's oil and gas reserves is hardly a secret, will be responsible for the country's security. On the face of it such an arrangement would appear, at minimum, to be somewhat awkward. In fact it is phantasmagoric. But the realities of realpolitik, UN-style, dictate. Australia, a member of "Five Eyes", the global espionage cooperative also comprising the US, the UK, Canada and New Zealand, will help ensure that the unpredictable guerrilla leaders of East Timor are kept on the right path.

East Timor is not Kosovo, or Srebrenica, or Rwanda, and flits in and out of international attention. But over 100,000 East Timorese perished in 1975 in the aftermath of the Indonesian invasion as the UN Security Council stood by and took no action to deter the Indonesian annexation, and thousands more East Timorese perished recently, and Dili was destroyed, due to the lack of adequate international protection. Is the stage being set for another betrayal of East Timor by depositing it into the interested arms of Australia?

2
VARIOUS ENTERTAINMENTS

The Wishing Star – A UN Day concert – A Louise Fréchette soirée – The inexpedient Hans von Sponeck – Off with Africa's head

The Wishing Star

Saturday, 16 October

I'm sitting on a bench in the Public Lobby of the United Nations contentedly sipping tea and reading the *New York Times*. I've come with my wife to an event she has helped organise with the Walt Disney people – celebration of the sixtieth anniversary of the Pinocchio film and presentation to the UN of something called "The Wishing Star." My daughter is all dressed up and has a role in the proceedings.

My wife arrives with Nane Annan. Other people turn up and surround Nane. I go over and say hello. Always beautiful, Nane has now assumed a near-permanent radiance.

My wife, Nane and enthusiastic followers go outside to the Plaza. I return to the *Times* and my tea. But it's a cold autumn morning and they soon retreat indoors in search of coffee. Nane asks me to join them and I find an excuse. Fool! When will I ever learn some harmless, courtier ways?

M, a relative, arrives. He's got a bunch of strangers in tow. I now remember that he had muttered something about wanting to introduce me to some friends of his. The friends are overwhelmed to meet me. They say they are sorry that I couldn't fit it in yesterday but this is as good a time as any. I look at M but he avoids my eye and hurries them away to take the UN tour.

The show is about to begin in the Plaza. There is quite a large crowd, gathered around a stage. Walt Disney characters troop in accompanied by kids from my daughter's school. The kids are in ecstasy. A, my daughter, walks with Cruella de Vil. Captain Hook, Peter Pan, Hercules, Mulan, Ariel and Baloo the Bear complete the crew. A girl in a mermaid outfit sitting on a half-shell is wheeled in. She is covered in goose pimples from the cold.

The show begins. Someone hisses indignantly, "That's not Cruella de Vil!" Someone else complains, "And that's not Hercules!" They are right. Naughty Walter. We've got actors playing the actors who played the characters. But wait a minute. That's not right. Don't we have actors playing the animated cartoon characters? What did the crowd expect? The real cartoon characters? My head begins to spin.

I turn to M for support but he has disappeared.

The Head of the UN's public information apparatus, a Japanese Under-Secretary-General, turns up to introduce Nane. He forgets her name. Hmm; I wonder if he'll last.

Pinocchio arrives and starts to hop around the stage. Nane Annan starts to hop around with him. I look frantically for my wife and pray, "Please, please darling; don't hop." My prayers are answered; she stands her ground.

A short, skinny kid with neat, blonde hair and watchful eyes bounds onto the stage. He is introduced as Haley Joel Osment who is starring with Bruce Willis in a hit film now showing called "The Sixth Sense." My daughter becomes very animated. Haley Joel is word perfect.

A returns triumphant, brandishing Haley Joel's autograph. I chant at her, "Crush, crush; you've got a crush on Haley Joel." She hotly denies it and threatens to call me "Popsy" in public every chance she gets unless I shut up. It's a shrewd thrust. I shut up.

We get ready to leave. Not fast enough. M's friends return. They press business cards, videotapes and beautifully printed brochures into my hands. I gather that we are going to make a fortune together in clean garbage disposal. Sounds like an oxymoron to me. I look around for M but he is not in sight. A perfect Saturday morning.

A UN Day concert

Friday, 22 October

The annual concert to celebrate UN Day is taking place this evening. It is being held in the General Assembly Hall. The room is awash with Ambassadors. The Duke Ellington Orchestra is scheduled to perform.

The President of the General Assembly makes a speech. The Secretary-General makes a speech. The President of the Duke Ellington Foundation makes a speech. Gillian Sorensen [American, Assistant Secretary-General in the Executive Office of the SG, Ted Sorensen's wife, responsible for relations with civil society] makes a speech. O, my UN you were ever thus. I decide I want to make a speech. I start to get up but L, my wife, the spoilsport, pulls me down.

Two black girls and one white girl appear and make their way to the top of the podium, which rises above the stage. They sit down and look around, and start to swing their legs.

Six musicians troop on and take their places; only the drummer is black. They warm up and begin to play. The sound system breaks down. The girls look around and swing their legs.

One of the black girls climbs down from the podium, grabs a microphone, and listens attentively to recorded music of the Duke Ellington Orchestra that is being piped into the Hall. From time to time, she sings along. The sound system breaks down again. I look around and start to swing my legs.

A white girl with a violin comes on. Now it's her turn to listen intently to recorded music being piped into the hall. Presently, she launches into an accompaniment of fiery gypsy music.

I gaze at the vaulted ceiling of the General Assembly Hall, straining to be the first to catch sight of the Duke as he descends to save the day; but the Duke has been delayed. We leave early.

A *Louise Fréchette soirée*

Wednesday, 3 November

Meeting to discuss Millennium Summit communications strategy. As a prelude, I've arranged for equipment to be installed to preview our website. A nervous Therese Gastaut, the communications focal point, is present. This will be her debut at a Louise Fréchette soirée.

The Deputy Secretary-General of the United Nations sweeps in, guarded. Her first broadside dispatches the website technicians before they have had a chance to realise that they are in a battle zone.

"I have not got the time for this. I know how to surf the web you know. I don't need to be taught how to surf."

I try to rescue the bemused technicians by babbling that I am responsible for this initiative.

Thump. "Yes, yes, I know very well that the Millennium Website is your initiative."

"No, no, I mean putting it on the agenda to get your views."

Thump, thump. "Let the technical people do their work; I deal with policy issues."

I wave the web people out of the room. It is now Therese's turn.

Thump. "What is this piece of paper? I do not approve projects." Therese has not yet caught on. She tries again.

"You know, Madame, we need at least your approval for the project to have the building lit for the millennium with the slogan 'UN 2000'."

Thump, thump. "I am not interested in the lighting. Put it up if you want. It doesn't matter to me."

Oh well.

The inexpedient Hans von Sponeck

Monday, 8 November

We had a curious incident this morning. Fred Eckhard [American, SG's Spokesman] was asked at a Press Briefing whether he had guidance on the Von Sponeck affair. He had replied that Von Sponeck would get a year's contract extension. Lamin splutters that he had in his hands the extension letter but had just been told by Riza to sit on it.

Hans von Sponeck, the UN Humanitarian Coordinator in Iraq, is in trouble again. He had previously attracted the ire of Washington and London for complaining publicly about the effects of the sanctions on the country. He has recently drawn attention to the damage caused by their constant bombing in the "no-fly zones", which has become so customary that it is now unremarked. [The "no-fly zones" are areas to the north and south of Baghdad, established unilaterally by Washington and London. They had not been approved by the Security Council and were considered by many international lawyers to be unauthorised.] Now, Washington and London have publicly demanded Von Sponeck's head. In direct response we had announced that his contract would be renewed. He had then been told to go and talk to the US and UK.

I interject: "The British and Americans are complaining about Von Sponeck's unauthorised remarks about their unauthorised bombing in the unauthorised no-fly zones?"

The Chef flaps his hand. So much for von Sponeck, I suppose.

Off with Africa's head

Monday, 15 November

Senior Staff Meeting. A Senior Colleague (SC) chairs and asks about the situation in Burundi (where there is a fear that the Rwanda experience could be replicated) and is told by Patrick

[Hayworth (Ghana), Director for African Affairs] that discussions are taking place on a successor to Nyerere, who had been serving as mediator. Mandela was being mentioned.

SC – "Why does everything to do with Africa move so slowly? Nothing has changed on this since Nyerere's funeral three weeks ago."

The SC looks around. Someone is surely to blame. But who should get the chop? Patrick? Mandela? Africa itself? Maybe that's it, the whole goddamned continent! Off with its head!

Patrick ducks his. We all follow suit.

Ah, the sweet crack of the whip!

3

A TERRIBLE BETRAYAL – AND UNRELATED DISTRACTIONS

The monstrous tragedy of Srebrenica – A touch of Kerry – It costs twice as much

The monstrous tragedy of Srebrenica

Tuesday, 16 November

9.45 a.m. – The focus this morning is on the Srebrenica Report, which was officially released today. It had been commissioned in November of last year, when the General Assembly asked the Secretary-General to prepare an assessment report on the fall of the town.

Srebrenica was a UN "safe area" in Muslim Bosnia, established by the Security Council and protected by UN troops. (The Council had been insistent on not calling it a "safe haven" since that would have conferred a greater degree of responsibility for its protection than Council members wished to exhibit.) A precautionary military arrangement was in place – the "dual key" – that allowed the UN, through Secretary-General Boutros-Ghali, to call in NATO air strikes to deter the Serbian marauders should they threaten the town. NATO held the other "key" and, thereby, the final say. When the Serbs attacked, the UN declined to call in air strikes and the Dutch defenders sat on their hands.

The graves of 8,000 men and boys have been discovered in Srebrenica. The UN may have acted in complicity by not calling for air strikes knowing that NATO did not want to suffer the embarrassment of having to refuse to turn the other key. This was due to the inadequacy of the troop strength on the ground and the

Dutch government's desire to minimise the danger to their troops.

It is a carefully-drafted report that, nevertheless, provides a comprehensive narrative of the events surrounding the killings. It is also a complex report, and this is to be understood, as the train of events is cloaked and circuitous. It is evident that there was constant disagreement in the Council as to how best to proceed during the Bosnian–Serbian war, that multiple levels of decision-making regarding the use of force were in place, and that a great deal of parsing of language in the preparation and making of decisions occurred when straightforward direction and swift responses were needed. In any event, the conclusion is plain. What happened is monstrous, and all are to blame, but the Serbs are to blame most of all.

The Report's conclusion is unambiguous about a despairingly dishonourable chain of events: "The international community as a whole must accept its share of responsibility for allowing this tragic course of events by its prolonged refusal to use force in the early stages of the war. This responsibility is shared by the Security Council, the Contact Group and other Governments, which contributed to the delay in the use of force, as well as by the United Nations Secretariat and the Mission in the field. *But clearly the primary and most direct responsibility lies with the architects and implementers of the attempted genocide in Bosnia.*"

It's a stern but oddly comforting conclusion. No one at the United Nations among the Member States or the Secretariat, no one on the Security Council or among UN personnel in the field, is to be held personally accountable for the tragedy. It's the Serbs who are to blame.

[Except for the Dutch, who decided that Dutch accountability needed to be delineated. After all, thousands of Bosnian Muslim refugees had taken shelter in the Dutch military compound, no doubt under the assumption that it was, indeed, a "safe area". The Serbs threatened to destroy the camp if the refugees were not expelled and the Dutch complied. Dutch soldiers then stood by and watched as the Serbs separated the men from the women and children and took them away to be slaughtered.

In 1996 the government of Wim Kok asked the Netherlands Institute for War Documentation to investigate "the events before, during and after the fall of Srebrenica". The investigation – "Dossier Srebrenica" – reported in April 2002. It found that Dutch participation was ill-conceived, that afterwards the army attempted to cover-up the true nature of events, and that the Dutch peacekeepers role was "tantamount to ethnic cleansing".

Upon receipt of the report the entire Dutch government resigned. The most senior Dutch general also resigned.]

A touch of Kerry

12.30 p.m. – I'm attending a "Friends of the UN" lunch in the Delegates Dining Room. I sit at a table with Leah Rabin and next to Senator John Kerry of Massachusetts. We are introduced. I ask when the UN dues will be voted on. He seems distracted, but he is the very image of a successful senator – tall, slim, handsome, fit, longish hair greying suitably. Also, without animation; also, very dull. It turns out that he is the keynote speaker. He speaks for a long, long time. Dullness is confirmed. He returns to the table. I extend warm congratulations on his speech. A radiant smile suffuses his face.

It costs twice as much

8.00 p.m. – Dinner at La Caravelle. At my invite we are reciprocating hospitality that we received in California this August from A and T. We had lunched at their beach house. A teeny place but apparently worth about a billion dollars. We are working with them to secure additional funding for the Millennium Summit in order to involve youth groups.

They are warm, generous and friendly people, but they are from California.

They bring another couple with them. A sits down and announces it is his dinner.

"Nonsense," I proclaim bravely. A commands the wine list and orders an expensive Rothschild. I begin to reconsider my position. A's guest leans over to me.

"Don't get into a 'Who-is-paying' contest with A; you'll lose."

I ask A what he has been doing in New York while our wives have been huddling together on millennium plans. He looks at me as if I am mad.

"I'm on the New York Stock Exchange," he shouts. Sensibly, I don't pursue this.

T tries to get A to take a bet about the presidential candidates.

"Hey, what's the point? If I win, I'll only be winning my own money!" It sounds like a well-worn line.

A warms to me.

"You know, Miles," he says, "I own so many buildings in LA that when I drive around the city I don't know which are mine anymore." I can see that this could be a problem. It preoccupies him for a while.

T arranges her hands on the table so no one can miss her jewellery. She has on the proverbial diamond as big as the Ritz and a ruby nearly as large. To show she's with the people though, she also has on a rubber band around her wrist. A explains patiently that he owns 104 buildings in California and his company's stock is traded on the New York Stock Exchange. Foolish me; I should have known.

A beckons again and orders an even older and more expensive Rothschild. His eyes glitter as he looks at me. He has raised the stakes. T sips the latest offering.

"Why, A," she coos, "This is even nicer than the first bottle." She has given him his opening.

"It better be," A bellows at me. "It costs twice as much."

I am defeated.

4
DIPLOMATIC CONVERSATIONS

A People's Assembly – Worrying about Burundi –
The travelling Secretary-General

A People's Assembly

Thursday, 18 November

3.00 p.m. – I've organised a meeting on the Millennium Forum. This is one of our reform-report ideas. The original proposal was to have a "People's Millennium Assembly" of civil society groups from all over the world as a companion event to the countries' Assembly. It's going ahead but under the less threatening name of Millennium Forum. It's quite a revolutionary prospect if we can pull it off. I've invited the Europeans, the US, Canada and Japan.

The briefing goes well until, toward the end, someone asks about recent, closed-doors meetings I've been taking part in on another, unrelated matter. I tell them all I know and distribute the background paper in my possession. It's a mistake. When will I ever learn that at the UN information is a tool to be employed sparingly, tactically, discreetly, selectively, astutely but never in a gush of goodwill as I have just done? They proceed to beat me up.

THEY – It's hard to believe that meetings involving Member States like this could take place behind closed doors.

ME – Actually, it was at the initiative of the South African Ambassador.

THEY – It's one thing for delegations to meet, but why are you involved in negotiations?

ME – I was asked to attend to provide technical support.

THEY – And why were so few people taking part?

ME – The South African Ambassador consulted the President of the General Assembly who approved the initiative.

THEY – It's your job to advise the President about proper procedures.

ME – I did. I spoke to his office. They didn't listen.

THEY – It's your job to make them listen.

Okeydoke.

Worrying about Burundi

Monday, 22 November

Morning staff meeting. It is being chaired by an SC. Burundi is on the SC's mind. After the recent killing of two WFP officials, the UN had decided on a Phase 4 Security Alert. The President of Burundi is upset about this. The SG had met him in Beijing last week.

Unusually, the SC is sitting all alone on one side of the conference table. The rest of us are arrayed in front. Discomforted, the SC takes aim.

SC – "I suppose the SG wasn't briefed when he met the President. He should have been briefed. Now we are going to have to send a long letter explaining our position."

Someone – "He was briefed."

SC – "I bet he wasn't briefed properly. Who did the brief?"

Someone – "Mr. Sy" [the UN representative in Burundi].

SC – "Well there you are; I was right."

Someone – "I've seen the minutes of the meeting; the SG seemed to have covered all the points."

SC – "He couldn't have. I bet he didn't touch on [this and this and this]."

Someone – "At least we have some good news: the World Food Programme is returning."

SC –"Really! And what are they going to do?"

Someone – "Distribute food?"

SC (throwing all caution to the wind) – "That's no use; that's not their main job."

The World Food Programme? Not their main job to deliver food? No one says a word.

The travelling Secretary-General

Monday, 29 November

The Secretary-General has returned from a long trip. He says, "It's good to see you all."

"It's good to see you!" someone rejoins with emphasis. We all laugh. The fact is he is travelling a lot. He relates his adventures.

He had first visited Japan. What struck him most was the hardening Japanese attitude about the lack of movement concerning their ambition to become a Permanent Member of the Security Council. He had discovered that this was no longer an ambition confined to the bureaucracy but had infected the Diet where withholding dues, *"A l'Americanne,"* in order to achieve the aim was being suggested. He had tried to calm them down.

He had met Yeltsin in Istanbul at the OSCE Summit. Yeltsin had let it be known that Russia was determined not to be bullied or lectured to about Chechnya. For his part, he had told Yeltsin that he expected Russia to cooperate with the UN on the humanitarian relief efforts.

In China, he had found that Falun Gong was the obsession. The UN party had been subjected to extraordinary security precautions designed not solely for their safety but also to preclude contact with Falun Gong petitioners. In his conversation with President Jiang, it had been made clear that the cult would be crushed.

"I made a mistake," Jiang had admitted by not taking them seriously enough at first. That was being corrected.

He had spent nearly two hours with Jiang who had conducted a rambling monologue. Jiang's aides were clearly accustomed to this, as most of them had nodded off. Jiang had complained about the criticism levelled at China for not being a democracy.

"Look at Switzerland," Jiang had mentioned in justification. He had paid a visit there recently.

"You don't even know who their President is. You call that a democracy?"

5
BOWING TO ZEUS

*Jesse Jackson – Being overheard – Briefing the SG –
Surviving Rwanda*

Jesse Jackson

Wednesday, 1 December

World Aids Day is being celebrated at the UN. It's an impressive programme. Hillary Clinton, Jesse Jackson, Queen Noor of Jordan, the First Lady of Haiti, Magic Johnson, Miss Universe, the CEO of Bristol Myers, former Mayor of New York David Dinkins, Isaac Hayes, the musician, three kids orphaned through the death of their parents from AIDS.

The whole event is very touching. People seem genuinely affected.

There is also a lunch in the Delegates Dining Room. Jesse Jackson is the keynote speaker. Still youthful-looking, albeit somewhat rotund, he is mesmerising. Words flow but not as a river; he is a bird, a hawk that swoops and swirls. We are his prey as he tempts, taunts, scorns, implores, and applauds us.

He begins by speaking softly and evocatively of, "those in the margins" of the disease that, "infects some, affects all"; of the indifferent among us, "suffering from attention deficiency disorder"; of the need to build a, "community of conscience." *Yea.*

"The fire is lit," he warns. "The wind is blowing. Your house will not be saved by your virtue." *Yea. Yea.*

I look around. My neighbour to the left, the Reverend Calvin O. Butts III, the Afro-American pastor of the Abyssinian Baptist Church, has begun to chant in counterpoint to Jesse's swoops and swirls.

"None of us is saved until all of us are safe." *Yea.*

"Magic Johnson lives because he has the money, the medicine, and the will. But how many are like him?" *Yea. Yea.*

He recalls the time when, "it was illegal to be black in America. But we have moved from Rosa Parks in the back of the bus to Kofi Annan at the head of the UN." *Tell them, tell them.* The Reverend Calvin is varying the routine.

"We must choose hope over the rhetoric of despair. Better to walk in dignity than to ride in shame." *Tell them, tell them.* Jesse's really rolling now.

"I worry about the lost sheep for the dogs are barking and the wolves are howling. Zeus was a freak."

(Huh?)

"Zeus was a freak. He was born fully formed. He was nurtured in no mother's womb."

(Cool it, Jesse)

"A being without feelings." *Yea, yea. Tell them, tell them.* The Reverend Calvin is undeterred.

Jesse senses he is drowning. He strikes out for safer shores. "Let us pray."

We bow our heads to Zeus.

Friday, 3 December

The Spokesman has announced that Nelson Mandela will be the Burundi mediator.

Monday, 6 December

The WTO talks in Seattle have ended in failure. Governments could not agree and the NGOs rioted outside the conference hall.

Being overheard

Wednesday, 8 December

Meeting of the Senior Management Group, which is made up of all UN department and programme heads. Rubens Ricupero [Brazil], the UNCTAD leader, briefs on the breakdown of the WTO talks in Seattle. He makes clear that despite the protests in the streets and the furore in the media the talks broke down for the same reason similar talks had stalled in the past – the unsuccessful attempt by countries like India, Argentina, Canada, Australia and Brazil to get freer access for their agricultural products into the heavily-protected US, European and Japanese markets.

Nafis Sadik, a Pakistani and head of the UN's Fund for Population Activities, complains about Clinton's intervention in the talks when he had advocated adoption of Western environmental and labour standards by the South as a condition for greater access to Northern markets; she says this was directly related to domestic political considerations. Catherine Bertini, the American head of the World Food Programme, becomes severely agitated and demands that Nafis' comments be stricken from the record.

What is she talking about? We are not allowed to say what every US newspaper is saying on the matter? Have we come to this? And what record? Obviously she does not share my assumption that the room we are meeting in – the SG's conference room – is bound to be bugged.

I turn to John who is sitting by my side and remark, "Doesn't she think we are being overheard?" Not wishing to be overheard, John keeps mum.

Ambassador Stewart Eldon, the British Deputy Permanent Representative, is spreading the rumour that I am opposing a new resolution on the Millennium Summit. Since I've been doing little more recently than trying to promote a resolution, it's an interesting rumour.

I don't trust Eldon. He has a wispy moustache of uncertain

colour. As a matter of doctrine, you can't trust a man with a wispy moustache.

Briefing the Secretary-General

Thursday, 16 December

I go to see the SG. I worry that I've chosen a very bad day. He had received yesterday the report from the inquiry team he had commissioned to review the events leading up to the genocide of over 800,000 people in Rwanda in 1994. The chairman is Ingvar Carlsson, the former Prime Minister of Sweden. The team had not given him any advance knowledge of its findings.

I think the SG and those involved had begun to worry about this. After all his wife is a Swede, the niece of Raoul Wallenberg and Sweden had been a strong supporter in his brutal battle with Boutros for the post of Secretary-General. He had been cooking spaghetti in the kitchen of the Swedish Ambassador's house when he got the news that the Security Council had selected him. At a meeting last week Riza had mused, "It's that 11 January cable that's the problem."

The SG had been applauded for launching an independent inquiry but, in reality, he could do little else. It had taken the General Assembly four years to call for an investigation of the Srebrenica tragedy but they had gotten around to it, and they would have gotten around to Rwanda eventually. The OAU [Organisation of African Unity] was undertaking its own inquiry, at the insistence of the unforgiving Rwandans, so it was best to pre-empt.

I haven't yet read the report or heard of any press leaks but there is unease about the house. Nevertheless, he greets me with warmth and affection. I thank him for his continued support. He waves his hand gently and dismissively as if to indicate that my gratitude is unnecessary though appreciated and I should never doubt his loyalty born of old connections and shared experiences. I brief him on my recent negotiations with the President of the

General Assembly to resolve the issues still stalling the key decisions on the Summit. He asks to be remembered to L and the "Princess."

Surviving Rwanda

Friday, 17 December

The Rwanda report is all that has been feared. The Chef's apprehensions are proving to be well founded. The UN is excoriated for its conduct with blame equally proportioned between the Secretariat and the Security Council.

The SG, who was head of peacekeeping at the time, is identified by name as having acted indecisively. Riza, his deputy then, is also prominently mentioned as most of the cautious cables cited in the report were actually signed by him on Kofi's behalf. Over 800,000 Rwandans, mostly Tutsis, were slaughtered while the UN stood by. It is the worst blot on our history.

The 11 January cable proves indeed to be a problem for Kofi and the Chef.

> "The inquiry believes that serious mistakes were made with dealing with the cable... First, the information contained in the cable, and in particular the information indicating the existence of a plan to exterminate Tutsi, was so important that it should have been given the highest priority and attention and shared at the highest level... Annan's and Riza's instructions to UNAMIR [the UN peacekeeping force in Angola] – and the caution which dominates those instructions – show that they did realise that the cable contained very significant information. However, they did not brief the Secretary-General [Boutros-Ghali] about it. And the Security Council... was not informed... Secondly, it is incomprehensible to the Inquiry that not more was done to follow-up on the information provided by the informant."

The media are not kind. CNN asks how it is that all those connected with the tragedy have been promoted? The BBC asks when the SG will resign. The SG issues a statement, which is widely interpreted as an apology and acceptance of personal responsibility. It is not quite that.

He states: "In 1994 the whole international community – the United Nations and its Members States – failed to honour that obligation [to 'prevent and punish' genocide]. Approximately 800,000 Rwandans were slaughtered by their fellow countrymen and women, for no other reason than that they belonged to a particular ethnic group. That is genocide in its purest and most evil form.

All of us must bitterly regret that we did not do more to prevent it. There was a United Nations force in the country at the time, but it was neither mandated nor equipped for the kind of forceful action, which would have been needed to prevent or halt the genocide. *On behalf of the United Nations, I acknowledge this failure and express my deep remorse.*"

So it is the UN writ large that failed, the UN as an institution – "On behalf of the United Nations". And, he says, the UN force could not have acted effectively even if it had tried to intervene. As for the Chef, I see a snippet of an interview with him on CNN. He says, "Mistakes were made... We have to move ahead." How do you move ahead from 800,000 mistakes?

There are no resignations. Boutros-Ghali, who was Secretary-General at the time, has already gone. He lives in Paris, courtesy of the French government, as head of the Organisation of French-speaking countries. The man then in charge of peacekeeping is now Secretary-General. His deputy at the time is Chef de Cabinet. The Rwandan desk officer, Hédi Annabi, has been made Assistant Secretary-General for Peacekeeping Operations.

It will be said that Kofi had Boutros for a boss so Boutros is to blame. It will be argued that if Riza and Annabi fall they are simply being used as scapegoats. It will be claimed that the killings went on for three months and yet the Security Council refused to act.

So no one at the United Nations involved in allowing the tragedy to take place, whether in the Secretariat or in the Security Council, whether at Headquarters in New York or on the ground, will be held personally responsible in the slightest degree.

6
HAIL THE PRO-CONSUL

Fun people – Richard Holbrooke – Red Alert

Fun people

Saturday, 18 December

8.00 p.m. – Dinner at Le Perigord at the invitation of Betty King. She is the Ambassador at the United Sates Mission in charge of economic and social issues. She claims that we are all her special friends, chosen to attend because we are lively and interesting – "fun people." I survey the field. The Austrian, Lesotho and Papua New Guinea Ambassadors are present. Betty you are telling fibs.

The evening wears on. I ask Betty about the negotiations on the next budget for the UN, which had broken down at 6 a.m. this morning. Apparently, many countries had refused to accede to Washington's demands. Betty gets upset at the memory.

"You know what's wrong with the UN?" she informs her guests.

"Those who should have no power, have power and those who should have power, don't. The UN should be run by the people with power and the rest should keep quiet."

I regard Betty with dismay. She is originally from my part of the world, a Saint Vincentian. "Brown Betty," I've always thought of her as from the ice cream parlour in Georgetown of my youth. She is lovely and graceful and is herself a "fun person." She had told me earlier that she is leaving in the morning to spend the holidays with her relatives in St. Vincent. She had been head of a foundation before accepting the post at the US Mission. She must be suffering from a touch of Holbrooke hubris, a hallucinatory condition. Let's hope that it is a temporary affliction.

Richard Holbrooke

Richard Holbrooke is the new United States Ambassador and Permanent Representative to the United Nations. He is a devotee of tough love. There was a report on a Holbrooke press conference that appeared in this morning's *New York Times* under Barbara Crossette's byline, which suggests the source of Betty's inspiration.

"At his news conference today, (Ambassador Holbrooke) took aim at the Organisation, which he said still needed a lot of reform – a theme that Congressional Republicans always like to hear. He is impatient with the chain of command and the complex relationships among United Nations agencies. The Security Council and the Secretary-General's office are on different wavelengths, he said.

"He made his point with an anecdote: the collision of an event that he had personally planned – probably one of many taking place around the UN that day – with a UN news conference to release a long-awaited report on mass killings of Muslims in Srebrenica, Bosnia in 1995.

"'On November 15 we had the three Bosnian presidents here, a historic meeting,' he said. 'In the exact middle of that event, you were summoned to a press conference to release the Srebrenica report. So I called up the Secretariat. I said, 'Why did you do that?' He found it hard to believe that UN officials claimed not to have known about his visitors. 'It happens all the time,' he complained."

Holbrooke's example of the lack of coordination in the UN and between the SG and the Security Council is an incident in which he got less press attention than he felt he had earned. Still, one would have thought that the fact of the agreement was the important thing. As for the media mix-up, he had not told us about his plans – that was fine. We had not told him about ours – that was wrong. For coordination with the Security Council and within the UN read, "Check with Dick first".

It would seem that we have a Pro-Consul now.

Red Alert

Thursday, 23 December

Western colleagues on the Floor are whispering that I am, "a mole for the Third World." They have gone on Red Alert. They're not quite right. My Third World friends in the delegations assert I've sold out to the West. They cite my support for the SG's reform programme. They haven't got it either. I just don't see why I'm obliged to be one thing or the other.

I think I am becoming a fossil. I think I may be Neanderthal Man.

PART TWO:
LOCKED IN THE GLASS HOUSE

"Assuredly, a lively scene!
And how pleasant, something green
With circling heavens one perfect rose
Each smoother patch of water glows,
Hence to where, o'er the full tide's Face
We see the Palace and the Place,
And the White dome. Beauteous but hot..."

Dipsychus

Arthur Hugh Clough

7
THE DAY OF FOLLIES

The $10 billion man – An invitation to Waldheim – Saddam Hussein – The Mouth from the South

The $10 billion man

Tuesday, 4 January, 2000

T calls. She's hot with news. Jane [Fonda, Ted Turner's wife] had spoken to her this a.m. She and Ted have separated. The story will break later in the day.

Friday, 7 January

The papers report that Ted and Jane had signed a "pre-nup." She'll get $10 million and some Time Warner stock.
   Not very much.

Monday, 10 January

AOL has merged with Time Warner. Ted's worth has risen from some $6 billion to $10 billion overnight.
   Oh well.

Wednesday, 20 January

Back to work to discover that the Iraqis are furious with me. The report that we had issued on a Beirut meeting held to hear Arab views about the Millennium Summit was supposed to contain the phrase, "The view was expressed that the sanctions regime against

Iraq needed to be changed." The phrase that appeared in the printed version had somehow become, "The view was expressed that the Iraqi regime needed to be changed." The Iraqis are not amused. They perceive a deep and dark conspiracy.

My staff want me to launch an investigation. They too discern conspiracy. But I won't do it. Witch-hunts lead nowhere. And anyway, I think it's rather funny. Someone in the typing pool must have a sense of humour (or, harbour a grievance, I suppose). We simply issue a correction.

An invitation to Waldheim

Next I find a note from the Chef. I look at it carefully. I turn it over. I turn it round and round. I turn it upside down. It still says what it says. "Please note that the Secretary-General wishes his three predecessors to be included in the invitations to the Millennium Summit." That means Boutros-Ghali, Pérez de Cuéllar and Kurt Waldheim. The SG wishes Waldheim to be invited to the Millennium Summit? What can possibly be going on?

Waldheim has been refused a visa to the US in the past because of accusations about his record in the Second World War, which was revealed after he was no longer Secretary-General. Specifically, he has been accused of knowledge of, and even complicity in, atrocities while serving with the German army in the Balkans. He had been placed on the State Department's "watch list" of suspected war criminals.

The Summit takes place in September on the eve of the US presidential elections. It is impossible to foresee that Washington would relax the ban on Waldheim at that time, if at all. Does this mean that the SG has private assurances from Waldheim that he would refuse such an invitation and not apply for a visa? But the simple fact of the SG issuing such an invitation would produce consternation among many governments and human rights groups not to mention the reaction among the American body politic that he has striven to cultivate. Moreover, Waldheim could certainly not be trusted to keep his word. Even if he declined he would do so publicly, proudly displaying this badge of respectability. No doubt the SG would like to be courteous to his predecessors and inviting Waldheim is in keeping with his sense of institutional propriety but this is surely folly.

Saddam Hussein

Meanwhile another act of folly is being played out. The SG has nominated Rolf Ekéus to be head of the new Iraqi disarmament body (UNMOVIC), established by the Security Council, which is to replace the discredited UNSCOM. I had heard that this was in the offing. The SG had floated some twenty names as possible candidates for the post but none had attracted the necessary support in the Security Council. Ekéus was supposed to be the ace up his sleeve as the former head of UNSCOM. But Ekéus is anathema to the Iraqis. They suspect he had worked with American, British and Israeli intelligence. The truth of all this is elusive. Ekéus has fiercely denied it but two former American UNSCOM inspectors, David Kay and Scott Ritter, have asserted that CIA operatives were inserted into the inspection teams.

I, in fact, knew Ekéus well. He had been the Swedish Deputy Permanent Representative at the UN during the time that I had been the Guyana Deputy Permanent Representative when Guyana was on the Security Council. We had gotten along and I liked him a lot.

Ekéus is being depicted as tough yet fair but it is inconceivable that Iraq will cooperate with him. Predictably, Russia, France and China are opposing his appointment. The American media condemn this stand as crass commercialism stemming from these countries' interest in receiving preferential treatment in the post-sanctions era in Iraq. Perhaps. But it is also political realism. Why propose someone you know that Iraq will not accept?

Saddam Hussein may be a monster but he is also a reality. In order to encourage the Iraqis to cooperate with the UN, punishment alone will not work. Incentives must also be provided.

Few if any incentives are being furnished to Iraq. Turkey crosses Iraq's borders with impunity in pursuit of the Kurdish Liberation Army. Iraq's protests at the violation of its sovereignty are ignored. The US and the UK have unilaterally established no-fly zones in Iraq without authorisation from the Security Council. Their warplanes patrol the zones and bombard the country as they see fit. And Washington has made clear that the sanctions will stay as long as Saddam Hussein is in power. To emphasise the point the US has publicly initiated a programme of support for the Iraqi opposition groups in exile. Where are the incentives?

The Mouth from the South

But the day of follies has not yet ended. I'm informed that in my absence Ted Turner has been offered the Honorary Chairmanship of the Religious Leaders Summit.

But what can they be thinking? One can speculate what has happened. Money is needed to underwrite the Religious Leaders Summit and so a deal has been struck. But Turner is not known as, "The Mouth from the South," for nothing. He may be a brilliant businessman and a far-sighted entrepreneur, but he is also capable of acting the buffoon. He could say anything. He has said anything. The press will dig this stuff up. I decide to dig it up first by perusing internet sites. It is even worse than I'd thought.

I find that Ted has offered much subtle public rumination on life and its discontents. His most recent is about the Pope and the Ten Commandments. According to press reports, he had appeared at a meeting of the National Family Planning and Reproductive Centre in Washington and made a speech advocating contraception. In the course of his speech he had proposed that the Ten Commandments be rewritten to eliminate the prohibition against adultery. He suggested further that the Pope should, "get with it. Welcome to the twentieth century." When Turner was asked what he would say to the Pontiff, who is Polish, Turner replied by kicking his feet in the air and saying, "Ever seen a Polish mine detector?"

I'd read a bit about this contretemps at the time. Now I discover that it is not his first foray into theological discourse. He is reported to have said in a speech to the National Press Club, "I am not much of a religious person, to tell the truth. I don't like 'isms'... 'Isms' have caused most of the problems in the world and I think religion is responsible. It's religion that, under the guise of religion, they murdered tens of thousands of women as witches – only a hundred years ago – burned them at the stake...I'd like to see a religion where everybody was good. Not just members of that sect. I mean I'm sick of it. Heaven is going to be a mighty slender place. And most of the people I know and like aren't going to be there. There are a few notable exceptions and I'll miss them. Remember, heaven is going to be perfect. And I don't really want to be there... But when we get there we'll have a chance to make things better because hell is supposed to be a mess. And heaven is perfect. Who wants to go to a place that's perfect? Boring, boring."

There is another report that in late 1989 Ted, in an earlier fit of theological speculation, told the *Dallas Morning News* that, "Christianity is a religion for losers." As for Jesus Christ dying on the cross, Turner is reported as having said, "I don't want anybody to die for me. I've had a few drinks and a few girlfriends and if that's gonna put me in hell, then so be it."

But it is not only religion that has attracted "The Mouth's" intellectual curiosity. In March 1997, Turner was shown by ABC News commenting on the "Heavens' Gates" suicides: "There are already too many people in this world. If a few crazy people want to get rid of themselves, it's a good thing." There is a Reuter's report that in a speech to foreign journalists in Atlanta in May 1996 he opined, "The United States has got some of the dumbest people in the world. I want you to know that. We know that. It's a disgrace. I mean there are times when I have been so discouraged about my own country."

And there is more. He has compared Rupert Murdoch to Hitler and threatened to, "squish him like a bug." He's said he supports a, "one-child policy" for the world despite his own brood of five.

(Questioned on this seeming contradiction, he revealed that he had apparently pondered a drastic solution so as to bring his paternal situation into line with his policy position but had decided not to go through with it: "You can't shoot them," he said in reference to his children.) And in another speech to the National Press Club in September 1994, he had condemned clitorectomy by employing a comparison that he evidently considered apposite: "While I'm in an angry mood, I'm angry at that too. I'm being clitorized by Time-Warner and the women are being clitorized by... that's exactly right. And I don't like it anymore than they do."

Where are the eagles and the trumpets?

8

AN AMERICAN FEAST

Jesse Helms – Keeping our eyes on the larger goal –
Weasel words – Africa Month

————◁◦▷————

"You don't need a weatherman
To know which way the wind blows."

Subterranean Homesick Blues
Bob Dylan

————◁◦▷————

Jesse Helms

Thursday, 21 January

Ambassador Holbrooke is President of the Security Council for the month of January and is introducing some innovations. He has invited Senator Jesse Helms, the UN's acknowledged foe in Congress and the man most responsible for delaying the payment of American dues to the UN budget, to take part in an informal meeting of the Council. A lot of people are upset about this because they abhor Helms and because it is precedent-setting. No legislator takes part in Council meetings in his or her own right because you can't have different branches of a government representing a state in the UN. It would make for some confusion. Anyway, such constitutional niceties have not deterred Holbrooke, who has produced Jesse out of his magic box and treats him like a prize heifer.

Helms is revelling in the moment. His voice is calm, his manner courtly. But at least he avoids disingenuousness. He warns right away what is to come. This will be no love fest between Jesse and the UN. The last Jesse who visited us was a preacher. This Jesse is a mortician.

"Now then, it may very well be that some of the things that I feel obliged to say will not meet with your immediate approval if ever." He takes a sip of water, reaches into his shirt pocket and wipes his nose with a scrunched-up Kleenex.

"Now I'm confident that you have seen the public opinion polls commissioned by UN supporters suggesting that the UN enjoys the support of the American public. That's all well and good but I caution you not to put too much confidence in those polls... Since I was first elected to the US Senate in 1972 I have run for re-election four times. Each time the pollsters have confidently predicted my defeat and they have been wrong." So much for public opinion polls.

Fortified by another sip and Kleenex wipe, he gets to the heart of the matter. Insults, like fat grapes, fall from his lips.

"I have received literally thousands of communications from Americans all across the country expressing their deep frustration with this institution... The UN lives and breathes on the hard-earned money of the American taxpayer... They have heard UN officials declaring, absurdly, that countries like Fiji and Bangladesh are carrying America's burden in peacekeeping... They see the majority of the UN members routinely voting against America in the General Assembly..." Sip, wipe.

"Most Americans see [the UN] as just one aspect of America's diplomatic arsenal and to the extent that the UN is effective the American people will support it... If it becomes ineffective, or, worse, a burden, the American people, through its elected representatives will cast it aside... The UN seeks to impose its utopian vision of an international law on Americans..." Sip, wipe. So much for international law.

"Americans reject the idea of a sovereign UN that presumes to be the source of legitimacy for the US government's policies, foreign or domestic... A UN that seeks to impose its presumed authority on the American people, without their consent, begs for confrontation and eventual US withdrawal." Sip, wipe. So much for majority decisions in the General Assembly and other UN bodies. So much for democracy.

Curiously, the reaction of Security Council members is muted. They disagree with some of his points but ever so gingerly. I'm told later that Holbrooke had spoken to each Council member in advance and asked that they exercise restraint in responding to Helms.

Afterwards I see the Senator leaving the elevator on his way out of the building. His fedora sits awkwardly on his head as he proceeds, this old man, slowly, painfully, step by step. For our nemesis is using a walker.

A memory comes with quick recall of a conversation a few days ago with a Pakistani friend. She had spent a weekend in Washington with friends of hers and had been surprised to find herself seated next to the Senator at a dinner. She had told him immediately that they should avoid the subject of the UN if he wanted to have an amiable evening. He chose instead to extol the virtues of American society. In retort she had suggested that there was some merit in the Third World approach to life.

"For example," she had said, "If my mother is old and ailing and has nowhere to live, I will take her in before putting her in an old people's home even if I only have a studio apartment. That is how we do it in Pakistan, Senator Helms. Now tell me," she continued, "I can see that you are getting on in years. Are your children going to take you in? That's not what is done here, is it?"

Jesse Helms had fallen silent.

Keeping our eyes on the larger goal

Monday, 24 January

Meeting to assess the impact of Helms' visit. Mortimer says that the whole affair was bad – bad for staff morale, bad as a public image of humiliation, bad for the SG as people will say they have come here to give him, their boy, his orders.

The many Americans around the table seem ready to accept this new humiliation as the price of doing business with the US Senate in the person of Mr. Helms. We are cautioned to continue to bite our tongues in the interests of the larger goal. We are admonished to remain "anchored in reality". Meanwhile the "Pro-Consul" has stepped up his attacks. He has taken to repeating as a mantra, "The UN is indispensable but it is deeply flawed. Deeply flawed." We are always "deeply flawed" squared and "deeply flawed" portentously. He has also taken to initiating regular and specific attacks on the Secretariat, while professing admiration and respect for the Secretary-General ("The best Secretary-General in the history of the UN"). Disorganised, bureaucratic, unproductive, the usual things. Ruggie remarks that he'd been told by a Holbrooke staff member that with Holbrooke you only get one chance. The Secretariat had blown its chance when we had inadvertently upstaged him with the issuance of the Srebrenica report on the day he was advertising the success of his Bosnia negotiations.

We were also interfering in Kosovo. We seemed to believe that we had a role there at the same time as Holbrooke was encouraging Kouchner [Bernard, French, head of the UN political operation in Kosovo] to strike out on his own. Our people feel that when Kouchner considers he is being inhibited by New York he complains to Dick. Shashi recounts that after a recent Security Council meeting, Holbrooke had gone over and hissed in his ear, "Corell is despicable. Despicable." [Hans Corell, the Legal Counsel, is one of those responsible for trying to control Kouchner's more extravagant impulses.]

(The Russians are, of course, upset about everything to do with Kosovo and that includes Kouchner. He had helped found the French humanitarian relief organisation, "Doctors without Borders". The Russians say that as far as they are concerned he is still behaving exactly like that – a doctor without a border.)

Anyway, we've still got to keep our eyes on the larger goal. But I've lost sight of what that is. When Kofi became SG he launched an unprecedented courtship with the US Congress in order to get the US to pay its arrears to the UN budget. Instead of dealing solely with the executive authority in the US, he also dealt directly with the legislature. This was a singular departure from custom and practice. He paid visits to Capitol Hill and went to see Senators and Congressmen in their offices. He was sometimes kept waiting while they went to vote.

The US Administration encouraged this venture; indeed they facilitated it. And why not? It absolved them of a considerable degree of responsibility. Let Kofi try. The humiliation of the Secretary-General of the United Nations going cap-in-hand to American Congressmen was another price we were supposed to pay keeping in mind the larger goal. He then launched his reform programme, important parts of which accorded with the known wishes of Congress at the time. The programme was dismissed by Helms and his staff as, "smoke and mirrors" and as "too little too late." Simultaneously, he attracted the suspicion of the Third World for playing Washington's game.

Finally, after three years, the US Congress agreed to repay two-thirds of the dues owed but only if the UN accepted a series of humiliating conditions. We still kept our eye on the larger goal. The SG said that he saw getting agreement on the conditions, "as a challenge to American diplomacy."

But what is the larger goal? To try and retain US support for the Organisation at any cost? And won't our gestures of appeasement simply bring forth further unpalatable demands?

Weasel words

Tuesday, 25 January

Summoned to see Louise who knows that I'd urgently left New York over a week ago because of a relative's serious illness and have recently returned. I prepare myself to receive the heartfelt commiserations that will surely be forthcoming.

Time-wasting preliminaries are eschewed. "I'm worried about this meeting, very worried."

I realise that this is in reference to a millennium event that had been cancelled. I take off my glasses, run my hands over my eyes and compose myself.

"What are you worried about... *now,* Louise?"

"Why hasn't the meeting been cancelled? I said it should be cancelled."

"It has been cancelled."

"No, I see here a letter from you suggesting it is still on."

"That is a mollifying letter which leaves open the possibility of it being rescheduled to assuage feelings."

"Weasel words. Weasel words. Who will notice those weasel words? I said it should be cancelled."

"I know you did. If you recall it was on my recommendation."

"Then why is it still on? Is this fellow (the organiser) a friend of yours?"

(I shudder inwardly at the indelicacy of this particular assault.)

"No, he was recommended to me by Gillian. If you remember when it was agreed to cancel it we also left open the possibility of folding it in to another meeting. It's that possibility that is raised in my letter."

"Never. Never. It was never discussed with me."

(It had been but what shall I say? *Was. Was not. Was. Was not.*) In between volleys, I fold my hands across my chest protectively. She fires again.

"You should have discussed this with me. Now people are complaining about your letter."

"I strongly recommend we let sleeping dogs lie for a few days. I don't think we really have a problem."

"What is the matter, you think I'll act rashly? I'm not rash, you know."

The telephone interrupts. I escape.

Wednesday, 26 January

The Security Council has rejected the SG's nomination of Rolf

Ekéus to head the new Iraq disarmament outfit. Hans Blix, former Director-General of IAEA, another Swede, has been selected instead upon the proposal of France.

Africa Month

"Africa Month" is at an end. An inspiration of Richard Holbrooke, the Security Council has spent the last few weeks debating Aids in Africa, and the conflict situations in Angola, Sierra Leone, Burundi and the Congo. This is the US's month to chair the Security Council and the "Pro-Consul" makes full use of the opportunity.

I think Holbrooke has benefited considerably from all this. He brought Gore to chair an Aids debate and Madeleine Albright to preside over a Congo one. For the latter, he had managed to get seven African Presidents to take part as well as the SG of the Organisation for African Unity, Salim Salim. He also arranged for Nelson Mandela, the mediator, to appear in the Burundi discussion and James Wolfensohn [World Bank President] to speak in the Aids debate.

Holbrooke has put on a masterly performance. It was his idea to stage this unprecedented show and he has pulled it off. I am also very impressed with his skill as a chairman. Before giving the floor to each speaker he has a few kind words to say often combined with a personal anecdote. Everyone is drawn into the world of Richard Holbrooke. It's a dictatorship but it's got a glossy face.

Everyone gets his or her reward from Africa Month. The profile of Africa's problems is undoubtedly raised and something may come of that. (I actually tend to think that, as has been reported, Holbrooke was genuinely affected by what he saw in Africa during a tour that he took last December.) The African Presidents get to take part in a big show. Nelson Mandela comes as a special guest and is on centre stage again. But Dick's the big winner. He pleases Gore and Albright by the prominence he accords them. He makes the Africans happy by paying them and their problems so much attention. And he increases his chances of getting his budget conditionalities through by so doing.

He has also done well with the Helms visit. He needs Helms for, like Albright before him, he will have to obtain Helms' approval when, as he expects, President Gore nominates him for Secretary of State.

To Helms he can say, "See, I've brought you here so that you can lash them in plain view. I will water your whip for you. But beware! They are slippery, they are stubborn. But, if I fail after you have shown them the way, how can you blame me?"

By revealing Helms in the flesh, he can whisper to his ambassadorial colleagues, "There. Look what I have to deal with. He is intransigent. He is inflexible. You have to help me out. You have got to give him what he wants or he will bring down the whole house of cards."

The SG, the first *real* African SG, has also benefited tremendously from Africa Month. (Boutros is technically the first African SG. But, as the *real* Africans like to say, "There are map Africans and there are black Africans". Boutros is undoubtedly a map African.) Holbrooke may have been the orchestrator but Kofi Annan has taken centre stage by dint of his position, origin and personality and has been confirmed as an international star.

9
THE REST OF THEM

Ekéus lives – Hans von Sponeck defiant – The importunate Theo-Ben – A small demurral – The rest of them

Ekéus lives

Friday, 4 February

Moncef [Khane, Algerian, my Special Assistant] is moving into temporary quarters with UNMOVIC, the new Iraq weapons-monitoring operation while our new offices are prepared. Since he is entering the former lair of Rolf Ekéus and Richard Butler, the previous heads, I feel that he needs some advice.

I caution him that security precautions there will be rigid but that I had come to learn the secret passwords for entry to the sacred chambers.

"Try 'Long Live Ekéus'," I explain helpfully.

"If that doesn't work, 'Butler will be back' will do the trick."

Moncef looks at me askance. I think he feels that an Assistant Secretary-General should comport himself with more dignity and decorum.

A little later he calls from below. I greet him with, "Ekéus lives!" I can feel him blanching on the phone. He tries to shush me by muttering darkly that one has to be careful of what you say on the phone at the UN particularly on some phones. We carry on until I end the conversation with, "Butler will be back!" and slam down the phone.

I dash up the corridor to discuss Moncef's paranoia with T, an Algerian friend. T, a former guerrilla fighter, who these days carries around his Viagra pills in a small, silver snuffbox, gives me a paranoid fish's eye.

"Did you know what took place when those offices were first put up?" he instructs me severely in a low voice.

"Well, a big team of CIA technicians came from Langley and installed all the equipment. Now any time you type on the computers in those offices, it goes straight back to Langley. The same is true for the phones."

Could that be right, I wonder, as I return to my own office deep in thought? Impossible. All these Algerians are paranoid. But....

Hans von Sponeck defiant

Thursday, 10 February

Hans von Sponeck, our Iraqi Humanitarian Coordinator, is at it again. He has made a public statement calling for an end to UN sanctions.

"As a UN official," he said, "I should not be expected to be silent to that which I recognise as a true human tragedy that needs to be ended." He went even further.

"How long should the civilian population, which is totally innocent on all this, be exposed to such punishment for something that they have never done?" he asked.

Naturally, the US and UK have complained again. Last time we had signalled a brave defiance by announcing that his contract would be extended for a year. I make a call and discover that in the end it had only been extended for six months. So now Von Sponeck is to leave, having resigned in protest against the sanctions regime. But he is going out with a little bomblet at least.

The importunate Theo-Ben

Friday, 11 February

We have had a meeting to try and make progress on the stalled preparations for the Summit. The current President of the General

Assembly, Theo-Ben Gurirab, the Foreign Minister of Namibia, convened it.

I'd known Theo-Ben in the 1970s when he was the SWAPO representative at the UN and Guyana was a member of the Council for Namibia. He had been one of those who used to be called, "cocktail-party guerrillas". I'd always thought the term was a bit unfair, tending as it did to suggest that the freedom fighters so described confined their battles to the scramble for plates at the buffet dinners held by supportive Western liberals and Third World diplomats. But there was enough truth in the charge to make some of the mud stick.

Theo-Ben was now a different man from the quiet, self-effacing one I used to know. He had acquired an air set off by a sort of ponderous presence tightly confined within dark three-piece suits and enhanced by a respectful coterie of aides trailing in his wake. But he knew the game and played it to his advantage. He was currently embarked on a high-stakes scavenger hunt. His term of office as President of the GA would end before the Millennium Summit. The newly elected President of Finland, a female Finn, was expected to succeed him. He appeared keen to see if he could muscle the Finn aside and get the Summit for himself or at least get into the game.

The Finns were already reeling from his onslaught. They had right on their side but it was not doing them much good. They had past favours and gratitude to call on as well for Finland had been among the strongest supporters of the cocktail party lads and it had been a Finn, Martti Ahtisaari, who had led the Transition UN administration in Namibia. The Namibians had recently begun to put forward a sly new argument certain to appeal to noble Nordic instincts partial to the chimerical lure of global solidarity. Why not have a joint presidency of Finland and Namibia to demonstrate North–South amity at this momentous Summit? But even though the Finns might be intimidated, others intend to make Theo work for his prize.

Theo-Ben has summoned some thirty Ambassadors to his

conclave. We are meeting in a room in the bowels of the UN, on the basement floor. The room is windowless and the walls are painted in dull brown. There are no pictures on the walls.

The meeting begins. I realise that it's going to be a long afternoon when they start to speak HIGH UNESE, a refined language in which compliments mask opposition and circumlocution disguises indecision.

Praise for Theo showers the room –

"Excellent initiative to call this meeting... most timely... opportunity to make progress..."

(Actually: Why has it taken you so long to hold it?)

Support is seemingly voiced for his co-presidency proposal –

"We will look favourably... open to proposal... good symbolic way of showing unity... ready to accommodate..."

(Actually: If you think you can simply call us here and shove this down our throats you are wrong.)

Theo sums up that the co-presidency idea is approved –

"While we can be flexible the rules of procedure must be observed... this meeting has no official status so a decision would be premature... have to work out how to arrange for two people to preside in the General Assembly Hall for the podium only has room for one..."

(Actually: Hold on. Not yet, not yet. You have to plead.)

My proposal to hold roundtables in addition to set-piece speeches is addressed –

"Valuable proposal... interesting new departure... of course attendance will be voluntary... of course the roundtables will not be open to the media."

(Actually: O God, let's hope my Head doesn't come. Can you imagine the problems such a visit will produce? And if he comes, let's hope he doesn't attend the roundtables where he will have to speak without a script... Who knows what he might say! And if he finds out by chance there are roundtables taking place and wanders in, let's make sure the world does not hear the stupidities he will surely utter.)

They discuss the question of NGO and citizens' group participation –

"Civil society involvement in the work of the UN is important... we have witnessed their participation at many UN conferences... question of how to properly arrange it taking account of short time available..."

(Actually: After the debacle in Seattle, are you crazy?)

We conclude with Theo's promise to call another meeting soon.

A small demurral

Wednesday, 16 February

The Chef's note asking me to prepare an invitation for Waldheim to attend the Millennium Summit still sits on my desk. The Chef asked me today to send him the draft.

Last week I'd asked Lamin [Sise, Gambian, Executive Assistant to the SG] to pass on my doubts to Riza. He'd come back to me to say that the matter had been discussed and a decision taken. I'd then voiced my misgivings to Louise who also took it up with Riza and got nowhere. Once more into the breach, I guess.

I send the Chef a note in which I warn that, "Such an invitation could provoke considerable controversy. Mr. Waldheim remains on the FBI's criminal, 'Watch List' on which he was first placed in 1986. It seems unlikely that the US would reverse its negative position on granting him a visa on the eve of presidential and congressional elections. Even if Mr. Waldheim declined the invitation, the fact of its issuance is bound to emerge." I continue by warning that, "an initiative such as this would be the sole responsibility of the Secretariat," and recommend, "that the question of an invitation to former Secretary-General Waldheim should be revisited."

It is a gently-toned disagreement but it will not be welcomed. They will feel that they have considered all this already.

The rest of them

Saturday, 19 February

There was a lovely photo in *The Times* yesterday of a tug moving purposefully up the Hudson, scattering the ice as it went. The Hudson is frozen over and the tug is making a pathway for the merchant ships to ply. And just outside my window, and down by the UN too, great slabs of ice break from the banks of the East River and begin a slow spiral to the sea. And last weekend, in the country, as I stood in the snow in my garden, a flight of birds appeared, fluttering irresolutely against the leaden sky, attempting a late emigration. They are very late, I thought, very late. I watched them sadly as they retreated, wheeling more east than south in irregular zigzags. One of their number kept falling behind, becoming detached from the flock, struggling to keep up. He's not going to make it, I thought. He will be left behind. But then, I thought, the rest of them, they are not going to make it either.

10
SADDAM'S GRAVEYARD

Weighing the cost – Honour bound – The perils of Iraq

Weighing the cost

Thursday, 24 February

The WFP Representative in Baghdad, Jutta Burghardt, has resigned in solidarity with Hans von Sponeck. In commenting on the resignations, James Rubin, Albright's Spokesman, says, "Good."

Monday, 28 February

Much continued twisting and turning about Hans von Sponeck who is expected to appear before the Security Council for a farewell briefing. Most members of the Council, we are informed, are in favour of giving him a hearing. If the matter goes to a vote the US and UK will lose since this is a procedural issue not subject to veto.

The ubiquitous Mr. Eldon [the UK Deputy Permanent Representative], provides the information about the Council's contortions. People on the floor seem to spend a good deal of time gathering information from him or, rather, being provided with information by him. He is one of the people, along with the Pro-Consul, who is regularly referred to in our staff meetings. Although we are in touch with all sorts of people, similar points of regular reference from, say, China, Russia, or the Third World do not exist. However, prejudice is not at work here since French, Dutch, German, or Japanese points of reference are also not to be heard.

Honour bound

Thursday, 2 March

The Pro-Consul has provided his measured judgement from abroad on the Von Sponeck conundrum.

"Stupid," he is reported to have pronounced during an interview in London with *Al-Hayat*. It would be, "Stupid to allow Von Sponeck to repeat in a closed session of the Security Council what he has already said to the international media."

This is an innovative new criterion by which to determine the receivability of statements to the Security Council. Nevertheless, it holds promise. If strictly applied Council meetings could become quite abbreviated which would be a joy to all.

Despite the Pro-Consul's pronouncement, Von Sponeck has been heard, albeit in whispers. As a compromise it was suggested that he should brief the Council at an informal meeting in the SG's boardroom. The compromise was eventually accepted and the briefing took place on Tuesday, Von Sponeck's last day as a UN staff member. This procedure was a win for the US and the UK. Russia, France and the others who had called for the briefing had wanted a formal Council meeting, held in the open for all to witness. They got instead a hole-in-the-corner, off-the-record affair.

So, after thirty-six years as an international civil servant, Count Hans von Sponeck, son of a German general executed by Hitler for disobedience, has paid the price for speaking his mind.

The perils of Iraq

Monday, 6 March

Lunch with the boys. Benon Sevan, the head of the UN's Iraq oil-for-food operation, and my friend of thirty years standing, is there. He is furious with Von Sponeck, who reported to him here at

Headquarters. He says Von Sponeck did little in Baghdad except to collude with the Iraqis. He also complains that the other German who resigned, the WFP Representative, had been on a sort of probationary contract that was not going to be renewed anyway.

If enough of this sort of talk takes hold any trace of heroism attached to the resignations will dissipate. Von Sponeck will then join the others in Saddam's graveyard. George Bush was led there after he won the Iraqi–Kuwait war but was unable to convince the US public that he was right to have stopped at the gates of Baghdad. The SG himself spent some time there. After his early success in averting the threatened bombing by Washington and London, a year later they bombed Iraq anyway and the inspection system was buried in the rubble. Ekéus had a good run but his reputation went into decline after he left. The Security Council rejected him when the SG sought to bring him back. Richard Butler [Ekéus' successor as head of UNSCOM] lost all credibility through his subjugation to American interests; he was fired. Von Sponeck's predecessor, Denis Halliday, was also his forerunner in reacting negatively to what he saw and what he was limited to doing in Baghdad; he too had resigned.

People keep explaining to Saddam Hussein that he has been defeated and humiliated. The trouble is he won't take a hint.

11
PREPARING FOR THE SUMMIT

*Theo-Ben triumphant – Our Big Brother – Unusual
apprehensions*

Theo-Ben triumphant

Wednesday, 15 March

I arrived at the office today and realised I'd really slipped up. The
General Assembly is set to adopt the resolution on the Millennium
Summit that I've been working on for months this afternoon. The
decision to take action today was finally decided on last night. I
have neglected, however, to warn everyone concerned that there
is money involved and that the Assembly will have to be told about
the costs at the time of the adoption of the resolution. I hasten
downstairs to see the President's men to explain the situation.

I encounter first Aboubakar Ajali, an itinerant Algerian and
sometime journalist, who is an Adviser to the President. I tell him
the news.

"Aboubakar," I say, "We will have to have a financial statement
about the resolution."

"It can't be done," he replies. "The resolution has to be adopted
today. And by the way, my name is Boubakar, not Aboubakar."

"Is it? Then why does everyone call you Aboubakar? My wife
calls you Aboubakar."

"No she doesn't; she has more respect. Aboubakar is an Arab
name. Boubakar is a Berber name. I'm a Berber. I hate those
Arabs."

"This is the first I've heard about this. I always thought you
were an Arab and your name was Aboubakar. I've known you for

over twenty years and now you are suddenly Boubakar the Berber instead of Aboubakar the Arab. Anyway MK [who is an Algerian himself] calls you Aboubakar."

"No he doesn't. He calls me Boubakar. I'd kill him if he called me Aboubakar. Come and speak to the President's Chef de Cabinet."

I wait around and am then escorted to see Theo's Chef de Cabinet.

The Chef, whose name is Harold, is unhappy.

"Where is Mr. Ajali?" he enquires. Ah, that's the way out, I think. That's the solution. Surname, use his surname.

"I don't know. But I think he has explained the situation."

Harold refuses to accept either a postponement or a reading of the financial statement. I tell him that it is not his decision and depart.

I've underestimated *Mr. Ajali*, however. He calls just about everyone he can reach in the Secretariat. In the end I get a call from Riza and we reach a compromise. No postponement but an oral financial statement.

The resolution goes through without incident. We finally have agreement on the dates of the Summit, what is to be discussed and that roundtables for the heads will take place. The oral statement is duly read without protest.

Afterwards I look at the final text more carefully and speak to Mr. Ajali. All the President's men are smugly content and I find out why they were so anxious to obtain swift passage of the resolution. For they have slipped in a formula for the co-presidency which is quite vague. Basically, it leaves it up to Finland and Namibia to decide whom to nominate to preside. When the Finns protested at the language, and said it should be made clear that only the Heads of State would be the ones to chair, the President's men demurred.

"What if the President of Namibia falls down the stairs on the day of the Summit?" they point out with sweet reasonableness.

"You mean then another Namibian could replace him?" I think I know whom they have in mind.

Monday, 27 March

A note from the SG on the Waldheim invitation.

"Do send invitations to Perez and Boutros."

Seems a little brusque to me. But the important thing is that I've won. Kurt Waldheim is not to be invited to the Millennium Summit.

Our Big Brother

Wednesday, 29 March

I am walking down First Avenue on a day when the forsythia has begun to flower as spring threatens to burst forth. Down past the Wallenberg memorial that already, so soon after its installation, seems shrunken against the backdrop of the new Trump World Tower, rapidly ascending on the other side of the street. Down a little further along to another symbol, the new, "Germany House", a steely-grey ode to might and magnificence with the black eagle on its shield surveying the passers-by from a lofty perch. Down the hill and up the little dale where the sumptuous restaurant "La Petite Marmite" once stood, with its ruby-red banquettes, I detour to Beekman Place where once I lived, so long ago it seems, and stop to watch the play of light on the rippling waves.

> ("And down by the brimming river,
> I heard a lover sing,
> Under the arch of the railway
> Love has no ending.")

Up the hill again and round the corner, retracing the paths of well-nigh thirty years, I arrive at the River Club swathed in memories wistful and sharp.

> ("In headaches and in worry
> Vaguely life leaks away

And time will have its fancy
Tomorrow or today.")

And so to lunch with the European Ambassadors with Portugal playing host.

It is a working lunch with Louise the guest of honour. They raise a wide variety of subjects with her and she responds admirably. She speaks without notes, is amiable, precise, and frank.

The luncheon livens up when the subject of a possible Summit meeting of the members of the Security Council comes up. This prospect is viewed with pleasure by some, with fury by others. One speaker in particular is driven to distraction at the prospect. The rationale for the opposition is ill expressed although "lack of consultation", "undemocratic procedures" and "detracting from the Millennium Summit" are among the evils cited.

Even the SG is not immune from his tirade. He is accused of promoting the idea in the first place.

"Who is he?" I whisper to my neighbour, the Dutch Ambassador.

"Can't you tell?" he sniffs. Unsure as to whether he is referring to the speaker's manner, the tenor of his discourse, or his accent, I enquire further. He sniffs again.

"Why the German Ambassador, of course."

The French Ambassador takes the floor. Short and slight with a shock of black hair and a monk's face straight from a sixteenth-century portrait, he explains that France has not proposed the idea but neither does it oppose it. It's a good line and the Brit, Sir Jeremy Greenstock, with his hawk-like air, seeming always to be straining against some invisible leash, follows suit. But the Dutch Ambassador has the best approach. He is all innocence. His government has taken no position on the issue, he has received no instructions, but, if you were to ask him, it may not be such a bad idea. I conclude that the French, British, and Dutch (currently a Security Council member) not only want it, but will campaign ferociously to bring it about.

Next it's the Italian's turn to rage. He chooses to speak in French, which I follow fitfully, but his tone and anguished countenance advertise his opposition. His fury, like that of the German, has no policy or substantive basis. Both countries are aspirants for Security Council permanent membership; indeed, they enjoy a fierce rivalry on this issue but they now unite against the possibility of their absence from the Council being so rudely exposed in contrast to the added prominence that a Security Council Summit meeting will provide the British and the French. They fear that the Security Council Summit will endow a special status on its fifteen participants, placing them well above the rest of the summiteers. They are right. Of course, no one has yet said what the purpose of such a Summit would be besides providing the "photo-op" of the Millennium Assembly.

It is left to the Spanish Ambassador to conclude the discourse with a taunting, crushing blow.

"We can discuss this as much as you like," he remarks. "Our 'Big Brother' is supporting it so it will take place."

Friday, 31 March

I dreamt last night that I was in Iceland. I was in a clearing surrounded by igloos. In the middle of the clearing was a pile of bodies. I noticed that some were moving and asked permission to take them to safety. The Icelanders agreed but Kurt Waldheim suddenly appeared and warned me against such a course of action. I don't remember what I did next.

12
GETTING IT RIGHT

Battling poverty at the Russian Tea Room – The Millennium
Report – Placating the Namibians

Battling poverty at the Russian Tea Room

Saturday, 1 April

Dinner with A and T at the Russian Tea Room, our first incursion since the famous renovation. The room is a riot of maroon and green and gold, all battling for predominance. Waiters in faux Cossack outfits hover intrusively. A genuine monument to vulgarity.

A eyes me challengingly but I'm declaring *nolo contendere*. He can pay. Gloomily, he orders an indifferent claret. I've spoilt the fun. When the wine arrives, he disdains the tasting ceremony. T announces that she must have Beluga caviar. We immediately launch into a discussion of youth poverty and the plight of deprived children around the world. The blinis arrive. T attacks. A regards his wife with admiration.

"Keep 'em coming," he prompts the waiter as the blinis disappear as fast as they are rolled.

A recounts a trip on the Concorde where each passenger was provided with an ounce of caviar on take-off.

"T ate my portion as well as hers," he recalls fondly. "Then we asked for second helpings and T ate those too," he continues. "Then she ate another ounce from the guy across the aisle. Five ounces!" They exchange affectionate glances.

They tell us about their visit to Egypt where the condition of the poor in the "City of the Dead" made them determined to rally support to alleviate the suffering of children. I can think of a few suggestions of how to go about this but my wife, ever alert in situations like this, casts a forbidding eye in my direction.

A covertly calls for the bill before we have a chance to order dessert. T explains that President Clinton will not be able to come after all to an event that she is helping organise at the UN. Hillary can't come either. Gore has also apologised. Seems like a lot of no-shows. But there is good news. T tells us that they are donating a million dollars to children's programmes in Israel. (But what about the Egyptian children of the City of the Dead, who inspired the concern in the first place?)

"Million and a half," A barks. "When it is your own money, get it right."

We prepare to leave. They are departing next day for London on the Concorde. Looking around as we walk out, A volunteers his culinary assessment.

"Never filled up," he mutters darkly.

"The place never filled up."

The Millennium Report

Thursday, 13 April

John's Millennium Report came out last week. It is a well-drafted, exhortatory, balanced effort in which governments are invited to adopt definitive targets dubbed "Millennium Development Goals", which represent a qualitative, ideological innovation even though clearly-defined means on how to achieve them are less readily identifiable. There are also a set of proposals designed to make use of internet technology, which are being stressed as an important aspect of the report.

John prepared the Millennium Report under Louise's direction and with the support of Andy Mack [Chief of the Policy Unit, Australian]. Edward Mortimer [British, Chief Speechwriter, former *Financial Times* correspondent] then edited it. Department heads were not consulted except on a handful of elements specific to their work. No one from the South on the floor had a hand in preparing the report.

An elaborate public relations campaign was launched to get good media coverage. The campaign was a success and much favourable press attention ensued.

Placating the Namibians

Wednesday, 19 April

The SG is to meet with the President of the General Assembly. This is the SC's idea with the aim of soothing feelings. I am asked to set it up with the Prez. The SG is to go to see him. I'm to accompany him.

I contact Harold in the Prez' Office. He tells me that he will have to wait for Theo-Ben's return from abroad before confirming.

I send an email to the SC relaying this information.

"You will have to check that the SG himself is ready to meet," is the reply. "I raised it again this week but I don't know where it stands."

After I've already contacted the Namibians as requested? Hmm, not bad, not bad at all. Maybe the SG might not like the idea, or maybe Theo-Ben will say no, or maybe the SG will say no and Theo yes or... So, now it's become my meeting and I have to get the SG to agree.

I spend two days squirreling between the SG's and the Prez' people. Finally they both agree to meet. A time is set.

The SG's office calls. They take it that the Prez is coming to see the SG?

Theo-Ben's people call. They assume that the SG is coming to see the Prez?

With diminishing confidence I go back to the SC.

"Both sides have now confirmed. Question is who is to visit whom? I have been non-committal but have assumed all along that the SG would pay the visit. Most grateful for your advice."

The SC replies decisively.

"I would not touch this question with a ten-foot pole!!!! (A lunch would have solved this tricky little problem.)"

Better and better. I'm responsible now for failing to think of arranging for them to have lunch together, which would have avoided the protocol problem.

I also raise the question of who should accompany the SG.

"The original idea was a tête-à-tête but I don't know how the SG feels about it. If he wishes to be accompanied I think you should go with him."

Failed again. Now where did I get the idea that I should go with him when, in fact, I should have ensured a tête-à-tête? But I might as well accompany him. And why not? It's my initiative after all even though I seem to have got it all wrong.

Fed up, I send a recommendation directly to him and he readily agrees. We will visit the Namibians.

I go to his office at the appointed time to collect him. Two minutes, five minutes, ten minutes late. He appears and we hurry off. Theo greets him pleasantly. Theo's entire staff troop into the room. They are a mixed bunch of African and other non-African staff. They are not introduced. They sit down and look at him.

The SG launches into our placatory scenario but is forestalled immediately by a call from his office. He goes next door to take it. Theo-Ben's men turn and look at me.

Two minutes, three minutes. Theo-Ben's men look at me. Four minutes, five. The SG returns full of apologies. He has been trying to make this urgent call all day. He relaunches the agreed scenario. His office calls again. He goes next door. Theo-Ben's men look at me. Four minutes, seven minutes. I tell a joke. Theo-Ben's men look at me. Ten, fifteen, twenty. I try to gauge the distance to the door.

The SG returns. More apologies.

"I hope you went over all the points while I was away," he says cheerfully to the Namibians, who look at me.

"Not *quite* all, SG," I reply. He and Theo then have a cordial chat and quickly go over all the points.

"Why did they look so glum?" the SG asks me in genuine bewilderment as we walk away, evidently unaware of the chagrin that his late arrival and subsequent comings and goings had occasioned.

"Are they always like that?"

"They did look a bit dour, didn't they SG," I reply. "They are like that sometimes. Must be a Namibian thing."

13

SHOOING THEM AWAY

Earth Day – A large French mirror – On going along –
Kurt Waldheim comes in through the window

Earth Day

Saturday, 22 April

Earth Day is being celebrated at the UN. My wife has arranged the programme with the help of J, a New York socialite. J has provided the celebrities.

There's a teeny-bopper singing group, "No Authority" ("O my God, O my God" my daughter said on hearing they would be coming), child stars from, "The Parent Trap," "Harriet the Spy," "Rip Girls," "Jurassic Park," "Home Improvement," "Stepmom," and the soon-to-be-released, "Michael Jordan Story." Apparently, they are all very famous. I have never heard of any of them. But the "Harlem All Stars," a Steel Band group, is also there and plays sweet West Indian melodies to open the event.

J had promised to provide Clinton, then Hillary, then Gore, later Bill Richardson or Andrew Cuomo, but they haven't showed. My wife is the MC and provides Nane who brings the SG as a surprise. He is greeted with warm applause.

The programme proceeds smoothly and the heavy rain that was forecast holds off. I am sitting with some friends in a front-row seat until a woman from my wife's office comes over, informs us that we are sitting in seats reserved for celebrities, and shoos us away. I stand grumpily at the side as a light rain begins to fall.

A guy with a camera and a ponytail, and a woman wearing a

scarf, make a dash for the newly-liberated chairs. I go over, inform them that these seats are reserved for celebrities, and shoo them away.

My wife thanks everyone and concludes the programme. J invades the stage and confiscates the microphone. She thanks the SG. She thanks Nane ("an angel"). She thanks L ("an angel"). She thanks Delta Airways and *Teen* magazine.

A bunch of people run from the back and colonise the chairs. I go over to shoo them away but they will not be shooed.

J thanks *Rolling Stone* magazine. She thanks my daughter ("an angel"). She thanks the New York Botanical Garden and the American Museum of Natural History. She thanks God for keeping the rain away.

I move over to the side of the stage to get a better view and take some pictures. A guy named Natabara accosts me and tries to shoo me away. I will not be shooed. He finds a security guard and demands my eviction from the premises. The guard whispers something to him. Natabara turns bright red.

J thanks SavATree, The Tree and Shrub Care Company, and Marders Landscaping Company. She will not be shooed.

We troop upstairs to the reception. Natabara sidles over and apologises profusely. He is redder still. I tell him to be cool.

The Steel Band begins to play. They are quickly shooed. J takes over the podium and thanks L again. She thanks every one of my wife's staff by name. She thanks the celebrities. The crowd loses interest and descends on the buffet.

J shouts, "I taught sixth grade so I know how to keep you people under control."

The crowd look at her sullenly. She thanks her own staff and calls them up to the podium.

A woman from J's staff refuses to go on stage and hides behind me. J spots the deception.

"Julie, I see you," she screams. "Come up here."

J thanks me for being L's husband. She thanks her husband for being her husband. Natabara turns up and explains that he wishes he had met me under different circumstances. I tell him it's all right.

A woman named Agapi Stassinopoulos comes over and introduces herself. She explains that she is Arianna Huffington's sister and wants to do something for the UN on women. I make sympathetic noises. She has written a book entitled, "Conversations with the Goddesses" about her chats with the Greek Goddesses. She speaks admiringly about my wife.

"She represents power and femininity," she confides.

I say, "You mean self-confident yet gentle?"

"Exactly, exactly," she answers. "I wish I'd said that."

I remember Oscar and think, "You will, Agapi, you will." Natabara comes over and apologises again.

J announces that No Authority will perform. They look startled. She announces that they will sing the American national anthem. Her staff, remembering that this is still the UN, run over to stop this. It is too late. The reception concludes with the Star-Spangled Banner. I stand and watch, uselessly aghast.

No country's national anthem is ever played within the walls of the United Nations. The only time anyone's national anthem is heard, and then only once, is when a country joins for the first time and a flag-raising ceremony takes place outside in the grounds. So I guess we are making history today.

But why be so priggish. The thing is done. And it's a pleasant anthem, after all.

A large French mirror

Monday, 24 April

I am staring with surprise at a large mirror over a fireplace decorated with twisted, dagger-like shapes in wrought iron. It's the dining room at the residence of the French Ambassador on Park Avenue where I have been invited to lunch along with Louise and John. It's a cavernous apartment, furnished with no great style. Another myth shattered. Another illusion destroyed.

Turns out to be a French/UN affair – only other guests are the Ambassador's deputy and a staff member of the Mission. Chirac will be the European Union (EU) President at Summit time, hence the intense French interest. The French grill us. Ambassador Levitte wants to know who prepared the report and is told John, Andy Mack plus two interns with selective review by some substantive offices once the writing was done. He says the report is "perfect" except for the proposal to have a nuclear disarmament conference. France opposes that and had made its views known to the 38th Floor.

The EU loves the report but will mute its praise for fear of putting-off the South. The problem is how to get Third World countries on board. The next two hours are spent on discussing tactics to suborn the South.

I say little. The fact that Europe is happy with the report is one thing. To covertly ally with Europe is another. To assume that I will go along with this is telling.

On going along

Wednesday, 26 April

I'm 57 years old today. I forgot who said, "The tragedy of old age is not that one is old but that one is young." Pound, Wilde, Eliot? Wilde, I think.

Some relatives and friends hold a dinner for me. I tell them indignantly about my experience on Monday with the French. They look at me pityingly. And Fayza [Abul Naga, later Egyptian Minister of International Cooperation, and later still National Security Adviser to Egyptian President Sise] an old friend of my wife's, who is here for the Nuclear Non-Proliferation Treaty review meeting, relates that a Secretariat document had appeared in connection with the event, which should have mentioned Israel by name as a non-signatory of the Treaty but did not. Egypt had protested to the Secretariat and had been told that the Americans had insisted that Israel should not be mentioned. The Secretariat had complied. Egypt had then talked to Washington, which was persuaded. Washington talked to the Secretariat. Only then was a revision mentioning Israel issued.

Kurt Waldheim comes in through the window

Monday, 1 May

I'm on a largish ship, a sort of tug-shaped vessel. I'm sitting in the dining room, which seems to take up all the available space on board. It's hard to see outside but I know that we are far north, with ice all around. I'm trying to reach someone, to meet someone but a revolving door gets in the way. I go outside to the deck of the ship and discover that we are stationary. We are suspended on a river and giant machines are tossing snow and ice on the decks and against the windows. Two steamboat wheels on either side of the ship twirl monotonously to give the impression of movement.

When I woke up I spied Kurt Waldheim trying to climb in through the bedroom window.

"Go away," I shout. "Go away."

14
KNOWLEDGEABLE, CRISP, WITTY AND SINCERE

Mismanaging Sierra Leone – Executive Outcomes – A long list of culprits – The Millennium Forum

Tuesday, 2 May

I'm on my way to speak at a UN Association meeting in Kent, Connecticut. I'm looking forward to it because I'm very good at such events – knowledgeable, crisp, witty and sincere.

The meeting is to take place in the auditorium of Kent School. It is said to have been widely advertised in Northern Connecticut. I'm sharing the stage with Ilona, a German Professor of Public Health from Yale. I'm to talk about the Millennium Summit, she about Aids. We hear that the North Connecticut UN Branch has been recently formed and now has 82 members. They must be taking a breather from pursuing international peace and mutual understanding because there are at most about seventy or so people in the room of whom only about ten are adults. The rest are kids from the school who look as if they are working off detention by attending.

We are introduced by the Academic Dean. He is to soften up the kids for us. He demands that the kids in the back row remove their caps and hats. "That means you too, Briers," he barks at a kid in the fourth row.

Now that the kids are properly softened up, I take the floor. I stare out at a sea of blank faces crammed into the central area of the auditorium to give an impression of mass. I start off by telling the kids that the UN is about to hold a "jamboree" in New York in early September. First Avenue will be closed for twenty blocks for three days and the FDR drive will be shut down as well. I warn against coming to New York at that time. The jamboree is designed to drive the residents mad.

Not a flicker, a smidgen, not a trace of a smile crosses the faces of the kids. I stumble on, explaining that this is the revenge that the UN has been carefully preparing for many years to counter the disdain with which we are viewed in the city. Nothing, no response, only the sea of blankness. I'm drowning fast but try to recover. I rush through the rest of my presentation.

I have a feeling that things might not turn out this evening quite the way I would want them to be.

Ilona makes her presentation. She is knowledgeable, crisp, witty and sincere. I can't help thinking that Ilona could turn out to be a very irritating person.

A fellow from WHO, a former staff member, suddenly appears and announces that he is taking over as moderator. He will control the flow of questions. He recounts how he had come recently to watch the ice hockey team practice, which takes him back to his days at school, which leads to his life in the army, then his career in WHO, how he met Ilona, how he admires Ilona, how he got Ilona to come tonight...

Finally, he allows some questions. I answer the first one. After I sit down, he announces that he disagrees with me. He spends a long time explaining why. Ilona answers some questions. She is knowledgeable, crisp, witty and sincere. I answer another question. Ilona jumps up to explain that I haven't given the full picture. She gives it.

Things are not turning out this evening quite the way I would want them to be.

I take some more questions. They are about the UN's role in the world, the future of peacekeeping, whither humanitarian intervention. Normally, I deal easily with these issues. Now I find myself providing, convoluted, complex, discursive answers. My own increasing confusion is no longer that easy to disguise.

After it's over, I am gratified that a little group gathers around me. Maybe it didn't go so badly after all, I comfort myself.

"I'm shocked that you gave that wimpy answer about US control of the UN," one guy says to me. "Everyone knows that the US is bossing you people around."

An earnest-looking Kent School student approaches and thanks me fervently for my traffic forecast. He insists on shaking my hand.

"Thank you, thank you, sir; I'll make sure to stay away from Manhattan during that time. And I'll warn my parents too." He is very grateful.

Another guy says, "I'm really sad about the situation. There are no more progressive forces active in the world." I mention cautiously the protests in Seattle [WTO meeting] and Washington [World bank/IMF annual meetings], which might suggest that something is stirring.

Having drawn me out, he pounces.

"Bunch of faggots," he hisses at me. "Bunch of faggots. Anyway, the Rockefeller Foundation will take care of them. Everyone knows that they developed the AIDS virus and let it loose. They've been trying to find an effective population control method for years. Now they've got it. Serve them right. Bunch of faggots."

Oh well.....

Mismanaging Sierra Leone

Wednesday, 10 May

The UN peacekeeping mission in Sierra Leone is falling apart. Some five hundred UN troops appear to have been captured by the rebel group the RUF, whose intentions are unknown. An undetermined number of peacekeepers have been killed.

This is a terrible humiliation for us. Following the disasters in East Timor, Bosnia, and Rwanda, it is unsettling that we should once again find ourselves in such a situation. We also seem to be unaware of what is occuring. While the capture of some three hundred soldiers has been confirmed, the whereabouts of two hundred Zambian peacekeepers is simply unknown; they are presumed to have been captured. We also don't seem to know how many troops have been killed. We announced seven, and then four but now it turns out that only one fatality can be confirmed.

We have made other mistakes. The mission's spokesman announcement that RUF troops were advancing rapidly on the capital caused panic. The announcement was subsequently withdrawn. Fred announced that we were preparing for a "pitched battle" while our whole effort has been to instill a sense that such a *denouement* was not imminent. The Force Commander, Major-General Vijay Jetley from India, is blaming Headquarters in New York for poor coordination of troop arrivals.

I was with the SG today when the incoming President of the Millennium Assembly, Harri Holkeri (a former Finnish Prime Minister) came to see him. The SG was quite distracted and, for the first time that I, at any rate, have witnessed, could not follow his brief. He has just returned from some extended trips, first to Rome for inter-agency meetings, then Florence to be lauded, followed by Paris to discuss Lebanon with the French, then back to New York for a week, then Cuba for the South Summit then a short interlude in New York before embarking on a regional African tour. Moncef had been on the Cuban leg and had confirmed the reports of other colleagues – that he maintained a steady calm, was always well-prepared, switched readily from subject to subject, from phone call to phone call (Barak on Lebanon, Mugabe and Cook on Zimbabwe and so on), sightseeing with gusto then returning to business without missing a beat. Against this background, his evident distraction at the events in Sierra Leone is disconcerting.

He has been making comments in recent days complaining about the quality and inadequate equipment of Third World peacekeeping troops. He wants those first-class, First World troops instead. He has asked the Americans to send in a rapid reaction force to salvage the situation in Sierra Leone but the Yanks won't go. I think he considers that his Secretary-Generalship is in jeopardy.

Executive Outcomes

Thursday, 11 May

Inspired by the disaster taking place in Sierra Leone, Edward Mortimer is advocating unorthodox solutions.

"Executive Outcomes", it is contended, is an alternative we should consider. It is being talked of in the English newspapers, he mentions authoritatively.

"Executive Outcomes" is a group of soldiers for rent who, I recall, are made up mainly of former South African security personnel, the kind whose task it had been to eliminate the opponents of apartheid by any means. Mortimer is proposing that the UN considers employing them.

A look of horror flashes across my face that does not go unnoticed by Riza. He smiles benignly, as one would if an idiot child had wandered uninvited into the dining room as dessert is about to be served. Shashi arrives to announce that William Shawcross had an article in *The Guardian* yesterday advancing the option. Since Shawcross had just produced a book on post-cold war, intra-state confusions in which the SG had emerged as something of a hero, Shashi reports that journalists are asking him whether Shawcross is flying a kite on the SG's behalf. He had denied this.

Lamin says, "There is a UN convention against the use of mercenaries, you know."

Louise flashes at Lamin: "They wouldn't be mercenaries if the UN employed them, would they?"

Riza hurriedly but elegantly cuts off further discussion.

"These are interesting intellectual speculations," he says with the same benign smile.

The correct response to the "intellectual speculations" is a mass withdrawal in protest from the room. But no one actually opposes this sinful proposition. No one from the North, and certainly no one from the South.

Not Riza, who must be appalled but will not show it, forever keeping his cards to himself, maintaining his reputation for impartiality, working for harmony and the avoidance of open discord, preserving the force of his arguments for his private conversations with the SG. Not Shashi, scrambling to retain his position as his ideological opponents on the Floor coalesce to limit his influence. Not Patrick [Hayworth, Ghana, Director for African Affairs in the SG's Office], increasingly lost in the Byzantine coils of the UN bureaucracy. Not Lamin, maintaining his lawyerly posture and less prone to the indignant outbursts that were once his forte. And certainly not I, offended by the spectacle of multiple desertions, fearful of losing control if I seek to utter, stunned by the bravura with which the Westerners on the Floor persistently advocate their agenda, and appalled at the accumulating drip, drip, drip of my own torturous prevarications.

A long list of culprits

Saturday, 13 May

A front-page interview with the SG appears today in the *New York Times*. The headline is: "UN Chief faults reluctance of US to help Africa." Throughout he identifies a long list of those who he holds accountable.

Washington has offered to provide transport to Sierra Leone for Nigerian and other Third World troops but they will not help for free. They want to charge three times that available to the UN by commercial charter. He complains about this.

But it is not only the Americans who are at fault. Few escape his censure. According to the article, he finds it "disheartening" to confront a continent with calamities from end to end and considers what this says about African leadership. He implicitly criticises the Security Council for not providing strong enough combat authority and proper equipment to the UN forces. Also the UN is not being supplied with adequate intelligence. He is "critical of the absence of authority from Sierra Leone's President, Ahmad Tejan Kabbah."

He casts doubts on the capability of his own Force Commander, General Jetley.

"There's tension in the command," he is reported to have said.

"Everybody who's met Jetley say that he's a very good officer. But some of the commanders complain that he just gives orders, implying that there is no consultation. The commander should be not only a good commander. He has to be a good team-builder."

He is not happy with his troops either.

"When a whole Guinean battalion on its way to Sierra Leone – 900 men with A.P.C's – said they were disarmed, you wonder. Did they sell them?"

Africa, already condemned for its leaders, apparently has another pervasive problem.

"Normally when countries are rich in natural resources, it is a blessing. But it's turning out to be a curse in the case of Africa. Diamonds, greed, war, political ambitions – this is a very poisonous mix."

It's a long list of culprits – the US, Africa, the Security Council, the Sierra Leone President, the UN Force Commander and the African peacekeeping troops. But shouldn't the UN Secretariat at Headquarters in New York, responsible for overseeing the mission, also have a place on it? Shouldn't he?

Monday, 15 May

SG is happier today, jaunty even. The British have sent in a force of some 700 troops, ostensibly to take control of the airport and remove foreign nationals. In fact, having first secured the airport they have gone on to secure the capital, Freetown, are sitting in on UN military planning meetings, and are advising Kabbah on the deployment of his troops. Of course, they continue to announce that they are only there to protect the foreigners. "This is one we cannot afford to lose," the SG states.

He admits that he has failed to persuade the West to provide him with a rapid reaction force but "the British force in effect has done so. The situation is now improving on a daily basis. Had the British troops not come in, the UN force could have unravelled". He mentions that he spoke to Madeleine on the weekend after his NYT interview had appeared. They had agreed on a "united front."

Tuesday, 16 May

The RUF are not a pleasant bunch. They gang-rape and murder with zest but they seem to relish most the intimidatory tactic of dismemberment – cutting off arms and legs not just of opponents but anyone, man, woman and child who cross their malevolent path.

It is impossible to speak of any saving graces in connection with the RUF but their *nommes de guerre* do attract attention.

The collection so far:

"One man, One bullet."
"Mad Bomber."
"Leatherboots."
"Razor."

Wednesday, 17 May

Today's RUF entries:

"Silent Killer."
"Boom, Boom."
"Mosquito Spray."

Thursday 18, May

Foday Sankoh, the RUF leader, has been apprehended. The crowd stripped him naked and turned him over to the Sierra Leone police. A former militiaman, who killed Sankoh's bodyguard and shot the rebel leader in the leg, effected his capture. The name of the hero?

"Black Scorpion."

The Millennium Forum

Friday, 26 May

The Millennium Forum is over. For a week civil society gathered here to speak among themselves with the hope that they will be listened to afterwards. Some 1,400 NGOs took part in the first forum of its kind. They want this to be the beginning of regular civil society gatherings, which will develop into a Global People's Parliament, linked to the UN.

The SG opened the Forum and received standing ovations at the beginning and the end of his address. He deserved the applause for his support for civil society as a force to promote change has been unwavering. But civil society will only follow him so far. His Millennium Report received scant reference in the final declaration while the hope had been that it would heavily influence their work. In fact the two most striking trends in the report are implied rebukes. Globalisation is characterised as "corporate-driven" and as such savagely attacked for being a force which "increases inequities between and within countries, undermines local traditions and cultures, and escalates disparities between rich and poor, thereby marginalizing large numbers of people in urban and rural areas... States are becoming weaker while an unaccountable, transnational private sector grows stronger." And throughout the declaration the call to guard against the unregulated activities of transnationals emerges as perhaps the major concern. The NGOs want some sort of "transnationals watch" modelled on "Human Rights Watch." They want the UN to enter into a "Compact with citizens" to match the "Compact with transnationals" as they call the "Global Compact."

It is a remarkably well-organised event with the NGOs managing to sort out their differences. Notably, NGOs of the stripe of "Ruckus", "Attack", and "Refuse and Resist," were not in evidence. This made the Forum tame and containable, but still valuable. Now we will wait to see what our Floor makes of it.

Monday, 29 May

Things are looking up in Sierra Leone. Through the intercession of Charles Taylor, the President of Liberia, the captured peacekeepers have been released and flow to Monrovia to be handed over to the UN.

Taylor is a long-time supporter of Sankoh with whom he is rumoured to be in business in the diamond trade, the chief export earner in the country, the stuff of dreams, and a motivating factor leading to much of the blood-spilling.

It is more than unfortunate that we have to treat with Taylor, a famous butcher in his own right, who bludgeoned his way to power in Liberia, and depend on him for rescue.

Friday, 2 June

The third round of the Cyprus proximity talks is set to start in Geneva. I estimate that the Cypriots can string this out for another ten years or so. After all, they have kept it going already for twenty-five.

15
REGRETTING THE RUFFIANS

Mugabe of Zimbabwe – Crown Princess Victoria of Sweden – An absence of dissent – Too long, too long – M. Henri Konan BEDIE is no longer the Head of State of Côte d'Ivoire – Untimely Arabs

Mugabe of Zimbabwe

Saturday, 3 June

It was decided yesterday that we would no longer be sending a mission to Harare. The mission was to have left today. Its purpose was to advise the government of Zimbabwe and its Prime Minister, Robert Mugabe, in particular, about a process of orderly land reform in that country.

Zimbabwe has undergone convulsions in recent weeks on account of approaching elections and the decision of Mugabe to either support, encourage or foster the takeover of white-owned farms in Zimbabwe. The white settlers, years after independence, still own 75% of the arable farmland. The "war veterans", landless participants in the struggle against Ian Smith, the Unilateral Declarer of Independence, have forcefully occupied hundreds of farms, threatened the owners and even, in a few cases, killed the white farmers.

The SG took an active interest in the crisis from its inception. He has been conferring regularly with Mugabe and Robin Cook. In short, he has been exercising his "good offices," an undefined but key attribute of his responsibilities. As a result of his persuasive efforts, Mugabe agreed to accept a UN mission to advise on the dispute. Now, twenty-four hours before the mission is due to depart, Mugabe has announced the nationalisation of 804 farms.

Private good offices are fine in regard to what is an internal matter for Zimbabwe. But because the white farmers, (all the while protesting that they are good, true and loyal Zimbabweans) also retain their British ties and passports, London is fully involved as the English media trumpet stories of black atrocities. So the British were keen to have Annan play a role. He suggested a UN mission led by UNDP. But the head of UNDP, Mark Malloch-Brown, *is white and British, with a Southern African background*, and he was to lead the mission personally. But we are surprised, offended and indignant about Mugabe's action in announcing nationalisation on the eve of the mission.

Crown Princess Victoria of Sweden

Tuesday, 6 June

The Crown Princess of Sweden is spending some time attached to our Floor and is attending our staff meeting this a.m. The idea is simply for her to sit in, to be part of the group, to absorb a little. Hers is supposed to be an unobtrusive presence. She seems a nice kid, just twenty-three, perky with a ponytail and defiantly ordinary, wearing a T-shirt-type top and slacks.

Iqbal presides. He welcomes her effusively. There is much *Crownprincessing*. He invites interventions as is customary but people aren't playing. Whether they resent being on display or are tongue-tied in the presence of the kid is hard to discern.

Fred, normally so voluble in the morning, is called upon first but says little.

"Crown Princess, Professor Ruggie is our brains trust, the author of all the SG's major reports…"

The "brains trust" passes.

Mortimer is summoned next. He passes. Iqbal is getting desperate.

"Crown Princess, Mr. Hayworth, our Director for African Affairs…"

The Director for African Affairs has come in late, missed the introduction, his cue and thus his moment. He passes.

The Chef seems a little irritated now. Iqbal, the Pakistani, turns to Shashi, the Indian, with whom he co-exists tenuously.

"Crown Princess, Mr. Tharoor, our Director of Communications. However, since he's always travelling, it's hard to communicate with him."

Not an encouraging introduction, this one. Shashi, grimacing, passes.

He turns to the senior Swede on the Floor, who is squiring her around.

"Crown Princess, Mr. Rolf Knudson, who as you know is Swedish, our chief political officer on the floor..."

The "Chief Political Officer," notwithstanding his battlefield promotion, passes.

"Rolf, you must have something to say about Lebanon?" Rolf mutters a few words.

"Crown Princess, Mr. Stoby, our Millennium Man..."

The "Millennium Man" passes.

"Crown Princess, Mr. Khane, who is in Mrs. Sorensen's office..."

This is news to MK who tries not to look surprised. MK passes.

"Crown Princess, Mrs. Lilia Amores-Mantas is the Administrative Officer."

Lilia rescues him.

"John, won't you tell us about the Security Council retreat?" John, prompted, complies.

A grateful Iqbal regains momentum. Revved up, he scoots around inconsequentially. In the end, everyone in the room is presented to the kid like debutantes at a coming-out ball. Before each introduction Iqbal inclines his head in a sort of half-bow in her direction.

"Crown Princess, Ms. Dissin who is Swedish..."

"Crown Princess, Ms. Saville who is half-Swedish..." He is unstoppable.

Afterwards a senior colleague says to me: "A sorry spectacle".

But I think that he is being too harsh. This was not a meeting to have missed.

An absence of dissent

Thursday, 8 June

Above all, what disturbs most is the absence of self-examination. And here, I think, we all bear responsibility for failing the SG. He has, after all, put in place a system of daily meetings of EOSG staff unlike anything done by his predecessors. Information is shared freely and respect for the dictates of confidentiality assumed and infrequently referred to. Twice a week the senior staff meets with the SG and twice a week Riza chairs a meeting of all the professional staff on the floor. In these open forums no restraint on informing about developments is apparent to me. This is admirable for it builds up a sense of community, trust and solidarity.

But the meetings have become exercises in self-restraint. We rarely, if ever, admit that something has gone wrong because of us, that we could have had more foresight, consulted more widely. Our attitude to the SG is reverential and this is truly mistaken deference. For he needs our views on whether things have been screwed up, on whether he has screwed up, misspoken, lent too far in one direction or the other, what the delegations think of what he is doing, saying. But none of this takes place. We do delight, nonetheless, in excoriating those off the Floor for their political clumsiness, indecision and lack of initiative, none of which sins adhere to us.

Since I am not part of the inner cell I do not know whether others dare to give voice in private conclave to the pointing out of errors and mistakes made by the Floor or by him. But I doubt it. There are simply not enough people in his office with the necessary political weight, independent position or sheer backbone to speak up. Those on the Floor are caught up in the delights of power and position, the pleasure of seeing the respectful look that colleagues not so fortunate so often assume, the thrill of being in-the-know, the seduction of a once-in-a-lifetime opportunity, the heady prospect of rapid promotion, the tactile pleasure in handling papers *first*.

But the price is to not offend, to sense the currents, the prevailing sentiments, to chart the curve of change and to be well in step.

Too long, too long

Monday, 12 June

It was Maurice Strong, in the Reform report, who called for an opening by the UN to civil society. The SG had taken this up enthusiastically and has pursued it vigorously.

When I circulated the draft declaration the Forum participants were working on, Louise looked at it, weighed it in her hand, flicked through the pages and pronounced, "Too long. Too long. No one will read it" and put it aside.

And she is right, at least where our group is concerned. No one on the Floor appears to have read it or to have any interest in it. Work is proceeding on drafting the Summit outcome and no attention at all is being paid to the declaration of the NGOs although the Forum was convened for the specific, announced purpose of getting their views.

And when we came to discuss the Forum's outcome someone complained that they had heard (without reading the damn thing) that the recommendations did not follow the SG's report enough. And that was it. All that really seems important is that the SG opened the Millennium Forum and was received enthusiastically having said the right things. There is no apparent interest in what the NGOs themselves have said.

M. Henri Konan BEDIE is no longer the Head of State of Côte d'Ivoire

Tuesday, 13 June

Eighty Heads have now said they will be coming to the Summit. This breaks down to sixty Heads of State, including three Kings, and twenty Heads of Government (Prime Ministers). Other indications suggest that some 170 in all are seriously considering coming. We are thus well on the way to the largest gathering of heads of state and government ever held.

Some of the replies to the SG's letter of invitation have a poignant quality about them. In a letter dated 25 November from Abidjan, President Bédié of Côte d'Ivoire assures the SG that he will, "personally take part." On 28 March we hear from the Ivorians again. They inform us that as a result of the "coup d'état of 24 December... M. Henri Konan BEDIE is no longer the Head of State of Côte d'Ivoire."

Franjo Tudjman, President of Croatia, writes on 6 September, "My commitments permitting, I shall be particularly pleased to accept your invitation to take part in this important gathering..." Alas, they will not permit. He has since died.

Bereft of poignancy but certainly to the point is the reply from Colonel Muammar Gaddafi, Leader of the al-Fateh Revolution.

He, "thanks the SG for the invitation to the Millennium Summit. However, he reiterates his opinion that the meeting should be held outside the United States, perhaps in Switzerland."

He concludes that he, "cannot travel all the way across the Atlantic to a country which is an enemy of the Libyan people and himself, to make a five-minute speech in the General Assembly."

Untimely Arabs

Friday, 16 June

Iqbal's just back from Syria where he represented the SG at the funeral of Hafez al-Assad. He tells us about the funeral arrangements in some detail.

(The Chef also tells us about his travel arrangements. He had to fly commercial. He had made strenuous efforts to get on the US delegation plane with Madeleine Albright but getting approval took time. He was already at Newark Airport when he heard he could go with the Americans on Air Force Whatever [Two? Three? Four]. It was too late.

Neither the Chef nor anyone else seems in the least disturbed at the prospect of his arriving in Damascus with the American party on a White House plane. The thought that this might bother the Syrians a bit [still a "terrorist" state according to Washington] and suggest a less than independent posture by the UN Secretariat in Middle Eastern affairs, is a quibble reserved for my hidebound, old-fashioned, traditionalist mind.)

The Chef concludes by remarking that the Syrians did their best but it nevertheless became a drawn-out and somewhat chaotic event. Unprompted, a SC intervenes.

"It was the same at King Hussein's funeral," we are alerted.

"It degenerated very quickly. Arabs just don't know how to organise public events."

I say: "Without exception?"

"Yes, yes," he replies.

"That is how they are. At airports, for example, they just turn up and stand around."

I say: "I think you should stop right there."

Another voice is heard.

"We are like that you know," Marta says coolly. "All of us, Latin Americans, Asians, Africans, Arabs. No sense of time."

16
TAKING WATER IN HIS WINE

Painful reminiscences – Richard the "Dark Prince" Butler –
A North-centred agenda – The Shebaa Farms

Wednesday, 12 July

The Pro-Consul has made another one of his appearances before
the Senate Foreign Relations Committee. He testified that "the UN
[is] flawed but indispensable." This is good news though because
we are making progress. Previously we were not just "flawed" but
"deeply flawed" and "deeply flawed" squared. He explains helpfully
that the improvements that have taken place have been the fruits
of his many labours on issues such as peacekeeping and a revised
system of budgetary contributions. We are surely in safe hands.

Sunday, 16 July

Two hundred Indian UN peacekeepers that have been kept in
confinement by the RUF have been rescued. Jefley, the corps
commander, sent in a group of Indian Special Forces to get them
out. There were a few casualties and one fatality. The British were
around – in an unofficial, advisory capacity of course. Actually
British SAS forces were heavily involved in directing the operation
and British Chinook helicopters brought out some of the captives.

Thank God this particular humiliation is over. We have looked
quite feeble in recent weeks with respect to Sierra Leone.

Painful reminiscences

Wednesday, 18 July

Lunch at Lutece given by John de Saram, the Sri Lankan PR, for Hans Dahgren, his Swedish counterpart who is leaving. The Algerian, Brazilian, Botswanan, and Polish Ambassadors also there. They are all tough, intelligent and fair people.

We drift into conversation about Boutros. Joe, the Botswanan, was on the Security Council during the war for the Secretary-Generalship between Kofi and Boutros. He recalls an encounter with Madeleine Albright.

She had summoned him to a meeting in the Delegates' Lounge to justify the continued African support for Boutros.

"He is the official African candidate," he had said.

"He is not an African," she had scoffed. "He is an Arab."

He had tried to advance her knowledge of geography.

"Egypt is an African country," he had pointed out.

"He is a francophone," was her next condemnation.

"He is an independent Secretary-General. We Africans like that," he had rejoined.

"He is too independent," she had said in final dismissal.

"He thinks he can run the UN independent of the United States. He will discover he cannot."

John asks Hans to recall his most memorable moment at the UN. "That's easy," he replies. He then recounts for us the time in December 1999 when the US and the UK were threatening to attack Iraq for non-compliance with the inspection system mandated by the UN. Richard Butler had submitted a report and the SG had offered his own recommendations. As the Council was in the midst of its deliberations, word arrived that the bombing had commenced. He recalls the shock and indignation felt by the other members of the Council, many of whom considered that this demonstration of brutal disregard for the Council spelt its death-knell. Others, of a less apocalyptic bent, were merely furious at the contempt Washington and London had shown to the Council and, indeed, the international system of collaborative decision-making based on UN institutions.

Richard the "Dark Prince" Butler

Richard Butler relates the same incident in his book that has just been published. But Richard, the "Dark Prince" (his British Secret Intelligence Service code name according to Scott Ritter, the former UNSCOM Inspector) is not offended by the affront to the Council. The British and the Americans did the right thing as they invariably managed to do during the entire phase of Richard's tenure as Executive Chairman of UNSCOM except for the odd occasions when they evinced a little spinelessness. Fortunately, they had the "Dark Prince" to guide them back to the true path.

Butler's book is devoted to explaining why he was always right on Iraq and everyone else was usually wrong. The SG is described as weak; Iqbal is a liar, Victor Gratchev, a Russian colleague working on the 38th Floor, is in thrall to Moscow, the Russians and the French are only concerned about their commercial interests in Iraq and the Security Council is indecisive. These are mere fly swats, however, compared to his description of the Iraqis – deceitful, offensive in their personal habits, and murderous in intent and deed. And he had not sought the job in the first place but duty had called.

This reference to having had heavy responsibilities thrust upon him is an unrelenting refrain throughout the apologia. But it jogs my memory about a conversation I had with the SG about Richard.

I had been in to see the SG soon after Butler's appointment had been announced. We were alone. He asked me what I thought. I had replied, "Some of us have been discussing this. I know Butler well. I think he will have the UN at war with Iraq within six months." (I was wrong. I had overestimated Richard. It took eighteen.)

The SG had laughed. "Richard does need to learn to take some water in his wine, doesn't he," he had said. Then he had become somewhat defensive.

"There was tremendous lobbying on his behalf," he had told me as if by way of explanation.

I had met Butler in the early 1970s when I was a junior diplomat representing Guyana at the UN. He was similarly positioned for Australia.

We renewed acquaintance twenty years later when, as Australian Permanent Representative, he was elected to the Presidency of the Economic and Social Council for which I was responsible on the Secretariat side. The decision on who should be President that year had also produced my first encounter with Louise, then the Canadian Permanent Representative to the UN. It was going to be ECOSOC's Fiftieth Anniversary Session. ECOSOC had never had a woman President and I thought it would be a fine piece of symbolism if a woman could be President in the anniversary year. I thus approached Louise who showed interest. Then Butler called me to say he would be the one.

During the lunch someone had remarked, "He always said that he had never lobbied for that post." But I remember a somewhat plaintive call from Louise to let me know that she had decided not to pursue the matter. Richard, that blushing bride, had lobbied early and had lobbied well.

A North-centred agenda

Monday, 23 July

Senior staff meeting with the SG. He has just returned from a thirty-two-day trip to the Middle East, Europe and Africa. He'll be at Headquarters for ten days before leaving on a three-week holiday.

He expresses concern about an event that he had attended while in Geneva during his recent trip. It had been arranged that he should launch a new publication called, "A Better World for All," which was the product of an unprecedented process of collaboration between the UN, the World Bank, the IMF and OECD.

The document was proving controversial not only for its content but because the UN had joined forces with organisations that are not favourites of many sections of civil society and, indeed, the Third World. Moreover, the OECD, an organisation of donors, had been party to the process but no organisation representing the recipients (developing countries) had been involved – none of the regional development banks or the UN's regional economic commissions, for example. Finally, neither of the UN's main departments handling development issues and headed by developing country nationals – UNCTAD [United Nations Conference on Trade and Development] and DESA [Department of Economic and Social Affairs] – had been part of the process.

The UN involvement was spearheaded by Mark Malloch-Brown, of British nationality, a former Vice-President of the World Bank, and appointed by Kofi a year ago to head the UNDP. DESA had in fact complained about the document as well as the draft of the SG's speech to be delivered at the launch.

Fréchette, Ruggie and Mortimer are absent. Shashi seizes the moment.

"Your critics are attacking you for this SG. The perception is that you have gone too far in taking the lead on a North-centred agenda."

The SG will not give ground. He argues that it is a benefit to everyone to have the Bank and the Fund accept UN goals and policies as he had sought to encourage through closer collaboration with them.

Shashi persists. He points to a meeting on the Global Compact, which is about to be held at the UN. The multinationals, which had signed on, will be there.

"The UN is being accused of 'blue-washing' [a cruel reference to the colour of our flag] the multinationals that the NGOs are criticising," he says.

The SG advances in retort the need to "take in the private sector," to "make multinationals responsible."

"In the process of bringing them in SG, you are perceived as having gone too far," is Shashi's reply. I speak up in Shashi's support drawing attention to the content of the Millennium Forum Final Declaration. But the SG will not be swayed.

The Shebaa Farms

The SG then announces that UN troops will begin deployment in the South of Lebanon immediately. This is the latest act in a drama that the SG has been drawn into.

Prime Minister Barak of Israel had come to power promising to remove Israeli troops from Southern Lebanon by 30 July. The SG had properly sought to anticipate the likely outcome of a precipitate withdrawal and had urged Barak to bring the matter to the attention of the Security Council. Barak had complied as a result of which the Council had authorised an increase of UN troop strength in Lebanon and the deployment of UN peacekeepers to the South of the country. The Israeli withdrawal and UN deployment were supposed to be phased and coordinated if at all possible. In the end, Israel withdrew in a hurry, well before the advertised deadline as the army of its Southern Lebanese allies disintegrated and Hezbollah moved in. The Security Council charged the SG with certifying the Israeli withdrawal.

Then Barak lost his majority in the Knesset. Even though the Lebanese protested vigorously that Israel continued to occupy Lebanese land namely the Shebaa Farms, which both Lebanon and Syria had historically claimed as their own at different times, the certification was issued overriding Lebanese and Syrian protests since the Syrians had announced that they had ceded their claim to Lebanon. Specifically, Lebanon called the certification invalid.

The history of the ownership of the Shebaa Farms area is muddled and contradictory. The area had never been properly demarcated and both Syria and Lebanon seem to have valid, historical claims. Syrian maps appeared to show that the farms lay in Syrian territory but there were also two maps from the 1930s in the possession of France which told the opposite story. In addition, the farmers themselves were Lebanese, who lived in a village in

Lebanon and travelled to the area to manage the farms, and had historically been accustomed to paying taxes to Lebanon.

What is uncontested is that the Shebaa Farms is not Israeli territory and that Israeli occupation of the strip is illegal. A practical and principled proposal to make at this point is for the Farms to be put under UN guardianship while a demarcation exercise is undertaken. Instead, by choosing to recognise as still current a dispute that the Syrians and Lebanese asserted had been resolved, the UN allowed Israel to retain a strategically-placed strip of land that Israel did not wish to surrender. Anticipating criticism, our line on the matter, in the words of Riza at one staff meeting, was that, "The Syrians had pushed the Lebanese into it."

[But who had pushed the UN into it? That question may have been unwittingly answered by Ambassador Nancy Soderberg, who was serving as the US Representative for Special Political Affairs at the US Mission to the United Nations at the time.

"When it was clear the Israelis were going to withdraw fully from Lebanon, Syrian and Lebanese officials fabricated the fiction that this small, sparsely populated area was part of Lebanon," Ambassador Soderberg wrote in a July 21, 2006, op-ed in the *Florida Times-Union*. "They even produced a crudely fabricated map to back up the dubious claim. *I and United Nations officials went into the map room in the United Nations and looked at all the maps of the region in the files for decades. All showed the Shebaa Farms clearly in Syria.*"

So the UN conducted a joint review of "all the maps of the region for decades" with a member state having no *locus standi* in the matter. How could the "United Nations officials" involved in this review not be aware of the impropriety of such an exercise? How could they not see that the integrity of the review would be compromised as a result of Ambassador Soderberg's covert participation?]

PART THREE: A CROWNING SUMMIT

"I am in love, meanwhile, you think; no doubt you would
     think so.
I am in love, you say; with those letters, of course you
     would say so.
I am in love, you declare. I think not so; yet I grant you
It is a pleasure indeed to converse with this girl...
No, though she talk, it is music; her fingers desert not the
     keys; 'tis
Song, though you hear in the song the articulate vocables
     sounded,
Syllabled singly and sweetly the words of melodious
     meaning.
I am in love you say: I do not think so exactly."

Amours de Voyage

Arthur Hugh Clough

17
MILLENNIUM PRELIMINARIES

*I'm sleeping well at nights – The Finnish-Namibian War –
We know who is sleeping with whom – The Holy Men –
A San Marino conundrum – The escape of Madeleine
Albright – A gulf appears*

August, 2000

Louise is chortling on the phone. "Good show, Miles. Good show," she says in reference to a problem that I have managed to resolve. I hope she doesn't keep this up. I don't think I can cope with a jovial Louise.

"My meeting is more important than your meeting!" Bawa Jain, the Religious Summit's Main Man is telling me. Actually, he is screaming at me. Bawa is really upset.

The General Assembly has decided to invite a representative of the Millennium Forum to speak at the Summit but has rejected out of hand a similar proposal in respect of Bawa's boys. I discern that I am somehow at fault. Bawa has also decided that he is in competition with me. ("Your meeting" is the Millennium Summit.)

"And my meeting will get more publicity than your meeting," Bawa shouts at me as he concludes our little chat. OK, Bawa.

"I'm sleeping well at nights," Louise announces in a meeting while looking at me benignly.

"Good show, Miles."

This bubbly Louise is driving me nuts.

The Finnish-Namibian War

The Finns and Namibians are now in open warfare. One tussle is over the seating arrangement on the podium of the General Assembly, which seats three. Mr. Jin, our Chinese Undersecretary-General normally sits to the left and acts as Secretary, the President of the General Assembly, sits in the middle and the SG to the right. Now we have the unprecedented situation of two Co-Chairs for the Summit. The sensible and obvious thing (which everyone expected when the decision was made) is for Namibia and Finland to share the podium and alternate the chairmanship. But they can't agree on how to do this and, in particular, who will chair first.

They ask whether another seat can be fitted on the podium. Both because it will cost a lot to construct as well as to nudge them to do the sensible thing – alternate chairmanship – I tell them it can't be done. But I've underestimated Mr. Ajali again. He manages to have the General Assembly decide that the three seats on the podium, "will accommodate the two Co-Chairs and the Secretary-General." This summarily disposes of Mr. Jin.

There is still one small problem, though. Finland and Namibia have agreed they will sit together on the podium but they still cannot agree on who should speak first.

The battle resumes.

We are putting up two temporary offices to accommodate the Presidents of Finland and Namibia as Co-Chairs of the Summit. (We have, of course, an office for the President of the General Assembly but we've a plethora of chairmen this time around. No stranger to our arcane ways would understand this and when I tried to get our legal people to explain to me how you could have any Chairs other than the President of the General Assembly for of a meeting that had been deemed "an integral part of the Millennium Assembly", I was told to keep quiet and stop causing trouble.)

Anyway, I'd sent the Finns and Namibians the plans for the offices months ago. Wisely, I'd arranged for them to be identical in size and appointments. The Finns had approved the plans but there was silence from the Namibians. Now I hear from them.

"The Finns have more offices than we do," Harold Urib complains.

What the hell is he talking about? Then I get it. The Namibians will be moving out of the President of the General Assembly's offices once the new Assembly starts and will only have one set of Co-Chairs' offices. Meanwhile, the Finns will have a Co-Chairs' set of offices for their President and the customary offices of the President of the General Assembly for Mr. Holkeri.

The Namibians, ripe with a passion unencumbered by the application of reason, are indignant. They demand that they be given both sets of Co-Chairs' offices. The Finns can squat anywhere as far as the Namibians care.

The Namibians have been taken to view their Co-Chair offices. Harold announces that they are unsuitable for a head of state and rejects them. I strike back quickly by taking the Finns to see their identical Co-Chair offices. They think they are lovely.

The Co-Chairs' offices are located in an area commonly know as the Chinese Lounge. However, I have discovered that the corridor leading to the Chinese Lounge also has a name. No one seems to know the origin but it is the official name. It is called, "The Vomitorium."

His indignant staff has taken Theo-Ben Gurirab to view the offending Co-Chairs' offices. He says they are fine. I've begun to think that Theo has been ill-served by the enthusiastic assassins around him and may not know half of what they are doing in his name.

Soon after Theo's concurrence, Harold is taken for another tour. All hell breaks loose again. It's discovered that the furniture that normally occupies the space in the Chinese Lounge is a gift from Finland. It is quickly removed. It is then discovered that there is a plaque on the wall recognising the gift. The plaque is removed. Harold then finds out that the Namibian Co-Chairs' offices are besides where the plaque used to be. We switch the offices.

When I left UNFIP, [the Turner Fund] a colleague had given me a lovely toy as a farewell gift. It's a model of a packing case and when you turn it on it starts to shake violently and you hear the voice of a man who is trapped inside begging, "Help, help. Let me out of here. Let me out of here."

We know who is sleeping with whom

I'm chairing a meeting of the UN/US Task Force, which I'd set up a few months ago. It has worked out well and we have received good cooperation from the American side. Today, though, we have a problem. The US Secret Service operates on the basis of a policy which has them providing protection only to heads of state and government. Thus, the some forty countries whose heads will not be coming will not get protection for the leaders of their delegations. Since this list of the unprotected will include the Crown Princes of Saudi Arabia and Monaco, the brother of the Emir of Kuwait and the uncle of the Sultan of Oman, I think they are being a little rigid. I tell them so but they are adamant.

I look more closely at the list and find that it is full of inexplicable inconsistencies.

"The President of Mali, the Governor-General of the Bahamas, the Prime Minster of St. Lucia are not to receive protection? But they are all heads."

The Americans tell me that they know what they are doing.

"But the President of Mali will be presiding over the Security Council Summit," I say.

The Americans say he has waived protection.

"That doesn't sound right," I say. "Why should he waive protection? And the President of Afghanistan – I've just noticed that he is not to receive protection either."

The Americans smile mysteriously and tell me that this is a political decision.

(What sort of political decision? Are they hoping that the guy will be bumped off?)

I look more closely and realise that it is President Rabbani, who Washington supports, and not the leader of the Taliban, who will be coming.

"But it's your man who is coming not the Taliban leader. Why don't you want to protect him?"

The Americans start to whisper among themselves.

I return to the Crown Princes and others who are to be unprotected and draw attention to the ire that will come the way not only of the UN but, more relevantly, to the US whose close allies all these people are.

Ambassador Betty King, leading for the US side, has had enough. I am questioning the competence of the superpower.

"We know who to protect. We know who our friends are," she tells me her voice rising.

I mention one of the royals again.

"We know all about these people," she says reaching a crescendo.

"We even know who is sleeping with whom."

Really? I think of the royal in question, a sweet old man in his late seventies, seemingly very frail now, but a bachelor. Gosh, you can never tell by appearances.

"Bravo to you, Your Highness!" I think admiringly. "Way to go. Way to go."

The Holy Men

The Religious Leaders Summit is underway. It was launched with the beating of traditional Taiko Japanese drums and a gospel rendition of "Amazing Grace" by Hope Campbell Owens of the United House of Prayer for all People. Fifty children from the Bochasanwasi Shri Akshar Purushottam Swaminarayan Sanstha welcomed the delegates with flower petals and a traditional Indian dance. Opening invocations were offered including "Blowing of the Conch," by Swami Bua, "An Inca Blessing" by Q'ero Elders from Peru and "Call to Prayer" by Sheikh Ahmed Tijani Ben Omar. Hindus, Muslims, Christians, Jews, Buddhists, Shintoists, Zoroastrians, Sikhs and Taoists, traditional African and Native American religions are all represented. Also present is a holy man in a full-feathered war bonnet whose religious affiliation is not immediately determinable.

The Honorary Chairman ("I am not much of a religious person, to tell the truth. I don't like 'isms'... 'Isms' have caused most of the problems in the world and I think religion is responsible") had a prominent part in the opening ceremonies. His entrance was greeted with thunderous applause. In his speech, Turner explained how he had once wanted to be a missionary but that he found his Christian sect "intolerant."

"It just confused the devil out of me because I said heaven is going to be a mighty empty place with nobody else there. So I was pretty confused and turned off by it. I said, 'It just can't be right...' We are all one race, and there is only one God who manifests himself in different ways... We're just one human race... we all came from Africa (cheers)... the bears in the North, the bears in the South are black... The religions that survive are the ones that build on love... technology ain't safe (you can't get Concorde out of Paris) (ecclesiastical giggles)... are nuclear missiles safe? Don't you believe it! (hysterical ecclesiastical giggles)... So maybe what we ought to do, what we have to do now is we have to work together."

The Honorary Chairman ("Christianity is a religion for losers") receives a standing ovation at the end.

I was right though to refer to the religious leaders as, "Bawa's boys." There is hardly a woman to be seen. Religion is pretty much a masculine preserve. Ah, if only that was all. There is a Muslim cleric who is walking around preceded by a phalanx of the faithful whose role is to remove any lusty members of the opposite sex from his path. Apparently, swarming women are waiting to ravish him. Then there is the Indian monk who we are told is a living saint. His eyes too cannot suffer the offence of a female. The UN is steadfastly opposed to this nonsense, or at least we are supposed to be. I begin to wonder what we will do if there is a clash between our principles and maintaining peace with these sensitive, holy men. I soon find out.

Those-whose-eyes-cannot-be-offended are seated in an area in the GA Hall designed to best avoid contamination. One day a female UN Security Officer is on duty in sight of the holy ones. She is immediately removed from the Hall. She is not the only casualty. A nurse who had been assigned to be ready to help if any of the holy-but-doddery ones fall ill somehow passes within sight of those-whose-eyes-cannot-be-offended. She too is dispatched immediately from the Hall.

A San Marino conundrum

The Ambassador of San Marino has discovered me. I have been hearing of his huffings and puffings for quite a while but have managed to lie low. Now he is sitting in my office, having demanded an immediate meeting, with his deputy in anxious attendance

"It is true we are not Sierra Leone," he says indignantly.

"Mr. Corell told me that when I spoke to him about our problem. He told me that the SG is busy with Sierra Leone."

I ooze empathy in return. I try to suggest by my posture and expression that as far as I am concerned, *he is* Sierra Leone. Meanwhile, I am trying to place San Marino on the map. I know that it is small. I know it is in Europe and joined the UN not so long ago but beyond that, I am stuck. San Marino?

"We are an ancient nation," he tells me. "Everyone in Europe knows about our situation. We never have this problem at European meetings."

Actually, just about everyone in the UN now knows about his problem, which is why I have been lying low. I want to be the only one not to know about his problem. He has approached the President's Office, and General Assembly Affairs, and Protocol, and the Legal Office and now he has washed up on my shore. A great deal of the time of a great many people have been devoted in this busy, tense pre-Summit week to dealing with the silly crisis he has created.

"Our constitution is quite clear. The Captain-Regents are co-equal heads of state."

Yes, it is true; San Marino is the only country in the world to have two heads of state. And both heads are coming to the Summit. So the Ambassador wants both heads to attend all events. Two Captains-Regents at the SG's lunch, two Captains-Regents in the group photo, two Captains-Regents speaking in the Summit debate...?

"I see. Do you want both of them to speak together?" I ask hopefully, suddenly perking up at the prospect.

Why didn't I get involved in this before, I chide myself? Maybe they can speak in unison? Or by paragraph? One reads a paragraph and goes back to his seat, the other reads a paragraph, she goes back, the other pops up... And at the SG's lunch, maybe one can have the first course, then leave, the other can come in for the second course, then they can switch...

No, he assures me they will not. Only one will speak. But they still need two seats for San Marino at all events. And so it is arranged.

San Marino is indeed an ancient nation, founded in AD 301 San Marino is 61 square kilometres in size. San Marino's population numbers 22,000. Yet, it has two heads of state, one more that every other country in the world, and it will now have one more seat than everyone else at the largest gathering of heads ever to be held.

San Marino?

The Religious Leaders Summit is almost over. The press has ignored the event, in spite of Bawa's predictions, happy in their ignorance of this, the more important summit. After it had been going on for three days, *The Times* managed to produce one article. (There was, of course, some coverage on CNN.)

This is galling to me. I expected the meeting to have loads of publicity because of, "The Mouth's" involvement. Where are the vaunted investigative journalists of the scandal sheets when you need them? Cursory research would have revealed his history of anti-religious pronouncements. I agonise over my options. An anonymous email to the *New York Post*? A quick phone call from a public call box to the *News*, handkerchief over mouth to muffle my voice? A collection of the internet articles slipped under the door of James Bone, the correspondent for Rupert Murdoch's ("I'll squish Rupert like a bug") London *Sunday Times*. What a pack of lazy idiots! ("Have you ever seen a Polish mine-detector?") Do they have to be spoon-fed? Damn, damn, damn.

The escape of Madeleine Albright

Tuesday, 5 September

10.30 a.m. – Madeleine Albright has escaped. She is rushing down the second floor corridor with Gianni Picco in despairing pursuit. A catastrophe is looming. Today is "Dialogue among Civilizations" day. A construct of President Khatami of Iran, the exercise is designed to launch panel discussions and other contacts with a view to fostering greater understanding and appreciation among representatives of various cultures and civilizations of each other's perspectives, values and strengths. The General Assembly has blessed the initiative and it has caught on to the extent of being the curtain-raiser for the Millennium Summit. The Director-General of UNESCO will be chairing a high-level meeting this morning, which the SG and some ten heads will attend.

I've arranged for the ten heads to gather in the Indonesian Lounge before the meeting and thereafter proceed together to the designated conference room. The SG will join them there. Now Albright has made an unexpected announcement that she plans to attend the high-level meeting. This is significant for it means that the Americans are sending serious smoke signals to Iran.

While the Iranians are not displeased to see the signals, they also do not want Albright to meet Khatami. This would be premature. They have asked us to make sure that she does not attend the pre-meeting gathering in the Indonesian Lounge. Consequently, Gianni Picco, the SG's Special Representative on the "Dialogue", [a confidant of Pérez de Cuéllar and author of the book "Man without a Gun" about secret missions to Lebanon to gain release of Western hostages during the worst days of the Lebanese civil war] has escorted her to the Security Council quiet room to await the meeting's commencement. Unfortunately for Gianni, nature calls and Madeleine has taken the opportunity to make a dash for the Indonesian Lounge.

Gianni tells me later that she reached her destination but he arrived in time to keep her away from Khatami.

"Two lives would have been lost," Gianni tells me dramatically. "The Iranians are eternally grateful to me for they said that two of them would have been executed if Albright had managed to meet Khatami."

Albright's precipitate intrusion could have seriously set back the delicate diplomatic two-step that the Iranians have been engaged in for the purpose of repairing relations with the US. For Khatami must be forever aware of the restrictive forces still in command of most levers of power in Iran who would delight in the sight of a picture of Albright greeting him.

A gulf appears

8.15 p.m. – Dinner at the SG's Residence. It is a Summit-eve affair to bring together the main actors in the coming attraction. The Presidents of Finland and Namibia, the Co-Chairs of the Summit are there. They chat amicably with each other having finally decided how to conduct the proceedings. (It is not a complicated decision since it was not a complicated problem. Finland will open the Summit and Namibia will close it. Bravo.) Also present are the Presidents of Algeria, Poland and Venezuela and the Prime Minister of Singapore, the Chairs of the Roundtables. The President of the GA is there too, as well as some lesser lights, like moi.

The Heads present agree rapidly that the main purpose of the Summit should be to strengthen the UN. But to what end? Poland refers to the need for a clear message to emanate from the Summit. Sam Nuoma, President of Namibia, feels that the Summit must conclude with a "clarion call to fight against poverty." Finland worries about lack of will: "When we go home, will we have the will?"

But the heart of the discussion is a subdued but determined struggle waged between the SG and three of the Third World leaders. The SG unwittingly initiates it with a reference to his report as providing the prescription for the manner in which the

UN should be strengthened and the direction in which it should proceed. Globalisation is now the main force in the world and should benefit all.

BOUTEFLIKA (Algeria): "Globalisation is an ocean in which many will drown... The UN is the only place where all countries have the right to speak without being scared or bombed..."

The SG talks about the importance of drawing in the private sector.

GOH CHOK TONG (Singapore): "The UN must be the protector to help the weak and the poor and to moderate the influence of big business..."

The SG talks about the critical role that civil society can play.

CHAVEZ (Venezuela): "We talk about strengthening the UN but for what? I have serious doubts about the capacity of the UN to put ideas into action... Our people will turn their backs on the UN unless it can make things compulsory..."

The SG talks about eliminating poverty, fighting AIDS and establishing democracy worldwide.

BOUTEFLIKA: "Democracy and human rights cannot be achieved overnight... The real problem for small countries is domination by the big powers..."

By the end of the evening it is clear that his UN is not the one the Third World leaders have in mind. Their UN is a place where the South can come for protection. Their UN remains the chief forum where the smaller countries can have some say in the running of the world. From what he has said, it is evident that this is not what he perceives the readjusted UN that he is seeking to fashion to be like. His UN would be a plac e where the pursuit of concord among all nations is the primary objective and where the interests of all nations, large and small, would be balanced. Respectful attention would be paid to Third World concerns but the voices of the powerful North would not fail to be heeded.

18
A MILLENNIUM SUCCESS

Man without a Gun – Another triumph for Kuwaiti diplomacy – Bill Clinton – Fidel Castro – Jacques Chirac – Kofi's achievement – Could this be love?

Man without a Gun

Wednesday, 6 September

The Summit has begun. And the US has sent more smoke signals to the Iranians. Clinton opened the Summit debate today as is customary – the US always speaks first as Host Country. Khatami was due to speak much later in the day. Then the US let it be known that Clinton wished to make a gesture by staying to listen to Khatami's address. So the Secretariat did a little juggling of the Speakers' List and set it up.

Gianni "Man Without a Gun" Picco carefully explained to me that he had orchestrated the dance.

"You know Miles," he says as we stand together in the corridor adjoining the GA Hall, "You just have to be ready for the breaks. You can spend months preparing an event [looking at me with more than a little disdain] but it is useless unless you are ready for the breaks. Picco," he concludes with satisfaction, "is always ready for the breaks."

Another triumph for Kuwaiti diplomacy

The Kuwaiti Ambassador is darting around a table in the Delegates' Lounge stalked by a suspicious Protocol Officer. He is checking every place card on the table where his Foreign Minister, Sheikh Sabah, is due to sit. He is moving really fast and it's hard for the Protocol Officer to keep up. He ought not to be in the room at all for this is the SG's lunch for the Heads and no lesser members of delegations are supposed to be here. Somehow he has slipped in. I'm standing watching by the side because I think I know what is coming. He is trying to make sure that Sabah is properly partnered at the lunch and, as it turns out, I am one of the partners. But sitting to my left is the still absent Sayyid Feisal, the head of the Omani delegation and uncle of the Sultan; he is clearly a more appropriate luncheon companion for the Sheikh. Abulhasan speeds up now. He is leaving the Protocol Officer in his wake. He pauses, looks around, quickly the hand descends... and the place cards are switched. Royalty will sit next to royalty.

Another triumph for Kuwaiti diplomacy.

The Summit's first session is drawing to a close. As I prepare to leave, I happen to glance up at the podium to see who is in the chair. Well, the Presidents of Finland and Namibia have left, and who presides in their place but Theo-Ben? One year's unrelenting diplomatic work has achieved its sinuous aim.

Bill Clinton

The Summit lunch is starting late. I'm concerned about this as we are in danger of upsetting the afternoon programme. The invariable practice at annual lunches like this (not quite like this: 150 heads of state and government have never sat down to dine together before but the SG does give a lunch at the beginning of every GA for the senior dignitaries who are in attendance) is that the SG comes in with the US head of state as the Host Country. It is a long-standing tradition with a clear institutional basis. But Bill is nowhere to be found. We sit down and wait for Bill. And wait and wait. I ask Nadia Younes [the Chief of Protocol] what is going on.

She shrugs. "He does this every year," she says with admirable calm.

The SG then walks in with Tony Blair. Tony Blair? If Clinton is not around then perhaps the President of the General Assembly, or the two Co-Chairs of the Millennium Summit, people with an identified institutional role at the UN. But why Tony Blair? There is no rational institutional explanation or justification for Tony Blair to be favoured above everyone else. What signal is this supposed to send? Must attachment be so obviously displayed?

Tony Blair? *Tony Blair!*

Eventually, having kept most of the leaders of the world waiting for some twenty minutes, Clinton turns up. Nadia escorts him. I overhear their conversation as he walks into the Lounge, swinging his hands and clapping them together.

"Gosh," he says, "They are all sitting down already. Nobody told me they were waiting."

I go over to explain something to the SG during the lunch. The SG introduces me to Clinton as, "one of the main organisers of the Summit."

Bill gives me the baby blues. He gives me sincerity, admiration, concern, gratitude all in one look.

"Thank you," he says to me. "Thank you. Thank you for your great work."

For him. I realise that he is thanking me for doing it for him.

Fidel Castro

The Summit lunch is over. There is a bit of milling around as the heads prepare to leave the room for the group photo. Many heads pass by Kofi's table where he stands to receive greetings and congratulations with Clinton at his side. Fidel Castro is in the line moving towards Kofi and Clinton. Fidel is obviously intent on greeting Bill. This would, to say the least, be historic. No US President from the time of Eisenhower has ever met Castro. What will Bill do? There is more than enough time for him to move away but he does not. Fidel approaches, they meet, shake hands and exchange a few words.

[This unprecedented event initially escaped the attention of the press. A few days after the Summit we were given instructions not to reveal the encounter to the media. Washington didn't want the story to get out and, naturally, we didn't want to discomfort the Americans. Eventually it leaked but was immediately denied by Joe Lockhart, the White House Spokesman. The White House then corrected itself and said that the President was cornered and was forced to be polite but no words were exchanged. Finally, the White House admitted words were exchanged but only pleasantries.]

Jacques Chirac

Jacques Chirac is walking towards the escalator to leave the building. He is accompanied by two aides and preceded by someone who is behaving as if his function is to secure and protect. It is a little crowded as some people prepare to leave while others arrive. Chirac's scout is waving his hands now, gesticulating for people to speed up so that the progress of his man is not impeded. Chirac leans forward, gently touches him on the shoulder and mutters a few words. The pace slows, the gesticulating stops.

I'm touched. I've seen the phalanxes preceding other heads, where you are in danger of being mown down. I'm very touched.

I am walking with Louise towards the General Assembly Hall when the Egyptian Ambassador intercepts us.

"Everything is going very well," he confides. "And (to Louise) you look very elegant. And Miles, he looks very efficient."

Louise (quick as a flash) "It's just as well it's not the other way around!"

This is the better side of Louise. She can't stand fluffery.

I'm sitting in on the first "Roundtable." This is something I dreamed up. It had seemed to me that, for the first time in UN history, we should get the heads to sit down and talk to each other instead of only giving set-piece speeches. So we had divided them into four groups of about forty each to discuss designated topics. Of course by the time the Roundtables were about to be launched, it was discovered that they were fortunate to have had the benefit of multiple paternity. Not to worry.

Iqbal pops in and sits next to me. He looks dazed.

"Not a hitch," he says wonderingly; "Not a hitch, Miles."

Friday, 8 September

The Summit is over. Louise hosts a celebratory drink in her boardroom. The SG is there and is cautiously congratulatory, as is his style. When I come in, Louise runs from the other end of the room, embraces me warmly, and showers me with compliments.

I swoon.

Kofi's achievement

Saturday, 9 September

The Summit has been a triumph for the United Nations and the SG in particular. He had pursued his Summit proposal resolutely over the last three years and has achieved an enormous success. He has been widely praised for his vision in convening the Summit, his Millennium Report, which formed the basis for the Summit outcome, the impeccable organisational arrangements and the innovation of the Roundtables.

"The Millennium Declaration", as the concluding document is called, is based on the Millennium Report. John and Louise did well to gauge what the traffic will bear – what set of propositions governments would be prepared to agree to. It is, in fact, a kind of synthesis document, which succinctly draws together the threads of common understandings that have emerged since the end of the cold war. Its enormous value is that it brings these themes together in one place.

Based on the Report the Heads reached agreement on how to proceed in the areas of: Values and Principles; Peace, Security and Disarmament; Development and Poverty Eradication; Protecting our Common Environment; Human Rights, Democracy and Good Governance; Protecting the Vulnerable; Meeting the Special Needs of Africa; and Strengthening the United Nations. The next step will be to find the means to achieve the lofty goals. But the authors have rightly assessed that they could go no further at this stage.

Nonetheless, the Millennium Declaration is a remarkable achievement. One hundred and fifty heads of state and government have met together and agreed to "free all men, women, and children from the abject and dehumanising conditions of extreme poverty". Louise, and especially John, deserve great credit for bringing us to this point.

Could this be love?

Wednesday, 13 September

Post-Summit assessment at a meeting of the Senior Management Group. The SG is lavished with encomiums. In turn, he thanks Louise, John and me. But Louise will have none of it. She talks about the "unsung hero" and is unsparing in her praise of me.

I swoon again. Could this be love?

PART FOUR:
LOST IN THE GLASS HOUSE

"Dulce it, and decorum, no doubt, for the
    country to fall, – to
Offer one's blood an oblation to Freedom, and
    die for the Cause;
      yet
Still, individual culture is also something, and
    no man
Finds quite distinct the assurance that he of all
    others is called on."

Amours de Voyage

Arthur Hugh Clough

19
A LUTA CONTINUA

The new blue helmets

Friday, 15 September

Richard Holbrooke has provided the US reaction to the Brahimi report. [The SG had set up a high-level Panel chaired by Lakhdar Brahimi, former Foreign Minister of Algeria, to look into the UN's peacekeeping operations. One of its major recommendations is for a substantial expansion in the amount of resources devoted to peacekeeping.] The Pro-Consul has let it be known that the US supports the thrust of the report while reserving the right to disagree with certain specific proposals. The "Pro-Consul's" conclusion?

"The UN is flawed but indispensable." Hmm.

Monday, 18 September

Senior staff meeting. We talk about Sierra Leone and a successor to General Jetley.

"What about putting the UN force under British command? That should be one of the options under consideration," Mortimer insists.

"Colonialism ended in the sixties," Lamin mutters sotto voce.

But did it?

The new blue helmets

Tuesday, 19 September

Bernard Miyet, the Undersecretary-General for Peacekeeping Operations, is leaving. It was announced some time ago and this is his last week in command. His successor is another Frenchman.

Miyet is briefing 38th Floor staff on his experiences as head of peacekeeping. His message is as clear as it is bleak. The Western media is the driving force in determining UN peacekeeping interventions. Such interventions will only work, however, if a permanent member of the Security Council offers support. (In reality he does not mean all the permanent members but those commonly referred to as the "P-3" – the US, the UK and France.) When they do so, it will be due to their strategic interests as with the British in Sierra Leone. NATO has nothing left to do. Consequently, when it is feasible, NATO will be utilised for peacekeeping purposes instead of the UN.

A UN peacekeeping operation needs "P-3" troops to enhance the likelihood of success. They have the training and equipment. Third World troops are often inadequately supplied and woefully short of transport. Still, it should not be forgotten that when the going got tough the Americans fled Somalia, the Belgiums ran from Rwanda and the Dutch stood by watching in Srebrenica. He was proud of the troops from Third World countries who had stuck it out in Sierra Leone.

Bernard Miyet is departing against the background of the UN's perceived inadequacies in conducting peacekeeping operations over the last three years. It looks as if he is to take the blame. I'd always liked him and am sorry that he is leaving.

Thursday, 21 September

The SG announces that India is to withdraw its troops from Sierra Leone. It will be a phased withdrawal and India has indicated that this does not signal the end of Indian involvement in UN peacekeeping activities. Jetley, the beleaguered commander, is to be relieved. India has also said that there is no connection between their troop withdrawal and his decision to relieve Jetley of command. He will come to New York to debrief the SG. India has told him of its concern, however, about having countries with strategic interests in Sierra Leone being involved in peacekeeping there. The SG concludes by mentioning that the US and the UK will be helping him with obtaining replacement troops. Nigeria is being mentioned. He will not have to do it alone though, as has previously been the case. He will be collaborating with Washington and London in regard to a crucial area of his authority.

Louise assures us quickly that Britain has no strategic interests in Sierra Leone. Mortimer tells the SG that the whole concept of strategic interests is wrong and outdated in this context. He will include a reference to this issue in a speech he is preparing for the SG to deliver on his forthcoming trip to Europe. All countries must be prepared to send their troops anywhere. (This view is in direct contrast to Miyet's who asserted without hesitation that Britain went to Sierra Leone for national, strategic reasons.)

Shashi points out that India's concern is that countries like Nigeria have special interests in Sierra Leone and Britain has a strategic interest. India was the only troop-contributing country there with no interests except restoring peace. Perhaps we needed to return to the era when countries with special or strategic interests were not invited to contribute troops.

"Haw!" says Louise.

The SG asks Shashi, "Are you speaking as a national, Shashi?" Then, sensing belatedly the severity of the cut he has inflicted, he seeks to salve the wound by recalling with appreciation India's contributions to the UN's peacekeeping activities.

I say quietly that having neighbouring countries, or countries with special or strategic interests, contributing troops creates difficulties for UN peacekeeping operations. I refer specifically to the P-3 (Washington, London, Paris) and contend that those troops and their commanders cannot be expected to have the right chain-of-command relationship to the SG. Their national interests will invariably supersede.

"Haw!" says Louise again, dangling her hand dismissively. (Happy days are here again. O, Cupid, Cupid, you fickle fiend: I think the elopement will have to be postponed.)

The SG informs me patiently that he does not necessarily disagree but that we have to proceed on a case-by-case basis. However, the key consideration has to be the capability of the troops particularly with regard to equipment and transport.

In the afternoon, I send Shashi an email. I entitle it, "Don Quixote." It reads:

"Well Shashi, my Pied Piper, now that we have lost on both development and peacekeeping, which quixotic battle shall we fight next?"

He replies: "Miles, *a luta continua*, as they used to say..."

"*A luta continua*," the slogan of the freedom-fighters in the Portuguese-occupied territories of Africa, later to become a revolutionary calling card for the idealistic, the restless, and the innocent.

Shashi is wrong. *A luta termina*.

I have become a fossil. I am Neanderthal Man.

20
MESSENGERS OF PEACE

A flock of celebrities – Not good, not good at all

A flock of celebrities

Monday, 23 October

We are holding a gathering today of the fifty or so UN Messengers of Peace and Goodwill Ambassadors. UNICEF launched the Goodwill Ambassadors arrangement in the fifties when Danny Kaye became the first one. Now UNICEF has a large number of Goodwill Ambassadors and the other UN agencies have joined the parade. The SG joined in too recently and has now appointed his own "Messengers of Peace."

This meeting is at Gillian's initiative.

UNICEF, UNDP, and the other UN agencies have a mixed and balanced group in terms of gender, region, and nationality. The SG's own Messengers number seven. All are from the North. Four are American. Three are European. Only one is a woman. We are not supposed to notice that all are from the North or that four are American or that only one is a woman. We are not supposed to notice that none are from the South. Alternatively, if we notice, we are not supposed to make anything of it. However, if all seven of his Messengers were from the South, or four were Arabs, or Africans, wouldn't it be noticed? Wouldn't people say that the SG is favouring Africans or Arabs? But we are not supposed to notice. So I don't.

The SG makes a speech. Then the Moderator, Riz Khan from CNN, our local TV network, takes over. He implores the members of the group not to make prepared statements. He mentions that the subject of the discussion will be "Celebrity advocacy in an age of cynicism." I look at the list of celebrities. I think Riz could run into a spot of bother with his topic.

Riz invites Peter Ustinov to start things off. Ustinov observes that the most important thing is respect. Then he launches into a series of anecdotes and jokes.

("I often had lunch with Dag Hammarskjöld. At lunch one day, he let me into a secret. He showed me a photograph of the famous occasion when Khrushchev banged his shoe on the table in the General Assembly. But you know what? He was wearing both his shoes in the picture. He must have gotten a shoe from some First Secretary. 'Ivanov. Your shoe.'") The audience smiles gamely.

Nadine Gordimer asks for the floor. She makes a prepared statement. A Japanese celebrity, whose name I can't quite catch, asks for the floor. He makes a prepared statement.

Seamus Heaney quotes from the catechism that he was taught in Sunday school.

A stunningly beautiful Somali woman speaks up. She is incomprehensible. Riz stands enraptured nearby and asks a number of unnecessary follow-up questions. She answers incomprehensibly.

Geri Halliwell, the lost Spice Girl, says that she doesn't claim to be the biggest intellect. (No Geri, no.) She sums up: "If you reach the poor, that's brilliant." I think Riz is running into a spot of bother with his topic.

I look for the SG to gauge his reaction but the SG is no fool: he has slipped away.

Muhammad Ali decides he wants to speak. But he cannot. He is shaking uncontrollably. A few sounds emit but it is a jumble of words.

"People are suffering... prostitution... God's law... people are suffering..." It is so sad. The audience greets his address with rapturous applause.

Susan Sarandon relates her experiences of visiting villages in Tanzania on behalf of UNICEF. She is intense but puzzled.

"How can you identify?" she asks. "What difference do you think you make?"

She relates that she had been bombarded with hostile questions from Tanzanian journalists at a press conference she held on her return from the bush. They did not seem to feel that her visit would make any difference, or that her involvement was anything more than temporary, frivolous and publicity seeking.

A Japanese woman called Tetsuko Kuroyanagi starts to speak. She is quite agitated and her voice grows louder and louder. When she concludes it is announced that the interpretation equipment wasn't working and she should speak again. She speaks again with equal intensity but louder and longer. Everyone has their earphones glued to their ears. We don't hear a word.

Geri Halliwell says, "We have to get marketing people in and re-hash it all." A little ripple runs through the audience.

Linda Gray says, "It must be heart through heart, not brain through heart, or statistics through heart." Another ripple runs through the audience, who are beginning to show strain.

There are other presentations. Danny Glover suggests that the problems we are dealing with are systemic and are the results of globalisation. Danny is a lone beacon of light. The representatives of the UN system explain why the celebrities should work closely with them. The NGOs explain why it is best that the celebrities work with them. Nobody really deals with the topic of "Celebrity advocacy in an age of cynicism", but the celebrities do spend a lot of time worrying about whether they are doing any good.

In fact, confused and disconnected as the discussion turns out to be, there is no doubt that these people do care and do want to do some good. How much good they do is arguable. Some of them help with fundraising. Some of these famous actresses may well be having an impact in their communities in drawing attention to the problems of poverty, disease and illiteracy. Ronaldo, the Brazilian footballer, surely has an impact among youth in Third World countries with his AIDS-awareness campaign – "Play Safe" is his slogan. But I think it is irrelevant to the lives of the Tanzanian villagers that Susan Sarandon came to call, or to the lives of the kids in another village in Africa that a famous violinist who they knew nothing about came to play an instrument they had never seen or heard before, or to the mothers in a run-down, ill-equipped hospital in Nicaragua that Linda Gray, of "Dallas" fame, dropped in. And I'm not too sure that the UN has thought through the implications of holding up some of these people to the world as role models through the stature we have conferred on them. "Fatal Attraction" Michael Douglas as a UN role model?

Gillian closes the meeting with a comforting conclusion: "The UN is imperfect but indispensable," she says.

Now where have I heard something similar before?

Not good, not good at all

Monday, 31 October

Senior staff meeting. The SG has been attending a retreat with the heads of UN organisations over the weekend. He reports that relations with the NGOs had featured prominently in the discussions. It would appear that Moore of the WTO and Wolfenson of the World Bank had been distressed at the depth of NGO opposition to the work of their institutions. They seem to be taking it personally.

The SG goes on to remark that the North was supportive of NGOs but that Third World governments were still very suspicious of them. Since most of these governments had now come to office through democratic means, they resented the criticism they were still receiving. I decide to plunge in.

"SG, Third World governments are also suspicious about NGOs for other reasons. We did a lot of work on reviewing lists of NGOs while preparing for the Millennium Assembly regional hearings. We discovered that some 75% of NGOs registered with the UN had their headquarters based in North America. And the North plays a funny game with NGOs. They say they are for them but only allow them to get involved at the UN with development, environmental and humanitarian matters. Let them play with the soft issues is the attitude. But they make sure that NGOs do not get involved with peace, security and disarmament issues. And there's another point. Heads and other officials from Third World capitals come up here for meetings and see the UN paying respectful attention to NGO representatives from their countries who they know have little or no political support there. So they ask: who do these people represent? Why is the UN listening to them?"

The SG looks at me but does not respond immediately. Shashi says, "I agree with Miles completely."

The SG regards me opaquely.

"Interesting," he says.

My spirits drop. I know him so well.

Not good. Not good at all.

21
FEARING FOR THE FUTURE

A Democratic redoubt – Waiting to see the SG

A Democratic redoubt

Thursday, 9 November

A Democratic redoubt has been discovered on the 38th Floor.

"Our fate hangs in the balance," Iqbal declaims.

"I hope Mr. Nader is feeling pleased with himself," Louise grumbles.

The US presidential elections has ended in uncertainty. It will take some time before a winner can be proclaimed. I discover that the resulting anguish of Gore is apparently also our anguish.

I'd always supposed that we were that way inclined, considering that it is a Democratic President and Secretary of State who had put Kofi in office. But this is a subject that we tiptoe around. Now, at this moment of uncertainty, the extent of our attachment, not just to Washington but particularly to Democratic Washington, is impossible to conceal.

"Shouldn't the Democrats be upset about the 50% of people who didn't vote rather than poor Mr. Nader's 2%?" I enquire. This is brushed aside.

I learn a lot from these exchanges. The senior staff in the Executive Office of the Secretary-General of the United Nations are discussing the American elections with fierce partisanship. It is somewhat indiscreet, especially at a formal meeting. But it is more than that. It is wrong.

Throughout the history of the United Nations, it has been an unfailing convention that the staff providing direct support to the Secretary-General should be international civil servants. The only exceptions have been for the very small handful of people, usually no more than two or three, who each Secretary-General has habitually brought in, usually from his own country, to be his personal, political confidantes. [Boutros brought in two Egyptians, Perez two Peruvians, Waldheim three Austrians.] Now, we are all being treated as political confidantes, not as non-political international civil servants, all presumed to want the same thing – a Democratic victory to enhance, if not ensure, the prospects of Kofi Annan's re-election at the end of next year.

"Thank God his statement was not picked up", Iqbal says with a sigh. It turns out that the Secretary-General, on another fruitless Cyprus negotiating quest, had extended congratulations to Bush on his victory upon arrival at Nicosia airport. What if the Gore people learn about this!

"Anyway," says Iqbal, "He did qualify his congratulations. He was careful."

We are all relieved.

Waiting to see the SG

Monday, 27 November

I'm waiting to see the SG. I haven't sought a meeting though. Elizabeth asked me last week if there needed to be a note-taker when I saw him, or whether it was to be a tête-à-tête. I'd told her carefully that I had not put in a request to see him. She seemed taken aback.

I'm waiting to see the SG to discuss my new appointment. I've received no sign, no signal as to what will happen next but I've not looked for any because I have not done the expected – I have not dropped hints with my colleagues, approached Fréchette, besieged Riza, taken Elizabeth to lunch, called on Shashi, complained to Lamin. I've not grumbled about the situation with my friends among the Ambassadors, I've not orchestrated lobbying efforts by them on my behalf. I've not approached other senior officials who have the SG's confidence to raise my "case" with him. No, I have not done any of this because I don't feel I should have to.

George Stephanopoulos recounts in his recently published book how close he was to Clinton and then the moment when something happened and it changed. He had gone too far in trying to influence the President on various policies, being one of the few liberal true believers left in high posts in the administration. And he had collaborated imprudently with Bob Woodward in a book about Clinton's first two years in office. He had also failed in his first assignment as Director of Communications and, to his enormous humiliation, had been replaced by David Gergen, a Republican who had served both Reagan and Bush.

Stephanopoulos could not stand to be omitted from the sort of policy meetings he had been accustomed to attending, could not stand not being in the know, and had embarked on a furious campaign of reinstatement. There was no favour he would not curry in order to achieve this.

He entitles the book "Ever so Human" and I suppose that title's purpose is to secure from the reader, in advance, forgiveness, or at least understanding, about the tale of myriad motives that he relates – a tale of arrogance and insecurity, good intentions and unscrupulous pandering, well-meaning mistakes and cowardly silences, a tale above all, about the licentiousness of power.

Being on the 38th Floor is to encounter daily that same licentiousness and to daily have to decide how to react to it.

I had never yearned to be on the Floor. I have enjoyed the exercise of authority when it came my way, have never avoided position, but the prospect of the 38th Floor has been something I have feared.

I have feared it because I was uncertain as to whether I had the combination of attributes that I thought essential to carry it off while retaining self-respect: confidence without cockiness, friendly without simper, eager but not pushy, firm but not stubborn, principled but not priggish. And I have been afraid of the effect of this proximity to power on me, not only in the well-known ways, but in the little things, in the words not spoken, the subservient gesture expected, the respectful look required, the requisite laughter at the apt moment, the careful cultivation of the inner circle. And so I set out, from my first day on the Floor, to thwart these courtier impulses, to be as natural as I could be, but I have not been good at this, and have not succeeded in effectively providing the measured, supportive, questioning that seemed so badly needed.

In the end, Stephanopoulos' efforts at reinstatement were rewarded and, by the end of Clinton's first term, he was back in favour. But something had been altered forever, some bond of mutual trust had been stretched too tightly, and so he left after the first four years amidst professions of everlasting affection and esteem.

Well, it's a tale to ponder over.

22
FA LA LA LA, LA LA LA LA

The irritating Third World – Does anyone know any Republicans? – Banquo's Ghost

———◦———

"Simba akujuwaye hakuli akakumaliza wote."
(The lion who knows you doesn't eat you all up.)

Old Swahili proverb

———◦———

The irritating Third World

Thursday, 30 November

The Secretary-General has been in a good mood recently.

At this morning's meeting, he is swathed in bonhomie. He mentions the situation in Indonesia where Wahid's influence appears to be waning. Megawati, Soekarno's daughter is the Vice-President and the one who would succeed if Wahid falls. He recalls a meeting with them both during a trip earlier in the year. He had tried to draw Megawati out but she had sat virtually silent throughout. He recounts a quip that Wahid, who is blind, had made.

"We make a good team", he had said. "I can't see and she can't speak."

But Louise is in a very bad mood.

"Algeria, India, Egypt, Libya and Syria are the ones causing all the problems", she complains.

These are familiar apparitions on the Floor, the ghosts of

Christmas past and of Christmas present. Now they have leapt out of the cauldron again, to cause confusion over the Brahimi proposals, one of which is for a substantial expansion in the amount of Secretariat resources devoted to peacekeeping. Developing countries have argued that in that case there should be a substantial increase in Secretariat resources devoted to development.

"They are the same ones causing trouble on human resources reform", we learn from her in reply to another enquiry from the Secretary-General.

"They don't realise things have changed. They still think governments control the UN", Ruggie says.

This is our standard now – hubris rampant on a white horse emblazoned against a field of blue. Ruggie reflects in this sentiment the objective the Floor has been working towards – lessening intergovernmental authority in the UN, particularly as exercised by the majority from the Third World, to the benefit of the authority of the SG, utilising outside actors such as the NGOs and the international business community as countervailing forces.

It is, for me, another sad discussion, replete with missed opportunities. No attempt is made to analyse why there is opposition to these preferred projects. Instead, the critics are dismissed as coming from the ideological loony-fringe, and a minority fringe at that, which should be silent. As for the Egyptians, not so easily dismissed as irretrievably loony, their motive is considered evident – revenge for the Boutros-Ghali humiliation. And so we content ourselves again with an equal mixture of virtuous self-justification and righteous indignation.

Does anyone know any Republicans?

Thursday, 14 December

"Does anyone know any Republicans?" asks Louise.

It turns out that we don't. George Bush has been declared the winner of the US election after a month or so of political and legal gymnastics. Louise is bewailing our fate.

"All our support systems, all our contacts are Democrats", she continues.

The Democratic redoubt on the 38th Floor is shaken. Gillian, Ted Sorensen's wife is silent. John Ruggie though, the other senior American Democrat on the Floor, has already arranged a new position for himself in the Kennedy School of Government at Harvard.

Iqbal clears his throat.

"The SG has asked for a meeting with Clinton", he announces. Louise eyes him with undisguised astonishment.

"I really think the next time the SG goes to Washington it should be to visit Bush, you know."

She is right and it is obvious. Iqbal smiles again, the man of the secrets, dying to reveal one but maintaining his discipline.

"Can't he see him after he gets to Chappaqua?" someone enquires. "It's nearby, actually."

"Well, maybe he can see him if Clinton is in New York in the next few weeks but we have put in the request and he will have to go to Washington if necessary." He chortles a little, hugging the mystery of this apparent imbecility to his bosom.

Then we fall silent as realisation dawns. The SG must be going to Washington to ask Clinton's blessing for his re-election bid and to urge him to recommend his candidacy to his successor.

But other realisations have begun to dawn, albeit a trifle tardily. Having discovered the Republican Party we have discovered too that there is a world outside of America and it is viewing us askance.

"We are too Washington and New York-oriented," Louise confides in us, by wonder of revelation.

This particular *coup de foudre* has perhaps been inspired by the disappointments she has suffered in recent weeks. Two major projects that she has been shepherding have run aground. Many aspects of the peacekeeping proposals have either been defeated or shelved. Meanwhile, the entire set of proposals for the human resources management reform that she was responsible for has been put aside by the General Assembly to be looked at again next year.

During the course of the discussion on these issues, the Secretariat has been supported by the North and especially by the United States. The opposition has come from the South and is too consistent and widespread to be dismissed any longer as the irrational spewing of the crazy states. Louise herself has, to her fury, been implicated as a result of the Canadians referring to the opposition at one point as "nitpickers". India, a leading nitpicker, had replied derisively to the Canadians by imputing Canadian support as stemming from the fact that the official in charge of this matter in the Secretariat was a fellow countrywoman.

We now have a complete reversal of the situation that once prevailed at the UN for decades where the South firmly supported the Secretariat. Despite having an African SG at its head, the Secretariat is viewed by the South as partial to the North and, particularly, to Washington. This should come as no surprise to us. Hitherto, however, we thought that we were fooling the innocent South or, even if they possessed the wit to work things out, it didn't matter since, as Ruggie likes to say, "They will fold".

Cosily positioned, the 38th Floor has failed to chart the trends.

Banquo's Ghost

Wednesday, 20 December

I go to see the SG to discuss my future. He walks around his desk to shake hands; he waves me to a chair.

He is in a very good mood. He looks sleek and elegant. He looks successful. He exudes holiday cheer.

"How are L and the 'Princess'?" he asks exuberantly, as I sit down in the chair in front of his desk. Oh, he is overdoing it, I think – bodeful, very bodeful.

Deck the halls with boughs of holly

"They are fine SG. How are you?"

He assays a bit of gloom.

"Actually, I've been fighting a cold since I got back. "Anyway," he continues, "I promised to see you but actually I haven't got much to tell you. I'd hoped for a post to follow-up the Millennium Summit but that didn't work out."

Fa la la, la la

He regards me reflectively.

"You did a good job with the Summit and with Reform. Pity the Turner thing didn't work out."

"Yes, SG; that was unfortunate."

"Has Louise spoken to you?"

Louise, Louise? Is my fate to be entrusted to Madame *C'est Fini?*

La la, la la

I deny it.

"I've asked Riza to look; Riza is looking."

First Madame *C'est Fini*, now the Chef. Am I to be outfitted for the role of Banquo's Ghost?

His smile grows warmer and wider. A delicate probe is coming.

"How long have you been in the UN now? Must be thirty years."

Not very delicate. Quite to the point in fact. Bloody hell, it's golden handshake time. Like the Cheshire Cat, I am beginning to disappear. Parry Miles, parry.

'Tis the season to be jolly

"No, SG, not that long."

We regard each other warily.

"I wonder if you can tell me what sort of options you are considering?"

He spreads his hands, which have been occupied with arranging and rearranging the leather in-and-out-trays on his clean desk.

"Well we haven't got to that stage."

"Then, if I may be so bold, I'd like to suggest..." (I name a department whose head has just left.)

The SG's face hardens. His eyes lose all their holiday cheer.

"It's true that we are looking for a new head. Let's see."

Fa la la, la la

The SG's smile returns, draped like a Christmas wreath.

"Well, all the best for the holiday season. And give my regards to L and the 'Princess'."

"The same to you, SG. All the best for the season."

La la, la la.

23
A HISTORIC TURNING POINT

The UN surrenders – The Pro-Consul's farewell –
Australia, looking after East Timor

———◦———

"I love the smell of napalm in the morning... It smells like victory."
Lieutenant-Colonel Bill Kilgore played by Robert Duvall

Apocalypse Now

Francis Ford Coppola

———◦———

The UN surrenders

Saturday, 23 December

The UN laid down its arms just before Christmas. It laid down its arms to Jesse Helms. Richard Holbrooke presided over the ceremony. It took place in the General Assembly. I did not attend.

The General Assembly agreed unanimously to lower the contribution of the United States to the regular budget of the Organisation from 25% to 22% and to the peacekeeping budget from 30% to 26%. The amounts involved are insignificant – about $34 million on the regular budget side and $100 million for peacekeeping – considering that it is currently being projected that the US federal budget surplus will be about $5 trillion over the next decade. The money is hardly the point. We are to be taught a lesson, shown who is boss, and reminded that at any moment, in disregard of national, or international public opinion, not to speak of international law and treaty obligations, the US government can do to the UN as it pleases and can punish us at will.

Each country's contribution to the UN budget is supposed to be based on one essential factor – capacity to pay. In essence, this is measured in relation to a country's share of the world's wealth of which the US share is currently around 29%. It will now pay 22% to the UN budget. Contributions to the peacekeeping budget are weighted to take account of the special responsibility, under the UN Charter, that Permanent Members of the Security Council have accepted for the maintenance of international peace and security. The US, which is the undisputed military giant in the world, with military power greater in proportion to the rest than at any time since the Second World War, has succeeded, at the moment of its martial pre-eminence, in having its share of the peacekeeping budget reduced.

Not only has the US succeeded in having its contributions reduced, it has succeeded unconditionally. No mention has been made by the General Assembly, in its articles of surrender, of the $1.3 billion in arrears that the US owes to the UN. The reduced US contributions have not been made conditional on eliminating the arrears; in fact, they have not been made conditional on any factors. The US can squeeze us any time it wishes and, as has been proved, once we are squeezed, we spurt.

(The French tried to have it agreed that the reduction should apply incrementally, one per cent a year over three years, subject to US repayment of the arrears, but the Pro-Consul said that would be an insult to the honour of the USA and that vapid effort went nowhere.)

The Pro-Consul has been in charge of the squeezing. As his imperial tenure draws to a close, he has surpassed himself. The following encounters have been reported.

Dismissively – to the Kuwaiti representative at a negotiating meeting, a middle-level diplomat, who protested and attempted to jump ship –

"I am not going to argue with you", he was admonished.

"I have made an agreement with your Ambassador. I am not going to argue with you."

Incredulously – to a Caribbean Ambassador who proposed that his country's contribution to the peacekeeping budget be reduced by 50% –

"We have to be serious here. What is your contribution now," rifling through a sheaf of papers.

"$11,000 to the regular budget, $4,000 to the peacekeeping budget. You want a 50% reduction on $4,000?"

Crushingly – to the Australian Ambassador who announced that her country would not agree to a reduction of the US contribution to 22% –

"What are you talking about? Your government has told me that they support the US position!"

It was, nonetheless, a difficult negotiation. Holbrooke had to bring to bear his full, persuasive armoury of cajolery, flattery, badgering, and bullying. If the matter had been left to the diplomats and ambassadors in New York, Holbrooke would have lost. The resentment against the substance of the demand was great and the Holbrooke style of persuasion did nothing to soften the concern. But the US spent as much time in capitals making their case as they did at the UN. And capitals, which are confronted daily with the political, economic, military and financial reality of American supremacy, are more susceptible to persuasion.

The issue that concerned UN ambassadors as much, or more, than the money was the demonstration effect. To give in would signal a collective weakness that they were reluctant to advertise. It would also damage them as human beings, damage them inside their pride. And they knew too about Helms, and not been seduced by his appearance in the Security Council.

In the end, the Pro-Consul's arguments were simple and the choices he presented were stark – do you really want to try and find out whether Jesse means what he says? Do you really think he will not act if we don't give him what he wants? Do you really want to risk the end of the UN? Do you think Jesse cares?

And so they gave in.

Wednesday, 10 January 2001

The papers report that the Pro-Consul has met with the US Senate Foreign Relations Committee to elaborate on his victory. It was a joyful occasion.

Jesse Helms said:

"Two weeks ago, Ambassador Holbrooke succeeded in cajoling, and maybe even a little browbeating, some of our friends at the United Nations into implementing several of the key reforms that lie at the heart of the so-called Helms-Biden legislation..."

"Through this debate, we have forced the United Nations to make much-needed reforms and we have protected the American taxpayer from unknown increases that might have happened and been contemplated by the United Nations and its supporters."

The Pro-Consul, commenting afterwards on the event, said:

"Today was really an amazing, unexpected day. This was a historic turning point."

He is right about that.

The Pro-Consul's farewell

Friday, 19 January

Emboldened by the fact and manner of his budget triumph (described by one Third World Ambassador as "brutal, absolutely brutal") the Pro-Consul is giving a new meaning to the term, "parting shots." (As a result of Bush's election he is being relieved of his post.) With him, it's parting bombs.

"The Non-aligned Movement is not Africa's friend at the moment," he volunteers at a farewell press conference.

"Africa is weakening its voice... by associating with a group that is dominated by non-African radicals, with one or two African members, which do not represent the interests of Africans and which weakens Africa's central agenda."

No head is safe from his whirling scythe. The General Assembly's decision to reduce the recommendations in the Brahimi report on peacekeeping is described as "appalling." The Department of Public Information is "a swollen mess." Member States oppose budget cuts, "because they are afraid that their friends or relatives are going to lose jobs." And, "we don't need 120 people in the (Dag Hammarskjöld) Library here in New York," and "we don't need 130 technologically outdated offices all over the world [the UN's network of Information Centres]."

Australia, looking after East Timor

May, 2002

The Age, Australia

Howard faces 'Theft' claims over Timor Sea

By Tom Hyland, Dili, with Jill Jolliffe.

May 20 2002

"Prime Minister John Howard has rejected suggestions that Australia has treated East Timor unfairly in negotiations over the carve-up of rich oil and gas reserves in the Timor Sea. Mr. Howard, who attended the fledgling nation's independence celebrations last night, declared that Australia's role in securing East Timor in 1999 was its most notable foreign policy achievement in recent years.

But at a news conference he was forced to defend Australia's tactics in negotiating the Timor Sea Treaty, which will be signed today in one of the first acts of the independent East Timorese Government.....

The treaty carves up shares to revenue from energy sources in the Timor Sea off north-western Australia. Under the deal, East Timor will get 90 per cent of the revenue from a joint development zone, with Australia getting 10 per cent.

Despite the apparently generous division, negotiations over the treaty have been marked by accusations that Australia has effectively denied East Timor the right to pursue claims to a greater share in the joint zone and elsewhere in the Timor Sea.

Oil and gas revenue is essential to the economic future of East Timor. The money will allow it to fund its budget without foreign aid by the middle of this decade....

UN officials and local politicians have accused Australia of taking advantage of East Timor's economic and strategic vulnerability in pressing for an early signing of the treaty.

It has also been criticised for its sudden announcement in March that it will no longer accept the jurisdiction of the International Court of Justice in maritime boundary disputes – cutting off East Timor's avenue of appeal following legal opinion that its entitlements are potentially far greater than those given under the treaty. Last month East Timor's Chief Minister, Mari Alkatiri, described the Australian decision as an "unfriendly act"....

Mr. Alkatiri will sign the treaty today, but said this did not resolve the issue of the final maritime boundary.

At a news conference last week, he said that once the new parliament had adopted a law on boundaries, it would seek to negotiate border agreements with Australia and Indonesia. He said the agreement on the shared zone in the Timor Sea was a "very temporary arrangement".

Any negotiations on a boundary, however, would take

years, while East Timor's economic needs are immediate. UN officials have warned the Dili government that there is a risk such negotiations could led to tensions between the countries, which East Timor cannot afford.

A senior UN official last week criticised Australia's negotiating tactics. 'We've been a little bit surprised Australia is playing such hard ball,' said the official, who asked not to be identified.

Adding to the controversy is an annex to the treaty covering the division of revenue from the Greater Sunrise gas field, straddling the eastern boundary of the joint development zone.

Australia had insisted on the agreement as a condition for finalising the treaty.

Under the annex, Greater Sunrise is deemed to lie 80 per cent in Australia's resource zone and 20 per cent in the joint zone. But East Timor's legal experts have advised that a permanent delimitation of the boundary could give East Timor most, if not all, of the field, likely to contain reserves worth tens of billions of dollars."

PART FIVE:
TURMOIL IN THE GLASS HOUSE

"So we cling to our rocks like limpets; Oceans
    may bluster,
Over and over and round us; we open our shells
    to imbibe our
Nourishment, close them again, and are safe,
    fulfilling the purpose
Nature intended – a wise one, of course, and a
    noble, we doubt not."

Amours de Voyage

Arthur Hugh Clough

———◄○►———

"Sea en got no back door."

West Indian proverb

———◄○►———

On the evening of Wednesday, 7 February, 2001, the Secretary-General of the United Nations took part in a discussion of "spiritual values" at the Marble Collegiate Church in Manhattan. The theme was "Morality and Diplomacy". He shared the stage, improbably, with Henry Kissinger, exemplar of a values-free approach to the conduct of foreign affairs.

We discussed it afterwards at our morning meeting, attended by the Secretary-General, and everyone was very happy. The SG had done a great job, he himself was happy that it had gone so well, but Henry had done a great job too, good old Henry, hurrah for Henry Kiss. Yet if all the blood from all the secret graveyards in Chile, and from all the fields and villages in Cambodia, Laos and Vietnam, if all that blood could well up in great spurts and settle in every room and corridor in our glass house, more than enough would still be left to spill out into the streets below.

This was no longer the Kofi I had thought I had known. That Kofi, I had come to realise, had really existed only in my own mind. I had assumed we were of like mind while in fact we'd only had some tastes in common, like cigars, and knew some of the same people. I had been arrogant in my expectations of him, for I'd expected him to think like me, and had been lazy in my perceptions, in my failure to grasp his political evolution, and in my sentimentalism about the past. Now, my attendance at staff meetings became sporadic; my journal entries dried up.

On the morning of Thursday, 22 March, Kofi Annan formally announced that he would seek a second term as Secretary-General. He announced it first in a cloistered gathering, at a meeting of our gang, and later to an unsurprised world at a press conference. He explained that he had been "encouraged" to do so, a reference to a recent announcement by African delegations urging him to run.

In making his announcement he appeared wary. He was no doubt uncomfortable because he was proceeding along the path that he most abhorred, the path of uncertainty, the path of possible ambush.

The re-election campaign was swift and efficient. He began with a number of enormous advantages. First, he had the backing of the Western three, especially, of course, of Washington and London. He had, after all, made himself acquainted with their needs. Next, he would have the backing of Africa, for although they might feel in their hearts that his was not with them, they would back him, as an African, against the rest. This characteristic lay deep in the African emotional consciousness, it was a solidarity of the skin which, while understandable in historical and racial terms, also led them to rally round even in defence of tyrants whom they should have rallied round to dispose of instead. Third, the world was used to him and he was undeniably competent and non-threatening. It took a lot for governments to change Secretaries-General, who, historically, stayed on, not least because the process of changing one meant bickering, and tedium and left wounds, as the Boutros battle had reminded.

Then there was his luck, which had held again. As it turned out we did not have to know many Republicans, we only needed to know two, and their names were Colin Powell, the new Secretary of State and Condoleezza Rice the National Security Adviser. Even without presuming a natural racial affinity, it would have been unthinkable for Powell and Rice, as African-Americans, to disavow him without damaging beyond repair their credentials as black people with the African-American community, as well as with men and women of colour everywhere.

The early announcement was meant to demonstrate supreme confidence and a sense of inevitability, thus intimidating any aspirants. Such aspirants could only come from Asia for there was a consensus that it was Asia's turn to provide the next Secretary-General. Here the key was China but China's tactic was, as always, to go along, never to expose itself internationally unless its vital interests were in play. China would not advance an Asian candidate, nor would it support one unless that candidate's election was assured. But there were no strong Asian candidates, and those that approached the Western three were told to bide their time. Through a combination of skill, timing, talent, and good luck, he was revealed to be unassailable.

On 29 June 2001 he was re-elected for a second term. A reception was held in his boardroom to celebrate. Champagne was drunk. I had waited until he was briefly unaccompanied and had then gone over.

"Many congratulations, SG, all the best. And good luck for the new term."

"Thank you, Miles. Thank you."

I had started to withdraw. He had called me back.

"Miles."

"Yes, SG?"

"Do you remember?" I was at a loss.

"SG?"

"Do you remember when you called and urged me to run?"

I had smiled and taken my leave. Yes, Kofi, I remember.

No Secretary-General in the history of the United Nations had been re-elected as early as this, half a year before his term was up. The pattern had been for the matter to go down to the wire with the fearing candidate having to wait into late December to learn the decision of his masters, the Member States. It was a historic triumph.

I, meanwhile, retreated. I had come to the 38th Floor in January 1997 with eagerness and enthusiasm. I accepted that we had to reassure Washington through sensible reforms in order to escape from the arrearages morass, and I had willingly contributed to that goal. In taking the lead role in steering his Reform Programme through the General Assembly I had found myself in alliance with

Annan's Western supporters and in opposition to my Third World friends. Ignoring the latters' barbs, I had been proud to be his arrow. Watching him close at hand during that year, I admired him without reservation.

The experience with Team Turner had sobered me but it had not affected my loyalty to and high regard for him. Rather, I was more inclined to consider that it was an exaggerated sense of propriety that had precipitated my departure. I had been happy to flee from Team Turner, and was grateful for the rescue net that Kofi had instantly provided. And it was no threadbare net but a silken one, organising the largest and most significant event the UN had ever staged.

During the following two years on the 38th Floor, my perspective slowly changed. It was not only that we responded first and best to the concerns of the West but that so many people in commanding positions on the Floor treated the Third World delegations as unreconstructed truants, and the Third World generally as a recalcitrant band that had to be force-fed.

Later that year I was appointed as the Deputy and Assistant Secretary-General in the Department of General Assembly Affairs and Conference Services. It was meant to be a soft landing, a job not thought to present many challenges, especially after the separate dramas of Reform, Turner and the Millennium Summit. The Department was responsible for running the meetings and conference apparatus of the United Nations worldwide. It had the largest budget in the Secretariat and the most staff. But it was considered a nuts-and-bolts job, without a policy dimension, and the Department was said to run itself.

Now, from a distance, I kept a less than vigilant eye on Kofi Annan. My sense was that he continued to gain in popularity and esteem, especially in the West. He was an African, a Third World man but without the brambles, without the resentments, without any lingering traces of cold war Third World rhetoric, or cold war, Third World thought; he was without Third World tics. But he had also gained in esteem in the South. He was now fully engaged in the myriad disruptions on the African continent, dispatching his Special Envoys on reconciliation efforts and organising UN peacekeeping operations. The UN held Special Sessions on HIV/AIDS and world conferences on Least Developed Countries, Ageing, Financing for Development, and, in reprise ten years after Rio, on Sustainable Development. (It also held a World Conference against Racism, Racial Discrimination, Xenophobia and Related Intolerance in Durban, South Africa, but this was not a success.) He took up the fight against HIV/AIDS with great zest, calling for a global campaign against the pandemic and proposing the establishment of a Global Fund to mobilise funds to battle it. East Timor attained independence after two years of stewardship by the United Nations and peace was restored in Sierra Leone, allowing for parliamentary and presidential elections. And at a session subsequent to the Millennium Summit, the General Assembly adopted a set of Millennium Development Goals, specific targets with dates established for reaching them, a signal and defining achievement.

As to whether his agenda continued to coincide with Washington's or, at least, to not veer in a contrary direction, I saw no sign of an assertive independence. I noticed, for example, that in his introduction to the annual report of the Secretary-General for the year 2001, he declared his priorities in phrases that had a familiar ring to them.

"Today universal ideas – the sovereignty of the people, accountability of leaders, individual rights and the rule of law – are spreading around the world. Yet there is no guarantee that these values will not be reversed, and that some nations will not once again succumb to tyranny and oppression."

It was not that there was anything inherently wrong with the sentiment. It was simply that in tone and emotional feeling, in the hierarchy of objectives expressed, in the emphasis placed on issues that the United Nations should address, it smacked of a paternity that was unmistakable. For support for the human right to development, elimination of nuclear weapons, democratisation of the United Nations through reform of the Security Council, and ensuring that globalisation did not become a unilateral encounter were not on his list of "today's universal ideas".

In any event the "universal ideas" were more aspirational, than universal, and were in fact the ones embraced by the West. While I myself largely held to them I did so in a broader context and it was hard not to be aware that they were being repelled, or at least disregarded, by a large portion of mankind. Moreover, at least one of those ideas, "the rule of law" had consistently been undermined throughout recent history and especially since the Second World War, by the same nations who so vociferously advocated it as they sought to retain, if not expand, their political, economic and military dominance.

But I was preoccupied with the responsibilities of my new position. Rather than belittling its lack of policy content, I found I welcomed its essentially technocratic nature and was determined to make something of it. Reform, I discovered, was still in my blood. For the next two years I took the lead in launching a thorough and vigorous reform programme, based on introducing widespread technological innovations, which in a short time, brought order to the UN meetings programme, and increased discipline to our documents production. The Department's budget, which had exceeded its limit by $34 million in the previous period, was kept under strict control.

The head of the Department (and my boss) was a Chinese diplomat, Chen Jian, whose last post had been Ambassador to Tokyo. The Department was the one designated for China. While being fully supportive of the reform programme I initiated, he was a holdover from another era. He represented one of the last (and the largest) totalitarian regimes in the world. He had been trained in the ways of that regime.

As a Chinese diplomat on loan from his government, Chen Jian saw the appointment and promotion of Chinese officials as one of his national responsibilities. Consequently, he intensified the Chinese employment programme begun by his conational predecessor. The SG's new staff selection system, that put virtually absolute power in the hands of the politically-appointed heads of departments, had, in the end, been passed by the General Assembly in virtually all its essentials and this facilitated the process. (Third World delegations had by then worked out that their heads of departments could bring in their people too.) Before very long, Chinese were appointed to senior and other posts in every part of the Department. I felt that, while some of these appointments were not without merit, many had been politically driven. I sought to temporise but ended up opposing his actions. I brought these developments to the attention of the 38th Floor; I could not confront China alone. But they chose not to intervene.

Chen's relations with me deteriorated. In the end, he did not want me to continue as his Deputy and I would not do so without a brake being put on his personnel actions. This the 38th. Floor was unprepared to do. I had just reached retirement age and, even though at my level that stipulation did not apply, it was clearly time for me to go.

"I'm sorry it had to end like this", Kofi Annan had said, with palpable emotion, getting up from his desk and coming around it to shake my hand at the conclusion of our final meeting. Quixotically, I found myself comforting him. "That's perfectly all right, Secretary-General", I had said. "We'll be fine".

Guyana against China: there could only be one outcome. For he had his multifaceted position to be mindful of while I only had my conscience to care for.

I had stretched the bonds of friendship to their limit. He had rescued me once before and was under no obligation to do so again. I had known the rules of the game and had chosen not to abide by them. And I had been a discordant voice for too long.

Immediately thereafter I took up the post of Senior Adviser on United Nations Reform to the incoming President of the General Assembly, the Foreign Minister of St Lucia, Julian Hunte. My responsibilities would encompass the area of continued efforts at renewal and reform of the United Nations' intergovernmental bodies, seen as more pressing following the marginalisation of the

Organisation on account of the Iraq disaster. I would also, once again, be in a position to be aware of the main activities occurring at the UN, to take part in some of them and to observe the flow of events. Hunte was a dynamic and ambitious man who was intent on employing the possibilities of his office to the benefit of the Organisation. He had gathered around him a staff made up of talented officials from across the Caribbean, thereby moving the presidency away from a nationalistic focus. I planned to do all I could to support him.

4 August 2003

24
DEATH IN BAGHDAD

Sergio de Mello – An inevitable involvement – A foot in the door – Working well with the victors

—◁○▷—

"...the hands of the sisters Death and Night incessantly softly wash again and ever again, this soiled world..."

Reconciliation

Walt Whitman

—◁○▷—

"We have entered the Third Millennium through a gate of fire."

Nobel Prize Acceptance Speech

Kofi Annan

—◁○▷—

Sergio de Mello

Tuesday, 19 August, 2003

A suicide bomber driving a cement truck destroyed the United Nations Headquarters in Baghdad today. Casualty numbers are unknown but people are dead. Sergio Vieria de Mello, the UN Special Representative there, is reported to be trapped in the rubble.

The UN Spokesman in Baghdad, Salim Lone, appears on TV and says, "Why did they do this to us? We only came here to help."

Friday, 22 August

Twenty-two UN staff have died in the bombing; a hundred more have been injured.

Sergio died. He hadn't wanted to go to Baghdad. He'd done East Timor and Kosovo, and was placed in a good spot as High Commissioner for Human Rights. He was a favourite of the Americans, and was being talked about as a future SG. They'd asked him to do it for them, and the SG had asked him to do it for him, but it was supposed to be a short-term assignment, and he was due to return in a few weeks.

Nadia Younes, his Chief of Staff died. Nadia hadn't wanted to go either but she was leaving her job at WHO and needed a transition post, and she'd worked in Kosovo as Chief of Staff to Kouchner, and the SG liked her. She was to take my old job, and she desperately wanted to come back, she knew how dangerous it was, and kept asking to be relieved. My old job was vacant since 1 August but she'd been told to grit it out a bit longer.

Rick Hooper died. An American, Special Assistant to the head of the Political Affairs Department, and an Arabist, he had gone in on a two-week temporary assignment. The media keep talking about him as the American who died, as if he had made a sacrifice for his country, but Rick Hooper was very UN, and was against the war.

Reham al Farah died. She had just arrived in Baghdad, also on a replacement post. She was waiting to get to Baghdad from Amman and there was no seat on the Monday plane for her but she had badgered the transportation officer and he had managed to squeeze her in and she had been blown up too. And many others died...

Benon Sevan didn't die. His office was on the second floor, immediately below Sergio's third floor office, and he had been holding a meeting in his office as that fearsome truck approached. They'd decided to move the meeting to the other end of the floor because, some say, Benon's office was too small, or maybe because the other office had a balcony where one could smoke cigars. So some five minutes before the blast they made their way down a corridor and they lived.

Salim Lone didn't die. He was supposed to be in the meeting taking place in Sergio's office when the bomb hit but he was working on a press release and it was Reham who had gone to Sergio's office to get the information for the press release.

An inevitable involvement

In September 2002, with the war drums already beating loud, President Bush had come to the UN to make his case. Taking the floor before him, Annan had spoken bravely from the depths of his UN convictions.

"I stand before you today as a multilateralist – by precedent, by principle, by Charter and by duty... Choosing to follow or reject the multilateral path must not be a simple matter of political convenience," he argued. "When states decide to use force to deal with broader threats to international security, there is no substitute for the unique legitimacy provided by the United Nations." He also called on Saddam Hussein to comply.

Kofi Annan did not speak out against the war although he did speak of the effects a war might have on the stability of the region and the great human suffering it would bring. Nonetheless, in a speech at William and Mary College on 8 February, 2003, his commentary on the approaching cataclysm was appropriately Annanesque. While warning that "war is always a human catastrophe," he argued that "the entire international community – first and foremost the leaders of Iraq themselves – have a duty to prevent this if we possibly can."

"But," he went on to say, "Our (UN) founders were not pacifists. They knew there would be times when force must be met by force... If Iraq fails to make use of this last chance and continues its defiance, the Council... must face up to its responsibilities."

His conclusions were clear. Iraq was in defiance of the international community. The responsibility for a war, if it came to that, primarily rested with Iraq's leaders. And wars were permissible and legitimate as long as the Security Council said so.

By the time the war arrived, he seemed unclear as to what options were available to the United Nations. He had not travelled to Baghdad to try to avert it as Pérez de Cuéllar had done in January 1991 before the first Iraq war or publicly asked both sides to show restraint as Perez had done in April 1982 before the Falklands/Malvinas war. He had not requested more time for his inspectors to do their work. He was regretful that the US and UK were acting outside the UN but he did not condemn their actions. He did not call the war unlawful only that Council sanction would have conferred greater legitimacy. He declined many opportunities to characterise a war without Security Council sanction as illegitimate although he commended "the unique legitimacy provided by the Security Council" and mused, from time to time, about whether the war was "in conformity with the Charter." (One reason for his forbearance from criticising the actions of the invaders was his own belief about Iraq's possession of weapons of mass destruction. Despite the finding of the IAEA that Iraq did not have a nuclear weapons programme, and the careful position of his own Chief Weapons Inspector Hans Blix, who refused to confirm that Iraq had biological and chemical weapons programmes only that Iraq had not yet satisfactorily accounted for their destruction, Annan could remark in Gourevich's New Yorker article, "They [the Iraqis] keep saying they have no weapons of mass destruction, which nobody believes.")

In a statement to the Security Council on 20 March 2003, the day the war began, he positioned himself.

"Today, despite the best efforts of the international community and the United Nations, war has come to Iraq for the third time in a quarter of a century. Perhaps if we had persevered a little longer, Iraq could yet have been disarmed peacefully, or – if not – the world could have taken action to solve this problem by a collective decision, endowing it with greater legitimacy, and therefore commanding wider support, than is now the case.

But let us not dwell on the divisions of the past. Let us confront the realities of the present, however harsh, and look for ways to forge stronger unity in the future."

A foot in the door

Kofi Annan preferred to wait for the war to reach its foreseen conclusion and to prepare himself, and the UN, to get into the post-war game. This could not be achieved by condemning the actions of the invaders. His contribution was to bide his time, anticipating that the UN would soon be needed by the victors to confer post facto benediction.

In this he was right. Once the bombardment had ceased, the victors had no choice but to come to the UN. Unpalatable as it was to the desk-bound combatants in Washington, the UN was needed for many reasons. It was needed to give them international recognition as occupiers under the Hague and Geneva conventions so that they could act in Iraq's name. It was needed to lift the sanctions imposed by the Security Council over a decade ago so that the economy of Iraq could be revived. It was needed to end the oil-for-food programme, which legitimised and controlled the sale of Iraq's oil so that the oil could be sold as thought best. And it was needed to provide international legitimacy and recognition to the paper Governing Council that the US had established and controlled.

Soon the Security Council gave the US what it wanted. Moreover, they accepted the US demand that they would be no restraint on the authority of the occupying powers. The schism that had led to the inability of the Council to either support the war or condemn it began to heal. There was little taste for a renewal of political battle on the part of those who had opposed the war and who were now anxious to restore their natural ties with Washington. In any event, there were hard facts to face. Iraq owed huge debts, billions of dollars, to the leading opponents of the war and the US now commanded the Iraqi treasury. Iraq had enormous economic potential and, with contracts and profits to be gained, it was time for realpolitik to reassert its hold. The indignant street protestors had, by now, exhausted themselves and the governments who earlier had dared not ignore those protests could return to the quiet making of shadowy deals.

Working well with the victors

Kofi Annan got what he wanted too; he got his foot in the door. The victors agreed to allow him to send a "Special Representative" to Baghdad but this person would have no role in the running of the country, or for that matter in its political and economic reconstruction. All that power and responsibility would rest undiluted with the victors. The Special Representative would coordinate the UN's humanitarian activities and peep from the sidelines at the unfolding political landscape. The Americans could shrug at the presence of the Special Representative. If he had ideas that were useful to the exercise of their authority they would take a look at them. Otherwise, he could be ignored. His presence did, however, provide another source of respectful acquiescence to their conquest. The opponents of the war did not mind the Special Representative either. Perhaps the poor fellow could establish good relations with the occupiers and play a mitigating role. But while the UN was needed in Iraq to carry on its humanitarian relief responsibilities, there was no need for a UN political presence in Iraq. There was no viable political role to be played. Worse, there was every likelihood that the UN would come to be seen as the handmaiden of the occupiers. The nature of the involvement was akin to an unsecured loan. The UN had lent its name and prestige but without a down payment of political collateral.

With the attacks on the occupying troops intensifying, Kofi Annan, on 25 June during a visit to London to consult with the junior victor, took part in a "press encounter".

Question: With regards to Iraq, was there any discussion [of sending UN troops in]?

SG: I don't think we discussed that and besides I'm not sure that UN troops are needed at the moment because you do have the coalition forces there, who are responsible for security on the ground... *But the UN is on the ground under the Security Council mandate to work with them and my representative, Sergio de Mello is working well with [Ambassador L. Paul] Bremer and [Ambassador John] Sawers* (emphasis added) and he has been around talking to Iraqi leaders and travelling in the regions... And of course it is absolutely essential that we assure a secure environment because without a secure environment, without containing the security crisis or problems, one cannot do all the wonderful things we want to do for Iraq, from reconstruction to the political process, which eventually will include elections and census and that sort of thing. So we need to continue the efforts to bring the security [back]..."

"Working well" with the victors. What signals did that send to the disaffected? Wasn't the UN supposed to be playing a neutral, broker's role? And the "wonderful things we want to do for Iraq" – that reveals much. George, Tony and Kofi would look after Iraq.

25

A LONG DAY IN WASHINGTON

Secosotus – Gary Cooper – Colin Powell

—◦—

"Juxtaposition is great, – but, you tell me, affinity greater."

Amours de Voyage

Arthur Hugh Clough

—◦—

Secosotus

Friday, 5 September

We're off today to see the Wizard, the wonderful Wizard of... Actually, of what...? He is, after all, Cole-in NOT Col-lin, Pow-well NOT Po-well, the Jamaican American, the fair-skinned black, the military diplomat, the diplomatist Supreme Commander, the Afro-American Republican, the General who is not running the Pentagon, the inevitable President who will not stand, the gentle charmer who promised "to cut off the Iraqi army, then to kill it."

He must also be SECOSOTUS, to Bush's POTUS. (Ah, SECOSOTUS, SECOSOTUS, SECOSOTUS – how the name trips off the tongue like the sound of a sucking plant.)

I ask our young State Department minder about this.

"So, he is SECOSOTUS, I guess."

"SECOSOTUS? "

"Yes, Bush is POTUS, isn't he – President of the United States, isn't that how he's called? And his wife is FLOTUS? So Cole-in must be SECOSOTUS – Secretary of State of the United States? "

"The President doesn't like POTUS."

"Really?"

"And in this building, the Secretary is 'S'."

"'S'?"

"Yes, and the Deputy Secretary is 'D'."

"'D'? I see."

I can't resist.

"And the Undersecretary for Political Affairs? He's got to be..."

"Yes, he's 'P'."

"'P'?"

"Yes, yes."

"Must be hard to go through life with people calling you 'P'."

Gary Cooper

This day in Washington is going to be a long one. It's at the invitation of the Americans but before we see "S" there will be lengthy prelude where we are to be prepped by assorted Assistant Secretaries of State.

The first is with the Assistant Secretary for African Affairs. We go to his office and wait around until Gary Cooper ambles in. Gary's operating incognito as one Walter Kansteiner, said to be a trader in African commodities before he left for Hollywood.

Gary seems mildly surprised to see us.

"Well, what do you see as your priorities?" he shrewdly asks Hunte, who answers institutional reform.

"Tough one, tough one," Gary replies, nodding sagely.

Gary remembers himself and gives us the pep talk. Liberia is now "in good shape", there is "good news out of the Sudan", the Congo "is moving in the right direction". All is well in Coop's world.

Hunte replies and talks about the Congo.

"Good. Great", says Gary.

Hunte talks about commodities.

"Good. Great", says Gary.

Hunte talks about the Human Rights Commission.

Gary yawns. He looks at his watch. Time's up.

"Thank you so much for stopping by. Wish you absolute best of luck."

We troop out. Gary shakes hands with Hunte then folds his as the rest of us file by.

"Go well," says Gary, "Go well."

— — ◄o► — —

Meeting with Assistant Secretary Roger Noriega, who is in charge of Western Hemisphere Affairs, which includes the Caribbean. Noriega is a protégé of Jesse Helms. He and Hunte spar genially but I'm distracted. We're meeting in the conference room of Noriega's bureau and there's a line of clocks against the wall showing the time in several countries of the hemisphere. There's a Washington clock, and a Mexico City clock, a Tijuana clock, a Buenos Aires clock, a Rio de Janeiro clock, an Ottawa clock, a Tokyo clock... Wait a minute – a Tokyo clock? I rub my eyes and look again. Yes, it's a Tokyo clock and it says 22:13. What's going on?

Noriega is chatting away but I can't keep my eyes off the Tokyo clock. 22:15, 22:20... Why a Tokyo clock? 22:22... Why a Tokyo clock in this room? Have I sussed out a covert op.?

— — ◄o► — —

Meeting with Elizabeth Jones, Bureau of European and Eurasian Affairs. Lizzie seems to be running most of the world – "my countries, my countries," she intones – and she's doing a damn good job too.

"All my countries are supporting us on Iraq."

France, Germany?

I nod off.

— — ◄o► — —

Lunch hosted by Kim Holmes, Assistant Secretary for International Organisation Affairs. This means the UN. Kim's our direct boss. He's just spent ten years at the Heritage Foundation.

It's a desultory conversation until the Heritage team brings up women. They seemed to have discovered them and want the Third World to do the same. They have also found out that women are being exploited. Everything depends on women, I gather. They are very intense about it. Well, there are quite a few women around the table but all of them have come with us from New York. Nary a State Department woman at this lunch. Still, the thought's the thing...

Colin Powell

Time to see "S". We are led, once more, down utilitarian-coloured corridors until, astonishingly, we step into a nineteenth-century world, a recreation of an antebellum America, huge chandeliers, damask sofas and colonial furniture, where "S" is waiting to greet us, serene amongst this disorienting splendour that his people had laboured unwillingly to sustain. They embrace; Hunte mutters something about intruding on his time.

"S" does his Caribbean bit.

"No mun; I was just sitting around lis'nin to some soca and caiso."

They spend some time on pleasantries and building bridges. For I've discovered that the St Lucians, all 160,000 of them, have been defying the Hyperpower. They have maintained their ties to Cuba, supported the Palestinians and attacked the WTO.

The crucial part for me is their discussion on UN reform. If Washington is inflexible on this, it will make our task much more difficult.

"S" is dismissive. He makes fun of the idea of Security Council reform, pointing out that the proposals he has seen envisage a Council numbering thirty or forty. His attitude is one of disinterest. But I don't sense opposition to the prospect. He simply doesn't take it seriously.

I'm impressed with "S". He is in command of his brief and

makes his points without evident threat. He must be a formidable negotiator.

He shakes hands warmly with each one of us as we leave. Good thing Gary's not around; I don't think he'd have approved.

26
TAKING A STAND

The Pro-Consul (Retired) redux – George W. Bush, Colin Powell and Condoleezza Rice – Terror and sex slaves

The Pro-Consul (Retired) redux

Thursday, 11 September

Taking part in a Council on Foreign Relations panel discussion on "The Future of the United Nations", the Pro-Consul (Retired) [Richard Holbrooke] demonstrates that he has lost neither his sense of timing, deftness of touch, nor sensitivity of tone. He has, moreover, his own vision of reform.

Thus:

> "We have 425 people in the peacekeeping division in New York. That is the UN's Pentagon. That's why they can't run anything in Afghanistan and Iraq... But there are 800 people in the Office of the Department of Public Information – a swollen monstrosity that should be blown up."

And:

> "The Non-Aligned Movement [comprising most Third World countries] should have been blown up a decade ago."

It is less than a month since the UN Headquarters in Baghdad was blown up. And he is speaking on the second anniversary of the destruction of the World Trade Centre.

George W. Bush, Colin Powell, and Condoleezza Rice

Tuesday, 23 September

9:15 a.m. – Meeting with Dubya just before he speaks to the General Assembly. It's being held in Hunte's small office behind the podium in the GA Hall. Dubya arrives with his people and a bevy of photographers. They all come in.

Cole-in, Condi, and Negroponte [US Permanent Representative to the UN] accompany Dubya. Andy Card, who must be the second or, at worst, the third most politically powerful man in the world, comes in as well. He's tardy, is Andy; Cole-in, Condi and Negroponte have slipped into the available chairs and are making sure they don't catch Andy's eye. Andy, who must be adept at this game in the White House, is demonstrably unskilled at UN presidential musical chairs. Outflanked, he retreats.

Cole-in assumes a genial pose. Condi's ready to assume poses on demand. Negroponte's got on a doomsday face, as if a chasm is about to open at his feet and suck him down below.

The photographers are calling for a handshake.

Dubya does his twitching trick that we've all come to know from TV; his shoulders shudder and his heads rolls about.

"I'll shake if he shakes," he promises.

Hunte tells Dubya he is looking forward to his statement; what the US says is important.

Dubya starts to twitch again.

"I'll tell you what I'm going to say when the press gets out of here." The press, taking the hint, withdraws.

Dubya tells Hunte that the US and St Lucia have had disagreements in the past, "but it is time to move forward". As for his speech, "The war on terror continues; I expect civilised nations to be tough on terror."

Then, without as much as a paragraph, a full stop, or even a comma, we are into, "sex slaves... women in bondage... thousands of women enslaved." I don't know what's going on; how did we get here; is it all part of the anti-terrorism terrorism agenda?

Without a break we go back to terror. It's a relief after the sex slaves.

"You will be held accountable when caught."

He looks straight at me. I am ready to confess and throw myself on his mercy there and then. This is one tough fella.

The twitcher returns.

"I love coming here to give speeches. I'm just a simple country boy from Texas showing up to do my job. "

(*Smile from Condi.*)

I'm beginning to catch on to the routine now. It's good cop, bad cop, all in one package. But what is disconcerting is the sudden change, without preliminaries, without preparation.

"We'll pay our bills." Now where did that one come from?

Hunte says we have to get back to the stage where US leadership is seen to be important for the UN and that has begun to happen.

(I'm realising that Dubya is nervous. The fingers of one hand drum, then the fingers of the other. I imagine he is not sure what sort of reception he will get when he speaks.)

Dubya's visage suddenly hardens.

"Some people think we took too strong a role last year. I love my country so much. I believe in freedom and human dignity. I will lead. Americans may not agree. If so, they will find someone else."

Drum, drum, drum. Left hand.

"I love freedom. When people are brutalised and raped, America will lead." (In which direction, I ponder; is he for or against?)

There's no twitching now. The Commander-in-Chief is laying down the law. And Condi's looking grim.

"When I say something I mean it."

Drum, drum, drum. Right hand.

Now it's our turn.

"Most Americans don't believe the UN is effective. The UN must show results to change that."

The face softens a bit. (*Condi smiles, but not a lot.*)

"Anyway, what else is on your mind? Here is your chance to tell us what to do."

Hunte launches an argument for reform and US backing for the process. He tells Dubya that it is obvious that "people regard this session as important. I hope that heads will come with proposals to show how relevant they think the UN is." Hunte goes on to appeal for flexibility on everyone's part.

Dubya, like Cole-in in Washington, is dismissive and unpersuaded.

"I won't be speaking about it in my speech. Powell and Negroponte will work the corridors on it though."

Hunte presses harder.

"A lot will depend on the resolve we show."

But Dubya has lost interest. He looks at one of our number. He starts to twitch.

"So your name is Missouri. Where did that come from?"

"I was born there and my father named me after the state."

Now Cole-in starts the twitching thing; a *bon mot* is at hand. Condi's twitching a tad too; only Negroponte retains his doomsday face. Here it comes.

"Good thing you weren't born in New Jersey!"

And then they are gone.

This is a man without guile who believes what he says. But after he does the tough guy bit, it's as if he has embarrassed himself and feels the need to become the joker. But the switch is so abrupt, from top cop to kid, that it leaves you bemused.

I still have the urge to confess but they've moved too fast for me. I won't run after them though. Condi might have me shot.

Terror and sex slaves

10:30 a.m. – Dubya's making his GA speech. I'm sitting in the well of the hall, among the Samoans, because there is no room by the side where we are supposed to sit. Opening day at the UN is a scramble. Anyway, it's time for George W. to offer his vision.

It's all terror and Iraq and Afghanistan and WMD; he lectures everyone on their duty which is simple – follow the US of A. Then the sudden segue into the "sex slaves" that he did in our meeting earlier before terrorising us again. The delegates can't follow this just as we couldn't earlier. He receives a cool reception. And that is pretty much it. So now we know what the international agenda is – terror and sex slaves.

Miles Stoby

Miles Stoby at a meeting at the United Nations

Secretary General Butros Butros-Ghali, Miles Stoby and Undersecretary General Rafeeuddin Ahmed

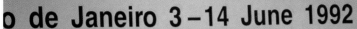

From right to left – Miles Stoby, President of Brazil, Fernando Affonso Collor de Mello, Butros Ghali, Secretary General, Maurice Strong, Nitin Desai

Foreign Minister Brandon Taitt, Ambassador Chris Hackett, Sir James Tudor and Miles Stoby, 1994

Miles Stoby with Prime Minister of Barbados Sir Erskine Sandiford, 1994, Bridgetown, Barbados

Miles Stoby and his wife Ambassador Lyutha Almughairy greeted by Prime Minister of Barbados Sir Erskine Sandiford and his wife at their residence, 1994, Bridgetown, Barbados

The Lloyd Erskine Sandiford Centre constructed for the occasion of the Global Conference on the Sustainable Development of Small Island Developing States, 1994, Bridgetown, Barbados

Fidel Castro among other heads of States who addressed delegates at the Global Conference for Sustainable Development of Small Island Developing States, 1994, Bridgetown, Barbados

Miles Stoby in the delegates lounge, United Nations, New York

Miles Stoby addressing the press

Miles Stoby, Secretary- General Kofi Annan, and his daughter Aisha Stoby at an event at the United Nations (this event is mentioned in the book in one of the early passages)

To Miles,
Many thanks for your contribution. *[signed]* Oct '97

United Nations Cabinet Meeting led by Secretary-General Kofi Annan

Miles Stoby presenting his credentials as Permanent Representative and Ambassador to Cari-Com to Secretary General Kofi Annan, 2005

27
A FORK IN THE ROAD

Cri de coeur – Australia, still looking after East Timor –
Why have the Arabs turned against us? –
It's happening in all the Departments

———◦———

"ANTI-BULLET CHARM FAILS. A traditional healer was shot in the head and killed by a client who was testing the potency of an anti-bullet charm the healer had prepared for him, the police in Central Benus State, Nigeria, said. To confirm its efficiency the healer tied the charm around his neck and insisted that the client fire a gun at him, a police spokesman said, adding, 'The experiment proved fatal'."

(Agence France-Presse)

———◦———

Cri de coeur

Friday, 3 October

The annual two weeks of General Debate at the United Nations is over. It has been dominated not by terror and sex slaves but by Kofi Annan's *cri de coeur,* delivered on the 23 September to open the Debate.

"Article 51 of the Charter prescribes that all States, if attacked, retain the inherent right of self-defence. But until now it has been understood that when States go beyond that, and decide to use force to deal with broader threats to international peace and security, they need the unique legitimacy provided by the United Nations.

Now, some say this understanding is no longer tenable, since an 'armed attack' with weapons of mass destruction could be launched at any time, without warning, or by a clandestine group. Rather than wait for that to happen, they argue, States have the right and obligation to use force pre-emptively, even on the territory of other States, and even while weapons systems that might be used to attack them are still being developed... My concern is that, if it were to be adopted, it could set precedents that resulted in a proliferation of the unilateral and lawless use of force, with or without justification...

... We have come to a fork in the road. This may be a moment no less decisive than 1945 itself, when the United Nations was founded. For my part, I intend to establish a High-Level Panel of eminent personalities... The Panel will focus primarily on threats to peace and security. But it will also need to examine other global challenges, in so far as these may influence or connect with those threats..."

Sitting amongst the delegates and feeling their hushed but admiring response, I feel a resurgence of my decades-long pride in him. Here was the man that I had known: admirable in his dignity of address, elegant in presentation, lucid in exposition, firm of purpose. Despite the diplomatic balance of his words, the message comes through; he has rebuked the American administration on behalf of the international community.

Friday, 10 October

Word's out that Coops resigned. I'm not surprised; he was having trouble with his lines the day we met him. "Good. Great," and "Go well. Go well," did not achieve the laconic sincerity he'd managed in "High Noon." He'll go West now, back to California and the Hollywood hills, back to the ranch and the thoroughbred stallions. I hope he finds a good new part soon.

Australia, still looking after East Timor

Tuesday, 14 October

"Anger in East Timor as Australia plays tough over gas reserves"

by

Jonathan Steele

The Guardian

October 14, 2003

Australia, which led an international peace force to help East Timor become independent last year, has become the greatest barrier to the country's hopes of breaking free from reliance on foreign aid, according to stark budget figures released yesterday.

Despite starting out as one of the world's poorest and most war-torn states, East Timor stands to benefit from huge gas reserves which lie under the sea that separates it from Australia. But harsh Australian negotiating tactics over disputed claims to the gas have forced the government to accept that long-promised revenues will not materialise for several more years, if ever...

News of the revenue shortfall came as Xanana Gusmão, East Timor's president, started an official visit to Britain. "We're not asking too much from Australia. What belongs to us is ours. We hope Australia can understand that," he told the *Guardian* in London.

Mr. Gusmão has been dubbed Asia's Nelson Mandela because of his long years in prison as leader of the armed struggle against Indonesian occupation, and more recently as a champion of post-conflict reconciliation. But he could not conceal his anger at Australia's behaviour. "They still haven't agreed when to start maritime border negotiations," he said.

The huge reserves of gas in question are known as the Greater Sunrise field. Although they are closer to East Timor than Australia, they were "awarded" to Australia under a treaty with General Suharto in 1989. Economic factors were a key incentive in making Australia one of the first countries to recognise Indonesia's illegal invasion of East Timor after the territory declared independence from Portuguese colonial rule in 1975.....

The Timorese government, with the backing of the UN, announced last year that it wanted to renegotiate the boundary line. Under normal international practice it would be fixed as the halfway mark, putting all of Greater Sunrise inside East Timor's waters.

Australia first announced it would not accept any decisions by independent arbitrators such as the International Court of Justice, thus leaving East Timor at the mercy of bilateral negotiations with its giant neighbour. Then it persuaded cash-strapped East Timor last year to agree that 20% of Greater Sunrise was part of a "joint production area", giving Australia a right to a share. Now Australia is declining to set a timetable for completing negotiations on the remaining 80%. By delaying production, the apparent aim is to press East Timor to soften its claim.

"We don't have to exploit the resources. They can stay there for twenty, forty, fifty years. We are very tough. We will not care if you give information to the media. Let me give you a tutorial in politics – not a chance," Alexander Downer, Australia's abrasive Foreign Minister, recently told East Timor's Prime Minister, Mari Alkatiri, according to a leaked transcript..."

Why have the Arabs turned against us?

Wednesday, 15 October

Today's main cartoon in the major newspaper in the occupied Palestinian territory newspaper, "Al-Quds" depicts the UN Secretariat building as a bloc in the separation wall being built by Israel. This comes after some two weeks of the regular spilling of blood in the region. The SG's Spokesperson has been reacting to the developments in his name.

4 October

"The Secretary-General *strongly condemns* the horrific suicide bombing that killed at least eighteen people in Haifa, Israel, today."

5 October

"The Secretary-General *strongly deplores* the Israeli air strike on Syrian territory today."

9 October

"The Secretary-General *strongly condemns* both today's suicide bombing at a police station in Sadr City, Baghdad, and the killing of Mr. Jose Antonio Bernal, a Spanish diplomat."

10 October

"The Secretary-General *deplores* the killing of Palestinian civilians during the Israeli incursion into Rafah in the Gaza Strip. Two children were among those killed when the IDF fired a missile into a crowded area."

15 October

"The Secretary-General *strongly condemns* the deadly attack on a United States diplomatic convoy in Gaza today. He views with alarm this apparently deliberate attack on diplomats."

On 3 June 2003 the Pew Research Centre for the People and the Press released its latest survey as part of the Pew Global Attitudes Project, conducted in twenty Middle East countries and the Palestinian Authority.

The new survey "shows... that public confidence in the United Nations is a major victim of the conflict in Iraq. Positive ratings for the world body have tumbled in nearly every country for which benchmark measures are available."

When he took office, the Secretary-General was determined to move the United Nations back into the Middle East negotiation. He and his people felt that they must, as a prerequisite, increase Israeli, and Jewish American, confidence in the UN. In those quarters, the conviction prevailed that the UN was an agent of the PLO. First, he had made clear his view that Israel, which was not a member of any regional group at the UN (since the Asian Group was the place it should be lodged but the Asians refused to accept that), should be allowed to belong to some group or other. Next he had gone out of his way to meet with Jewish groups in New York to show that the UN was without horns. During his visit to Stockholm to receive his Nobel, he had met with a Jewish group seeking the return of missing Israeli soldiers, resulting in that meeting being prominently featured in the documentary film made of the occasion and shown around the world.

In late August of this year, just after the Baghdad bombing, the UN brought together the heads of the UN public information offices in the Arab world, along with a number of Arab journalists, to discuss the UN's image in the region. I learnt that the comments made had been brutal: in essence the UN was considered to be a stooge of the Americans and the Americans were considered to be an ally of Israel and the enemy of the Arabs. This had been reported to the SG who had come himself, at the end, to meet with the group. Though delivered with more restraint, the same perspectives had been made available to him. The UN was no longer liked or trusted in the Arab world. The meeting concluded, however, that the fault was with the messengers not the message; the information people had to do a better job.

In a featured interview in the September issue of *UN Chronicle*, Salim Lone had this to say:

"Ours was the first civilian plane to land in Baghdad at the newly reopened airport... You know, just two days earlier, two staff in UN cars had been targeted and killed, and another one with the ICRC. Two were badly wounded. So it became clear that the UN was being targeted...

As the Director of Communications for Sergio, I had called a meeting of the other information officers of UN agencies. They had talked to as many Iraqis and Arabs as they could to get a feeling for what the situation was, and I discovered right away that for most ordinary Iraqis the UN and the Coalition Provisional Authority (CPA) were seen as one. They didn't distinguish between the two. It is not that they hated the UN: they were saying the UN should be helping them, that it should not be working with the Coalition... We thought if we could convince the ordinary Iraqis of the UN commitment to Iraq, this would deter the extremists who were targeting the UN and other innocent civilians. In hindsight, I can say that we were grasping at straws. ... It was a difficult role for the UN and, you know, what the UN was being asked to do in this phase was not easy to implement... because the UN could not point beyond the Iraqi Governing Council to concrete events and steps that showed that military control was going to end soon, that jobs and security and services were being restored. The other problem was that most UN staff, feeling the tension in the city and the resentments of even ordinary Iraqis, leave alone the extremist threats, felt that there were too many international professionals in Baghdad. They were really worried that there would be a big attack."

The resentment with which the UN was generally viewed in the Arab world, and in Iraq in particular, was thus no secret to the policy makers in the Secretariat. Yet when Israeli Jews were killed in Haifa on 4 October, the Spokesman of the Secretary-General of the United Nations *"strongly condemns"* it, while merely *"deploring"* the killing of Palestinian Arabs in Rafah, including children, a few days later (10 October). The denunciation, such as it was, did not even rise to the level of "strongly" deplores.

Five days on, the Spokesman *"strongly condemns* the deadly attack on a United States diplomatic convoy in Gaza... and views with alarm this apparently deliberate attack on diplomats." One would have liked him to have "viewed with alarm" the attack on Palestinian children.

The Spokesman is more forthright about the Israeli breach of Syrian airspace on 5 October and the bombing of a sovereign state. He *"strongly deplores"* it. The Syrians announce no casualties but they still prosper more than the Palestinian children; Syria is favoured with a "strongly." The Israeli action is against everything the Charter stands for, everything that the UN is pledged to uphold; sovereignty is violated and unprovoked military action taken but, nevertheless, the incursion fails to rate a condemnation. So the internal security circumstances within the states of Israel and occupied Iraq call forth swift condemnation, but the breach of international law, and the killing of Arab children, inspire nothing more than the wringing of hands.

"Why have the Arabs turned against us?" they ask on the 38th Floor. Why indeed!

It's happening in all the Departments

Friday, 31 October

While walking on the first basement floor, where the meeting rooms are, I bump into Wagaye Assebe, an old and dear friend and a close confidante of Kofi Annan, who works as his Personal Assistant in his Executive Office.

We embrace.

"I'm sorry things didn't work out," she says.

I freeze. Don't do this to her, I think. She is a lovely person.

"What was going on was a complete scandal," I say. "Chinese were being appointed to posts all over the Department without regard to due process. It was a disgrace."

She opens her hands wide and shrugs her shoulders.

"What's the difference," she says. "It's happening in all the Departments. But you can be proud that you stood up for your principles."

We re-engage and chat about our children before we part.

"It's happening in all the Departments."

Where are the eagles and the trumpets?
Buried beneath some snow-deep Alps.

28
APPOINTMENT IN SAMARRA

Lethal miscalculations – The elusive buck –
A chat with Louise

———<o>———

"Help him. Help him.
Help *who?*
Help the bombadier.
I'm the bombadier; I'm all right.
Then help *him*, help *him.*"

Catch 22

Joseph Heller

———<o>———

Lethal miscalculations

Monday, 10 November

The United Nations and its associated humanitarian organisations – UNICEF and the like – had not been frog-marched into Iraq. From early in the year, the SG had ordered that a contingency planning mechanism be put in place under Louise. Contact was established with Washington and plans were drawn up for the UN's own, unwitting "appointment in Samarra." The SG himself had personally lobbied for post-war UN involvement. In March and April he had asked to meet with all the regional groups of States and had advocated, and requested, support for such involvement.

The humanitarian organisations did not resist. They were in the forefront of the stampede. Like religious institutions, humanitarian organisations are driven by entwined motivations. There is, supremely, the demand of conscience, which commands people with a calling who wish to do good works. But there is the equal need, as with the religious proselytisers, to satisfy the bureaucratic motivation, to do, and to be there.

If you were a UNICEF or one of the NGOs – Doctors without Borders etc – a humanitarian crisis, like the one anticipated in post-war Iraq, held a compelling attraction. It was what they did, after all. Someone was certainly going to do it, and the humanitarian world is not without competitive instincts. The humanitarian agencies have to keep proving themselves to their donors, and that cannot be done from the sidelines. And the truth was that Iraq seemed set to be a humanitarian bonanza.

The Secretary-General's determination to be in the political game in Iraq (and the Middle East generally) meshed nicely with his humanitarian lieutenants' determination to be in the relief and reconstruction game. The rush into Iraq thus began. The consequences are described pitilessly in the "Report of the Independent Panel on the Safety and Security of UN personnel in Iraq", issued on 22 October, that Kofi Annan had felt obliged to establish in response to internal staff disorder and media stories about inadequate UN security precautions.

The report points out that, "There is no record of a security assessment prior to the return of the UN staff to Baghdad." Moreover, the Steering Group on Iraq, made up of the heads of the Departments and operational agencies involved and chaired by Fréchette, did not discuss the security implications and requirements of the decision. The staff returned to a security environment that the Coalition Provisional Authority itself described as "hostile," meaning that humanitarian assistance organisations should not enter.

Nonetheless, on 1 May the UN Humanitarian Coordinator and twenty-one international staff returned to Baghdad from Amman. Thereafter, the floodgates opened. De Mello and his staff arrived on 2 June and, by the time of the attack, there were some 600 UN personnel in Baghdad, despite the fact that a decision had been taken by the UN security team in Baghdad that a ceiling of 200 staff should be established. But, as the report points out, there was "constant pressure from agencies... to provide clearances to non-essential staff, particularly after the arrival of [De Mello and his team]."

The report describes a rapidly deteriorating security situation from June onwards. Not only were the occupation forces under escalating attack, but there were also fifteen incidents that affected the operations of the UN, including grenade attacks on the WFP office in Mosul, and gunfire directed at the UNDP office in Baghdad. Notwithstanding these developments, the UN assessed the risk to De Mello as a direct target as "low..." In the same vein, UN senior management in Baghdad asked the occupation forces to withdraw the heavy equipment and other fortifications around the building.

Following the 19 August attack, the security rating of Baghdad did not change. Indeed, flights continued to bring in more personnel. In Rio for a memorial to De Mello, Annan said at a press encounter, "The option of withdrawing is not something we can consider. The people of Iraq need us; they want us to stay. And the fanatics and the violent people who took Sergio and Nadia, Rick Hooper and other colleagues from us are not going to dictate what happens in Iraq."

On 2 September, two weeks after the Iraqi headquarters bombing and the deaths of De Mello and the other staff, the Security Coordinator in Baghdad recommended the withdrawal of all international personnel from Iraq. The SG, whose decision it was, demurred.

On the morning of 22 September a second attack was launched on the UN compound. The explosion killed several Iraqi police officers. That same day the senior UN staff in Baghdad recommended the evacuation of all UN staff. This was immediately endorsed by Fréchette's group in New York. The SG demurred.

The report excoriates "the haste with which the UN returned

to Baghdad... The re-entry of the UN team to Iraq on 1 May was characterised by a series of breaches of the Organisation's own security regulations." It further points out that the UN failed to adequately or accurately assess the attitude towards it.

"The UN system is viewed by many [Iraqis] to be at the origins of the imposition of the longest and most stringent sanctions regime ever, the deployment of the most invasive weapons inspection programme and the conduct of the oil-for-food programme, which for over a decade the UN system controlled much of the income of the oil production of Iraq."

The Panel report concludes, "The UN system failed to provide adequate security to its staff prior to the attack. Despite attempts to address the situation, UN staff continue to be at risk in Iraq."

On 25 September, the Secretary-General announced that UN staff in Iraq would be "downsized"; in deference to the occupiers it was made clear that this was not an "evacuation." Within a week, there were only some fifty staff remaining in Baghdad. But, despite the report's findings, it was not until 6 November, two weeks after the Panel had reported, and following an attack on the ICRC headquarters in Baghdad, that Kofi Annan finally relented and, unable to withstand the internal pressures any longer, withdrew all UN staff from Baghdad.

The elusive buck

Asked during his press conference on 22 October to say whom the Panel held responsible, Martit Ahtisaari, the Chairman of the Panel [former President of Finland, former UN Under-Secretary-General] did not hesitate: "The buck always stops with the Secretary-General." (This remark did not find its way into the official UN press release on the briefing.)

On Friday, 24 October, UN Day, the Secretary-General dedicated a memorial in the UN gardens to staff who had died in the course of duty. The dead of Baghdad were uppermost in everyone's mind, particularly after the Ahtisaari report. With the controversy about the destruction of UN headquarters in Iraq continuing to intensify, and his own role increasingly being called into question, he addressed the question of where the buck stopped.

Speaking of UN personnel serving in missions abroad he said:

"Let us never forget that those men and women serve as a result of decisions taken by Member States of our Organisation. And that for them to carry out their mission as effectively and safely as possible, we need Member States to give effect to the resolutions they adopt... "

Evidently, the buck stopped there. His advocacy in the spring, after barely a week had passed from the war's commencement, when he had lobbied Member States to let the UN go in, no longer counted.

On Friday, 31 October (Halloween, a badly-chosen day) the press was advised that the SG had written a letter earlier that day to all staff in which he said he was gravely concerned about the findings of the Panel and that he was taking immediate steps to implement its recommendations. By this time the anger of the staff at the security ineptitude and political game-playing exposed by the Ahtisaari report required a more concerned and sensitive response than the first, defensive reflex. Nonetheless, it was announced that Fréchette would be in charge of a strategic reorganisation of UN security management. This was greeted with some surprise, and even incomprehension, considering that she had, according to the Panel report, played a leading role in the rush to Baghdad.

Question at the press briefing: "Now the Deputy Secretary-General is one of the senior officials mentioned in the Ahtisaari report who basically formed part of the complete failure of management that exacerbated the outcome of the bombing, how does the UN square that circle that someone implicated in management failures is in charge of a review of security management?"

The question went unanswered. The questioner persisted.

Question: "But you haven't answered the question I asked."

Associate Spokesman: "Which is?"

Question: "Which is that the person in charge of the details of looking into the strategic reorganisation of your security management is also one of the officials implicated by the Ahtisaari Panel in the systematic failure of management. How does the UN justify that?"

Associate Spokesman: "Right now, the current system is under the responsibility of the Deputy Secretary-General so, it's natural that this evaluation be done under her leadership. Yes, David?"

On 4 November surprise turned to dismay when, as a follow-up to the report, an Accountability Group was set up to determine responsibility for the lapses in a security system that the Panel had described as "dysfunctional." Simultaneously, it was announced that the UN Security Coordinator and the UN Humanitarian Coordinator in Baghdad, who was the Designated Official in charge of security there, had "asked to be relieved of their duties." Apparently, accountability had been determined well in advance of the accountability investigation.

Question at press briefing: "It seems a bit of an unusual coincidence that Tun Myat [the UN Security Coordinator] and Ramiro [the UN Humanitarian Coordinator in Iraq] both decided voluntarily to temporarily ask to be relieved of their duty. Were they asked? Were they presented with basically a choice of having this imposed on them, or accepting it voluntarily? And also, the fact that the Secretary-General has asked the Deputy Secretary-General to organise or to oversee the reorganisation of the security system – is that an indication that he thinks that the Deputy Secretary-General and the Steering Committee handled the security issue well? They have come under some criticism, as well, in the Ahtisaari report. Does he not believe that the criticism was warranted?"

Associate Spokesman: "The Secretary-General reiterates his full confidence in the Deputy Secretary-General and she will continue, as I have said, with the responsibility she's been assigned. As for Ramiro Lopes da Silva and Tun Myat, as you know, Ramiro was the designated official on the ground with responsibilities for security for UN personnel in Iraq, and Tun Myat is the UN Security Coordinator in charge of overall security coordination...."

Question: "Were they asked to voluntarily step down?"

Associate Spokesman: "What I have is that they both volunteered to be relieved of their duties while the investigation was going on."

So, on the one hand, the review of the security system is kept tightly under the control of the 38th Floor and, on the other, the 38th Floor distances itself from responsibility for the security lapses in Baghdad by essentially indicating where the blame lay. "Asked to be relieved." Few gave credence to this assertion but if they had, indeed, asked to step aside, shouldn't the requests have been turned down in the interests of the obvious desirability of waiting for the outcome of the inquiry before rendering implied, public judgement?

A chat with Louise

Tuesday, 11 November

Louise has called and asked me to brief her on General Assembly reform; she says she wants to be "supportive." I'd only talked to her – sort of – once since I'd left the Secretariat. I'd been standing in the corridor leading to the General Assembly Hall.
　"Hello, Louise."

"Still working, I see," she had said as she'd sailed by. I hadn't been quite sure how to take that but I suspected that there was a trace of sarcasm tucked away somewhere in the remark; as I'd become accustomed to doing with Louise, I'd let it ride. Now, as customary with the 38th Floor, they know little of what delegations are considering and needed to catch up.

Arriving at her quarters I move, with well-remembered step, towards her waiting room, when, intercepted, I am ushered, instantly, into her chamber. She hurries around her desk to greet me, and guides me to an easy chair. A pleasant contrast this to days of yore. Then one was parked in her boardroom, unaccompanied, to await her arrival, until, guarded by two or three attendants, they together faced one, phalanx-like, across the broad, bare expanse of a shiny wooden table. But a presidential cloak is woven with a magical thread.

She professes herself relieved that the pressure of the recent Iraqi incidents has abated; she asks how she can be helpful. I welcome her interest and try to find out what is happening about a rumoured panel that the SG is considering setting up to deepen the reform agenda. She deflects me and tries to find out what is happening with Revitalisation. We offer each other nebulous indiscretions. We talk about the relationship between SGs and GA Presidents; we recall the time of Theo-Ben. She reaffirms her wish to be helpful.

It has been an orgy of hypocrisy. I am ashamed.

29
ISSUES OF CONSCIENCE

The revolt of Kofi Annan – Supping with Sasakawa – The Panel to save the world – The Americans say no – Lunch with "The Boys"

————◄○►————

"The time has come," the Walrus said,
To talk of many things:
Of shoes – and ships – and sealing wax –
Of cabbages – and kings –
And why the sea is boiling hot –
And whether pigs have wings."

Alice in Wonderland

Lewis Carroll

————◄○►————

The revolt of Kofi Annan

Saturday, 15 November

Following the destruction of the UN Headquarters in Baghdad, the United States and Britain returned to the Security Council to seek enhanced legitimacy and, even, expanded support for their conquest and occupation of Iraq. Whereas, hitherto, the opponents of the war on the Council could view with distanced and even ironic satisfaction the post-war travails of the invaders brought about by the guerrilla activities of the Iraqi paramilitary forces, (or, rather, terrorists, Baathists, fedayeen, Osamists, al-Quaedists, rumpists, dead enders, Iranians, Syrians, Chechnyans, Uzbeks, Muslims) the alliance judged that the moment was propitious for the international community to finally conclude a concordat in respect of the future of post-war Iraq.

For Kofi Annan, the new initiative brought him, inescapably, to his own "fork in the road." He had precipitously sought UN involvement in Iraq and had accepted a feeble and ill-defined mandate for the Organisation. He had no doubt expected that, in time, the situation on the ground would force a reappraisal on the part of the coalition leading, in turn, to an augmented UN presence.

The actual shape and content of the UN's activities in Iraq were matters that, without the bombing, could normally have been deftly obscured behind a waterfall of words in silkily-drafted reports. But the bombing in Baghdad had revelatory effects. It reminded the world that the UN was not beloved by Iraqis who had endured a decade of sanctions, bombardments and intrusive inspections for which they held the Organisation indisputably responsible. And its horror released the anguished survivors from any requirement of discretion about the reality of the UN's role in that country. They returned with angry tales of the marginalisation of the UN Iraqi mission that the Americans there had instituted.

In response, he initially pursued his favoured path of closed-door conciliation. He convened a meeting of the Foreign Ministers of the Permanent Five to be held at the UN offices on 13 September in Geneva, away from the brittle political atmosphere of New York. As for its purpose, he declared, "My own sense is that Iraq is of such importance that all of us will have to find a way of working together to stabilise Iraq."

The day before this meeting, he consulted with the heads of the UN humanitarian organisations, in company with his own political advisors. The ensuing discussion must have come as a shock for the humanitarian heads were vehement in their opposition to an early return to Iraq and caustic about the UN's stance. "We have no policy," he was told. (The theme of this consultation had been foreshadowed by a meeting of the survivors with senior UN officials in late August in Amman, Jordan, to which they had been "relocated." Many took the view that their "bosses" had put the mission ahead of their safety and might do so again.)

The P-5 meeting in Geneva made no more than marginal progress in reconciling the war's proponents and opponents – France, Russia and, more discreetly, China. He put the best face on it afterwards "I think it was a very good session." The model that Kofi Annan had in mind for a UN involvement in Iraq was the Afghanistan experience where the UN was not administering the country, or providing peacekeeping troops, but had been given the leading role in promoting political reconciliation and arranging for the putting in place of democratic institutions.

"We have had very good experience in facilitating political processes, helping countries that have been in difficulties in re-establishing democratically elected governments, helping them draft a constitution and a whole range of activities that we have had experience doing and would be able to do," he stated.

But Iraq was not Afghanistan. Iraq represented a major strategic interest for the West and, foremost, for the United States. Afghanistan had provided the opportunity to harass the Soviet Union through support for the mujahideen but, once the Soviet presence had been removed, it became again a country worthy only of neglect. The events of "9/11" refocused attention on Afghanistan. With the subsequent removal of the Taliban from power and, as a consequence, the end of that country as a terrorist bazaar, Afghanistan diminished as a political priority. Iraq, though, at the centre of the Middle Eastern vortex, would be a long-term American investment. Iraq was to be moulded to conform to, and exemplify, the US view of what Arab countries should look like in every sense – their internal constitutional arrangements, political and economic dependence and military and security reliability. The United Nations would not be permitted to tamper with these objectives.

The UN – for it was not only Kofi Annan but his lieutenants as well – had never learned the value of abstinence. They did not seem to see that sometimes it was better to stay out. They had, by now, become accustomed to going in to tidy up after the US, and NATO, had taken military action. So it had been in Kosovo and Afghanistan.

By mid-September, as the negotiations intensified, it was re-confirmed that the UN would not be granted a significant political role in Iraq. The victors wanted the UN to return as soon as possible but on the basis of the earlier mirage of a mandate. Kofi Annan was left with no further room to manoeuvre. Finally, after seven years, he emerged to take a stand in sharp, public opposition to Washington and London.

At a lunch for Security Council members on Wednesday, 18 September, the Secretary-General announced that he was not prepared to expand the UN presence in Iraq unless he was provided with a revised mandate, which clarified and extended the UN's role. He also demanded assurances of protection for UN staff in Baghdad and advised that he would delay appointing a successor to Sergio de Mello.

By late September he was going even further. He told Washington that a provisional government should be established in Iraq within three to five months to which political power should be transferred. He was now openly advocating the Afghani model and threatening, furthermore, to keep the UN out of Iraq unless such a model was adopted. He was, however, bypassed and the US produced a draft resolution that paid no heed to Annan's remonstrances. He acknowledged as much at a press encounter on 2 October by commenting, "Obviously it's not going in the direction I had recommended." That same day, at another Security Council lunch, he reaffirmed that he would not restore the UN political presence in Iraq without a strengthened and clarified mandate. Moreover, he indicated that there was no point in the UN returning in full force before a more representative Iraqi government was in place.

Unused to such intransigence, the US quickly let its views of Annan's position be known.

"Unusual", "unhelpful", and "surprising" were some of the epithets delivered.

"Is the Secretary-General exercising a sixth veto?" was another unattributable quote.

"We just have a basic difference with the Secretary-General on this," that ubiquitous "senior administration official" was reported as saying.

"He has the model of Afghanistan in mind, but that's not the right model."

On 16 October the US got their new Iraqi resolution, and got it by unanimous passage. The resignation that had attended the acquiescence to the first post-war resolution found full expression in a text that gave the US and the UK control of the country until a handover to an Iraqi government, sanctioned the occupation of Iraq by indicating that the "coalition" forces were serving as a multinational force under US command, and called on countries to contribute to the reconstruction of Iraq. Even though France, Germany and Russia immediately announced that they would not supply troops to the coalition forces nor should substantial reconstruction funds be expected from them, the US had acquired full *post facto* benediction of its conquest.

Nor was there any redefinition, clarification or expansion of the UN's political responsibilities for Iraq; having said that without this he would not permit a full-fledged UN presence in Iraq, the victors accepted his conditions and left him to his tent. Annan would appoint a new Special Representative "as circumstances permit." The UN would return, "as circumstances permit." It would carry out its tenuous mandate "as circumstances permit."

Kofi Annan's latest defiance was of a kind with his calling for an enlarged Security Council, taking to task the US and the UK in the General Assembly over the invasion, establishing an Eminent Persons Panel, and now opposing the new Iraq resolution. The consequence was to find himself sidelined. The price of opposition turned out to be the punishment of exclusion, the verdict he had feared most.

My friends view with scepticism this refurbished Annan and mock my admiration for his latest stands. They claim that he has only altered his position since a Republican administration, uncomfortable to work with, has taken over in Washington, while before he had been content to reach out to and please the Democrats who had put him in office, especially Secretary of State Madeleine Albright. But I make no apologies for praising his new course of action. People bob about and you need to see them whole. And didn't Whitman write, "Do I contradict myself? Very well then I contradict myself. I am large, I contain multitudes."

Now the markers were well drawn. The UN would only return when Iraq had a more representative government. It would not return until security of its staff had been assured. It would play no political role under the prevailing conditions.

These were positions to be applauded. The test would be whether they could be maintained.

Supping with Sasakawa

Wednesday, 19 November

We are on the way, this evening, to an annual event that I've been invited to regularly for many years. I've regularly managed to get out of it, but have finally succumbed out of loyalty to a friend.

The event is being held at the New York Historical Society, which has inconveniently chosen to locate itself across town. The organisers, for their part, have chosen a night where the gods are very angry, for we can barely see to drive through the indignant rain.

The gods may have decided to provide their public commentary because of some slight annoyance at yet another tribute being offered by the United Nations system to the memory of the late Japanese multimillionaire and indicted war criminal Ryoichi Sasakawa.

By the time we park and enter the Society we are drenched from the rain. Klaus Töpfer, the Executive Director of the United Nations Environmental Programme, and the man in charge of the tribute, meets us at the door.

"Klaus," I say. "How nice of you to come to greet us."

Klaus bows graciously before admitting that he had really come to await the arrival of the main speaker and honoured guest. I'm crushed but I forgive him and we go in.

Sasakawa was one of eventy indicted "Class A" Japanese war criminals who were due to be tried at the Tokyo Trial, the Japanese counterpart to the Nuremberg Tribunal, after the end of the Second World War. The seventy were divided into three groups. The first group of twenty-eight were the major political, military and diplomatic leaders. The second group of twenty-three, and the third of nineteen, were industrial and financial magnates and other devoted supporters of the Japanese war machine.

The event we are attending is the annual ceremony held by UNEP for the awarding of the Sasakawa Environmental Prize, worth $200,000 and described by UNEP as "one of the most prestigious environmental awards in the world... sponsored by The Nippon Foundation and founded by the late Mr. Ryoichi Sasakawa [and] awarded annually since 1984..." The Nippon Foundation's President is now Mr. Yohei Sasakawa, son of the distinguished founder.

With the onset of the cold war and the civil war in China, General MacArthur decided to abandon the Tokyo Trial as of lesser importance to the imperative of re-establishing Japan as a reliable bulwark against the Soviet Union and the emerging Chinese communist state. As a result, only the first group was tried, and the rest were set free, in 1947 and 1948, to return to their pre-war tasks of forging an omnipotent Japan.

The event was set to start at 7 p.m. but we are late and it is now half past that. The other guests have already sat down to dinner and have finished the first course. They don't appear enthused, maybe because there is no sign of the second course arriving. Meanwhile, a long discourse is being provided by the Honourable William K. Reilly, Chairman of the World Wildlife Fund, who is present to add his own tribute to the once-indicted Ryoichi Sasakawa.

Sasakawa was well known as one of the most fervent advocates of a militant and militarised Japan. A member of the Diet, he founded the "Fascist National Essence Mass Party" in 1931, and organised his own private army of 15,000 men, clad in black shirts, in emulation of his idol Benito Mussolini. In 1939 he flew to Italy to meet Mussolini who he called the "perfect fascist." Sasakawa called for war with the United States.

The honoured guest arrives. He is the Secretary-General of the United Nations who has come to play his part in this ceremony to the memory of Ryoichi Sasakawa. He is to present the awards. Töpfer rises to introduce him, and the event. Töpfer speaks without notes for a long time. By now it is 8.30 p.m. and the plates from the first course are still on the table. There are also wine glasses on the table but the waiters aren't serving the wine. I look for comfort in the bread rolls, but our companions have eaten every one.

After his release Sasakawa re-established his empire from profits from his gambling enterprises, notably the Japan Motorboat Racing Association, which, due to its origins, helped fuel the suspicion that he was connected to the political-criminal enterprise known as the Yakuza. He was on the board of the All-Japan Council of Patriotic Organisations and supported a number or other right-wing organisations. He was said to be a major, silent backer of the Unification Church of the Reverend Sun Myung Moon. He was a participant in the World Anti-Communist League, notable for having among its members former Eastern European Nazis and present-day Latin American politicians with right-wing, death squad connections such as General Jorge Rafael Videla, the Argentine dictator, and El Salvador's notorious Roberto D'Aubusson.

Töpfer finally calls on Kofi Annan who makes a brief, graceful speech and presents the awards to a Chinese and a Brazilian. The Chinese takes the floor and speaks for half an hour. It is now approaching 9.30 p.m. I get up and go over to the bar at the far end of the room and wrestle a glass of red from the bartender. People look angrily at me as I return to the drinks-free, detritus-laden table where the plates from the first course still reside.

In 1962 Sasakawa started the "Japanese Shipbuilding Industry Foundation" to provide assistance in the development of maritime affairs and vessels. It afterwards metamorphosed into the "Sasakawa Foundation" before settling down to a splendid run as "The Nippon Foundation" dedicated, as a non-profit-making organisation, to a global agenda to alleviate suffering. The original foundation was financed from revenues from motorboat racing; in short from gambling profits generated, according to published accounts, with the connivance of the Yakuza.

The Brazilian takes the floor and speaks for half an hour. The tables are decorated with coloured glass beads and people are starting to play with the beads. Two people have made noughts-and-crosses patterns with the glass beads and are engrossed in the game. Another guy is piling up the glass beads into little mounds. A woman is surreptitiously wrapping up a stock of beads in her napkin preparatory to smuggling them into her handbag. Yet another guy is putting the glass beads, one by one, into his empty coffee cup and trying, intently, to set them alight.

Originally intended to advance Sasakawa's maritime interests, the Nippon Foundation soon became the means to his international rehabilitation. The Nippon Foundation began donating money to many worthy causes, but the target it soon set its sights on was the mother of all good causes, the United Nations itself.

The Brazilian finishes his speech and reaches behind him to produce a huge Brazilian flag, which he waves back and forth. It is now ten o'clock. People are looking for a back door to slip away but others, more boldly, are marching out the main entrance. They must have taken a look at the menu where the second course looks likely to be a meat-eater's punishment – "Trumpet Mushroom Crushed Talapia and a Sauté of Root Vegetables Julienne" accompanied by a "Saute of French Beans with Red and Yellow Pepper Confetti in Lemon Butter."

The organisations of the United Nations were unperturbed by the affiliations, ancient and more recent, of Ryoichi Sasakawa. They readily scooped up his tainted largesse. The World Health Organisation was a special beneficiary. By the year 2002, the Nippon Foundation had contributed $60 million to support its activities including the "Sasakawa Health Prize", established in 1985. In gratitude, a bust of Sasakawa was placed in the lobby of the Headquarters of WHO in Geneva. UNEP was proud of its annual $200,000 Sasakawa Environmental Prize. And the United Nations, through its Department of Public Information, headed by successive Japanese, accepted millions from Sasakawa's foundations. Money from these gifts went to put up a memorial to the dead of Hiroshima and Nagasaki in a prominent area in the UN Visitors Route where the world could view relics from the nuclear holocaust as an evident rebuke to the victor in the Pacific War, the United States, all courtesy of its former enemy, the late Mr. Ryoichi Sasakawa.

Not tempted by the advertised repast in view, we begin to sidle out. Töpfer turns up again and, before I can explain the sidling, launches into his own apology.

"The Brazilian spoke for much too long," the man who spoke for too long, without notes, complains. "I told him he shouldn't speak without notes."

In its Obituary on Sasakawa (20 July 1995), The Independent of London commented: "The last of Japan's A-class war criminals has died, a nonagenarian multimillionaire. Ryoichi Sasakawa stood out as a monster of egotism, greed, ruthless ambition, political deviousness and with a love of the limelight equalled in his time only by his fellow right-winger Yukio Mishima."

In 1982, Secretary-General Pérez de Cuéllar presented the United Nations Peace Medal to the distinguished philanthropist, Ryoichi Sasakawa.

The Panel to save the world

Friday, 21 November

The Secretary-General announced the names of his Panel of Eminent Persons who are to save the United Nations about a month ago. I've been waiting to hear reactions. I've now heard. The panel to look to the future is drawn solidly from the past.

It is a sixtten-person Panel, full of formers, such as Anand Panyarachun, a former Thai Prime Minister and former Ambassador to the UN who is its chair, Gro Harlem Brundtland, former Norwegian Prime Minister and former Director-General of WHO, Salim Salim of Tanzania, former Foreign Minister and former Secretary-General of the OAU, David Hannay of the UK, former PR to the UN, Brent Scowcroft, former US National Security Advisor, Gareth Evans, former Australian Foreign Minister et cetera, et cetera. Of the sixteen, there are only two, Amre Moussa, the Secretary-General of the Arab League, and Enrique Iglesias, President of the Inter-American Development Bank, who are still fully in the game. The "formers" are just hanging on – state senators, international consultants, members of boards, honorary university officials, occasional advisors.

Not one member of the Panel was born after the end of the Second World War, and many were born well before it began –

the Japanese (1927), the Frenchman (1928), the Chinese (1928), the Russian (1929), the Brazilian (1931), the Thai (1932), the Brits (1935), the Indian (1936). A number are shy about publicly revealing their ages but are known to be in their seventies – the Pakistani, the American, the Uruguayan. The youngest member is fifty-nine. A university professor has calculated that the average age is 69.5. "Relics reforming a relic," is the winning *bon mot.*

There was quiet incredulity among delegations when the names became known. It was immediately renamed "The Geriatric Group," and those even more disrespectful began to take wagers on how many of its members would still be around when the Panel concluded its work. Certainly, it seemed inopportune that an Old Boys (and Old Girls) kind of club was to be asked to render judgement on a new twenty-first century UN. Wasn't this supposed to be the century of the young and the vibrant? Shouldn't there have been, at minimum, a mix of the old and, if not the young, at least the not-so-old, the experienced with the visionaries, the employed with the pensioners? One wondered too where "We the People's" had gone to? After years of proclaiming that the UN was an instrument to serve the world's citizens who should have more say in the running of it, they had been ostentatiously overlooked. Where too were the businessmen, the "Global Compactors," without whom the UN was previously felt to be isolated and self-absorbed, why weren't they in evidence on the Panel?

The setting-up of the Panel could have been better handled. Yet Kofi Annan is right to have considered that the UN has reached a fork in the road and is to be commended for trying to do something about it. The backdrop is, nonetheless, quite daunting. The Organisation's record in addressing major crises since the end of the cold war when amity was supposed to reign is one of endless failure – Rwanda, Bosnia, Afghanistan, Iraq. The UN had either been unable to forestall tragedy or meddled ineffectively. Can a panel of this sort really prompt the necessary institutional change to avert in future any more such disasters?

The Americans say no

Wednesday, 26 November

1.15 p.m. – Hunte is holding a lunch today as part of our campaign for a General Assembly reform resolution. We're concentrating on seeing if anything can be done to make the General Assembly more efficient and more relevant.

As a matter of fact the Assembly has been looking into this regularly for the last ten years without much success, which suggests what is wrong with the General Assembly. The UN has some 170 items on its agenda every year, nearly all of which are repeat items, and nearly all of which result in some 200 reports, which require repeat resolutions following repeat speeches by the same repeat delegations.

This reality is freely admitted by delegates when they meet privately. A few of them are even prepared to admit it publicly, but they are looked at as mavericks, or people who are coming to the end of their posting at the UN and can therefore afford to stray. For the last two months I've been attending a series of these sumptuous affairs, breakfasts, lunches and dinners, where there is much bemoaning about the situation, the waste of energy and money that the annual rote entails, and much hesitation about doing something about it, as we tuck into our two-to-three hour repasts which, to give us credit, we do not hesitate to enjoy.

"These fellows are all jokers," Hunte likes to say. "They're happy with the situation just as it is."

At many of these affairs I've come across a sense of hopelessness as to whether anything can be done. Delegations have been trying for so long to reform the way the GA works that they have no confidence in their own ability to agree and to act. I keep telling them, not originally, "You succeed by doing."

I've drafted two papers on the matter, which we circulated, and have now prepared a draft resolution that we are to talk about at lunch today.

All the representatives of the various groupings of states are at the lunch, as well as the big boys of the P-5. The mood and tone is positive, which is a good sign in this kind of activity, and just about everyone likes the text subject to some adjustments. Almost everyone. The Americans, who call most for UN reform, do not seem to like the draft at all.

"This is unacceptable," Negroponte keeps saying about various aspects of the text.

"This must be changed." Well, let us see.

Lunch with "The Boys"

Tuesday, 2 December

Lunch with the boys. It is a reduced group now, from the original core group of eight, all of whom had once worked together on the same floor in the Secretariat in the early seventies, and who had maintained our ties. There are only four of us today. Two have passed away. We reminisce.

Benon recalls the time when he had been in charge of administering the building and had received a peremptory summons from Mrs. Boutros Boutros-Ghali.

"Benon, come down here right away."

"Come down where, Mrs. Boutros-Ghali?"

"Come down to the Ladies Room in the first basement."

"I don't think that is a good idea, Mrs. Boutros-Ghali."

"Why not?"

"I don't think we should be meeting in the Ladies Room."

"And why not?"

"People might talk."

"But the toilets are all blocked."

"I'll send a repairman, Mrs. Boutros-Ghali."

He remembers too when he fell afoul of the privileges police. As you move up in the Secretariat, countless little, but crucial and, best of all, distinctive benefits accrue. There are the office windows – two, three, four and then the ultimate, five at the most senior levels. (The SG has six.) And there is more; halfway up you get one water glass, with flask; then two (with flask and ice) until the summit of three is attained. But it is the carpet space that most defines. Until you are quite far up, you get no carpet. At one point, Benon had finally achieved carpet status but the only room available for him was larger than his entitlement. Undaunted, he moved in. Deeply offended, the privileges police struck. Workers were sent with carpet cutters to trim a neat, exact space around the room to return him to preposterous compliance. Even though his room entitlement might have been exceeded, he would at least be restored to carpet regulation.

I contend with the Great Bathroom War. When Dadzie became Director-General [Kenneth K.S. Dadzie of Ghana, Director-General for Development and International Cooperation, a precursor post to that of Deputy Secretary-General, a wonderful man for whom I worked], a suite of offices had to be prepared for him as it was a new position in the Secretariat. He asked for a toilet to be provided. This request produced consternation, then resistance, and finally anger: the battle commenced. For, until then, only one person had a toilet in his suite in the building and that was the Secretary-General. The SG's men of the time would not allow this barefaced attempt at hierarchical equality. Senior officials were entitled to washbasins and that was quite enough. I acted as Dadzie's point man in the struggle and leapt gleefully into the fray. The fight went on for months until finally resolved by a historic UN compromise. The SG had his toilet. Senior officials had washbasins. The Director-General was below the SG but above the senior officials. He would get a pissoir.

(Louise's arrival as the second-most senior official was a happening blissfully unforeseen by the privileges police; it constituted both awkwardness and a challenge. But they gritted their teeth and did the bold thing: they gave her a lavatory.)

30
SOME SORT OF ACHIEVEMENT

America alone again – A stab at reform –
The Great Smoking War

America alone again

Friday, 12 December

We are convening today the third of a series of informal meetings of the General Assembly to discuss our reform resolution. Since Hunte's lunch we have adjusted the text somewhat while retaining all its essential features. By now we have most countries on board, including, importantly, the South, the Europeans, and Japan. Russia has a few quibbles but they can be easily accommodated. We are now waiting to hear from Washington.

Ambassador Cunningham, Negroponte's Deputy, takes the floor and douses the whole enterprise with customary cold water. He reads out three pages of complaints and specific changes to a text that has been under consideration for a month and which are of a breath and magnitude not previously advertised. It is America alone, America resplendent. They have done this in other instances this session and have insisted on votes on resolutions, which everyone else has agreed to. In two recent votes, the scores have been 154-1 and 153-1 but they appeared to be undeterred.

Afterwards, I speak to friends in the US Mission who are touchingly embarrassed by both the content and the timing of their intervention. They tell me that Washington has just woken up.

They engage in gallows humour.

"Don't worry," they confide. "If it comes to a vote, we'll have Palau, Micronesia and the Marshall Islands with us."

A stab at reform

Friday, 19 December

The General Assembly today adopted unanimously our Reform resolution. The text has only been marginally modified from the one the US dismissed a week ago. In essence, we called their bluff.

We made it clear to the US delegates that we would not go along with their radical amendments. Their friends, especially the British, spoke to them too and must have convinced them to desist. They were left with the prospect of being totally isolated on a matter on which they should have been supportive, given their traditional harping on the need for UN reform. They have misjudged the political mood, and simply misunderstood what the text was proposing. Finally, there was the astonishing ineptitude of the US negotiating posture. It was driven by ideological rigidity and unrealistic estimations of the extent of their influence. There are limits to the capacity of even the US to bully the world successfully.

After the resolution was adopted, the US delegation makes an ungenerous statement in which it explains that it has only grudgingly gone along but continues to consider the resolution to be inadequate and insubstantial.

I don't think they are right. We have managed to enact potentially far-reaching changes in the way the GA does its business. The provisions of the resolution call for a drastic reduction in the UN's agenda, a sharp cut in documentation, a greater focussing in deliberation, the introduction of more informal and interactive modes of discussion moving away from the endless formal speech-making, and a rebalancing of the relationship between the Security Council and the General Assembly to the latter's benefit. If properly implemented, this result should be something of a success.

The Great Smoking War

Tuesday, 23 December

On 11 August 2003 an announcement appeared under the Secretary-General's signature stating: "No smoking shall be permitted in any of the United Nations premises at Headquarters." The ban was to take effect on 1 September.

Reaction to the SG's pronouncement was slow in coming. This was the doldrums month at the UN, when it was emptied of delegates and staff alike. The first response came from Sergei Lavrov, the Russian Ambassador, and a chain-smoker, in an interview with *Izvestiya* on 9 September.

"The UN Secretary-General can by all means tell his underlings what to do but not members of diplomatic missions. The new rules are not binding on anyone," he said. "The UN building is owned by all the member-nations while the Secretary-General is just a hired manager."

By the middle of September, with the reopening of the General Assembly, the cohorts returned. At the very first meeting of the Assembly's budgetary and administrative committee, which up to that point had thought it had oversight over the matter, the counter-attack was launched. Costa Rica's representative requested the inclusion of an item on smoking at the UN.

"The problem is not a smoking ban," she stated, "but who has the authority in this respect. The answer is clear – it is Member States."

The next move came from the Secretariat. Workmen removed the glass ashtrays from the lounge areas at the UN where smoking had been allowed, and tore down the metal ashtrays placed on the walls outside the conference rooms. The smokers improvised by employing coffee cups as ashtrays. Member States addressed questions to the Secretariat in the Fifth Committee about the cost of removing the ashtrays.

Impervious to the gathering rumblings, the Secretariat pressed on. Workmen painted over the notices on the walls in the lounges that advertised smoking freedom as well as those in conference rooms advising, "Smoking discouraged." Replacement signs warning, "No smoking" proliferated. Member States raised questions in the Fifth Committee about the cost of repainting the walls and putting up the new signs. The Chairman of the Committee, Ambassador Kmoníček of the Czeck Republic, said, "I will make sure, because I am also a smoker, that we will be given our explanations from the Secretariat."

At the annual UN Correspondents' Association dinner on October 22, Nane Annan chose to make light of the growing brouhaha.

"One of your favourite ambassadors has already told you that the 'Secretary-General can by all means tell his underlings what to do, but not members of diplomatic missions'." she said. "I guess the ambassador must have been fuming at the time." The mocking of Sergei Lavrov may have been ill-advised.

On 29 October a UN security guard attempted to "physically" enforce the ban on the Acting Mexican Permanent Representative. The attempt failed. The following day, in the Fifth Committee, the indignant diplomat stated, "The matter is not whether people should or should not smoke. The question was who decided the matter... Those concerned are mature adults and diplomats not minors."

The UN security staff had been charged with enforcing the ban. Member States addressed questions in the Fifth Committee to the Secretariat as to whether the responsibility given to UN security staff to enforce the ban had required additional recruitment, or extra overtime costs.

Member States of the United Nations were now enveloped in the smoking crisis. Sergei Lavrov, especially, had not been biding his time. Sergei's cigarette smoke was to be spotted far and wide at UN Headquarters. Sergei puffed in the areas where smoking had habitually been permitted. Sergei puffed in areas where smoking had habitually been forbidden. Sergei puffed as he strode up and down the corridors of the building. Sergei puffed during Security

Council meetings. Sergei could be seen happily puffing during Security Council press conferences. And Sergei's gathering band of mutineers all puffed too.

Confronted by this sustained defiance, the Secretariat adjusted its tactics. A new policy was enunciated. Security guards would no longer try to physically impede smokers but would "note the name and department/mission of individuals smoking in the building. The list would be submitted to the respective heads of department/mission concerned. It would be up to them to take whatever actions were required." This was a disciplinary policy reminiscent of the mentality of high-school Puritanism and smacking of the techniques of an informant totalitarian state. Sergei, for one, had a succinct view of why the ban was imposed in the first place.

"The ban was obviously designed to please New York Mayor Bloomberg" he observed. "Imposing the code of a city on the UN building is absurd."

Sergei's implication was evident – Annan's Americanised Secretariat, was following the directions of the American Republican Bloomberg. This was a surly cocktail of resentment to concoct.

What had begun as a quixotic, marginal, and, even, mildly comic affair was now consuming the attention of the Assembly and was in danger of developing, unnecessarily, into a confrontation between the Secretariat and Member States. Secretariat intransigence had been answered by delegation muscle flexing, nurtured by years of accumulated grievances. The Fifth Committee did have some other items on its agenda, such as considering a new two-year Budget for the Organisation and approving a new scale of payments for countries' contributions to the UN, but these passing distractions were not being allowed to impede the focus of delegations. This was acknowledged in a UN Press Release of 3 November: "In a debate that threatened to overshadow the agenda items on the [Fifth] Committee's work programme, many delegations... addressed the legality of the Secretariat's administrative instructions on a total ban on smoking at the United Nations premises."

But a perfect denouement was at hand.

At the end of the year, the General Assembly confirmed its previous resolutions regulating smoking in the UN building. The Secretariat maintained its smoking ban. The warning signs stayed up. The security guards were told not to enforce it. No one had won. No one had lost. It was the best of all UN endings. And Sergei, and the mutineers, smoked on.

[In March of the following year Sergei was appointed Minister of Foreign Affairs of the Russian Federation. Meeting him at the UN not long afterwards, I enquired (after the necessary congratulations), "Sergei, so the policy of the Permanent Representative of Russia on smoking will now become the policy of the Russian state?" Twinkling, and hugely pleased, Sergei replied, "It was always the policy of the Russian state, Miles."]

31
RETURNING TO THE FOLD

Back to Baghdad – Dictating democracy

Back to Baghdad

Wednesday, 14 January, 2004

UN Will Send Team to Iraq To Prepare for Possible Return

By Warren Hoge

New York Times

"United Nations, Jan.13 – The United Nations said Tuesday that it had decided to send security advisers to Baghdad to study safety provisions in preparation for a possible early return of staff members to Iraq...

The move could be a first step in the organisation's reconsidering its determination to stay out of Iraq until the scheduled transfer of power to the Iraqis by June 30."

Wednesday, 21 January

On Monday, 19 January, Martin Luther King Day, Secretary-General Kofi Annan met with the occupying powers of Iraq, and their designated surrogates on the Governing Council, to be briefed on their plan to delay the institutionalisation of democracy, through free and fair elections, in that convulsed nation.

The US had reached an "agreement" with the Governing Council to transfer sovereignty to Iraq by 30 June 2004. No role for the UN was identified. Sovereignty would be transferred to a provisional government to be selected following establishment of an interim assembly chosen under a nationwide "caucus" system. The US had ruled out the holding of elections to choose the assembly and thence the government. Iraq was deemed not to be ready or, perhaps, too ready since an election seemed sure to result in bringing to power the Shiite clergy or their representatives which, bearing Iran in mind, was a denouement that the victors were resolved to frustrate. Most critically, the US intended to transfer power well before the American Presidential elections in November and, concurrently, to conclude arrangements for a continued military presence in Iraq with the reliable government, which the caucus elections, a form of "guided" democracy, were designed to ensure. However, Grand Ayatollah Ali al-Sistani, the most influential Shiite leader, had called for direct elections. The victors now saw a suitable role for the UN – to serve as the means to convince the Iraqis that elections could not be organised before 30 June.

On the day that Kofi Annan met at the United Nations to discuss the delaying of democracy in Iraq, Grand Ayatollah Ali al-Sistani sent 100,000 followers through the streets of Baghdad to call for direct elections. This was no doubt intended as a broad hint to the occupying powers that his opinions should be taken account of. It may also have been his way of initiating a dialogue with Annan, who had written to the Chairman of the Governing Council in December to say that he did not think "fair and just" elections could be organised before 30 June. Upon receiving Annan's negative assessment, Sistani is reported to have commented, "We did not ask Annan to issue a fatwa from New York..."

Dictating democracy

At the Martin Luther King Day meeting, the Coalition authorities and their Iraqi surrogates requested Annan to "quickly send a technical mission to Iraq to advise on the feasibility of elections and, if not, what alternatives might be possible." While popular commentary held that this request put him in a difficult position, his options were, in reality, not complicated. He could, persuasively, decline in the light of the precarious security situation and the fact that the UN had not been a party to the agreement calling for a managed selection by 30 June. He could, without dispatching a team, announce that it would be best to reschedule the election to later in the year to ensure optimal electoral circumstances in the country since he was already on record as harbouring doubts as to whether elections could be arranged by 30 June. Or he could do as the occupiers desired and send a team to provide cover for their plans. In fact he could have, at the meeting, discouraged the making of the expected request. That he had not, revealed that he both wanted to be approached and intended to cooperate. The unwelcome burden of abstinence was about to be removed.

Equally uncomplicated were the motives of the occupying powers; they were intent on installing a compliant Iraqi government. They would explore all and every option to achieve that objective. And, failing that, they would assure compliance through the bitter device of fostering division among the major Iraqi groups in order to keep that country weak and discombobulated. For didn't Thucydides relate in the Melian Dialogue that the Athenian representatives negotiated with their Melian counterparts thus: "The strong do what they can and the weak suffer what they must"?

32
NEW ENTERTAINMENTS

The Big Leak – Returning to Iraq –
Eavesdropping on Annan

The Big Leak

Thursday, 23 January

"Your paper's leaked," President Hunte said to me accusingly.

It was at a morning meeting, in November of last year, and he was referring to a paper I had written on Security Council reform; it was the most sensitive matter we were tackling. We had a measure of success with General Assembly revitalisation but Security Council reform was something more profound. The leaking of my think-piece could undermine our efforts before we had even begun. It was most disturbing.

"Well, I didn't leak it", I say.

The leak produced consternation in our office. After quickly absolving ourselves of responsibility, we were left to a familiar (and comfortable) Third World explanation – a conspiracy was afoot. Meanwhile, a colleague in the office whispered to me, "I'd like to talk to you about this," but, in my agitation, I had paid no attention.

Hunte instructed us to be vigilant about security. We should be careful on the phone. We should not leave papers lying around when we left our rooms. We should lock our desks at night. And we should be cautious about what we put on our computers since those were probably being monitored too. Meanwhile, my colleague said, "I've got to talk to you about the leak," but I could never get around to chatting with her.

It was a really big leak, and it was not being treated surreptitiously by anyone. The Italian Ambassador, President of the European Union at the time, sent out my paper to all EU members with a cover note identifying the origin. Ambassadors approached me smilingly and gleefully announced, "I've seen your paper." Others approached me grumblingly and predicted it would never fly. I would mutter something about "early drafts" but I was unconvincing. Our thinking on one of the most sensitive subjects the UN had before it for consideration had spread throughout the building, while I was suspected within my own office of having initiated the dispersal.

At our first staff meeting after the Christmas holidays, the President warned us sternly that leaks were unacceptable, that we should all be careful in our dealings with delegations, and be aware that our activities were being monitored.

Today, I had coffee in the Delegates' Lounge with the Liechtenstein Ambassador, one of our Facilitators on Security Council reform. There were two of them and their job was to keep in touch with delegations on Hunte's behalf.

"I don't know where we go from here," I complained. "Since the paper leaked, the whole process has stalled."

"Maybe you could redraft the paper," he'd replied. "I've made some suggestions to the President on it."

"You have?" I had asked. "How did you get the paper?"

"Why, the President gave it to me in November and asked for my views. But," he went on, "I didn't leak it."

"So, both Facilitators were given the paper by Hunte?"

"Yes, didn't you know?"

This afternoon, I met the colleague who had been trying to talk to me about the leak. I relayed to her what I had heard.

"I think I've discovered the source of the leak," I said. "It's Hunte. The President is the leaker."

"I don't know about the delegations but I know about the press," she had said.

"The press?"

"Yes, I was in a meeting with him when he gave a copy of your paper to a reporter."

Oh well.

Returning to Iraq

Monday, 26 January

The UN sent a two-person team to Baghdad over the weekend to assess the security situation as international media reports were seemingly felt to be insufficient and incomplete. The team was greeted on arrival by roadside booby traps that killed four US soldiers and five Iraqis. Today, mortar fire was directed into what is presumably the most secure installation in the country, namely the Coalition Headquarters within the Green Zone. One mortar exploded near to the heliport that is customarily used by Paul Bremer, the US Administrator.

I have already learnt that this is where the UN mission will be located if all is felt secure for the return of UN staff.

Tuesday, 27 January

Kofi Annan this morning announced that he would be prepared to return the UN to Iraq in the person of an electoral advisory mission if the coalition authorities could provide adequate security arrangements and assurances.

Attacks on the coalition forces today resulted in the deaths of six US soldiers, four Iraqi policemen and two CNN local employees.

Eavesdropping on Annan

Thursday, 26 February

"GOD SAVE THE QUEEN." I address this remark to the air conditioning vent in the ceiling in Hunte's office. News has come out of London that the UN building is bugged and I am taking no chances.

I had first learnt about this when awakened this morning to BBC News and heard Marrack Goulding, a former British head of political affairs in the Secretariat, give a little background and perspective.

"Devices," he explains, had been discovered more than once in the offices of Secretaries-General. It had sounded a bit louche to me and it had taken me some time, in my drowsy state, to realise that Marrack was not exposing the sex secrets of my previous bosses.

"AND I WISH PEOPLE WOULD STOP CRITICISING PRESIDENT GEORGE W. BUSH ON IRAQ. AS FAR AS I'M CONCERNED, HE DID THE RIGHT THING." Now I've gone close to Hunte's desk and am speaking loudly in the direction of his phone.

The British work a fascinating scam at the UN. Everyone knows that they will, in the end (or often from the beginning) follow the US but they are expert, in a tempting, sinuous way, at holding out the hope that they won't. They do not see themselves, as so many do, as a flea on the back of the American dog, satisfied with going along for the ride. They contend that they are the restraining, nay civilising and mitigating force to the blind American buffalo. Without retaining the confidence of the US, they argue, they will not be in a position, at defining moments, to rein the beast in. They play this game particularly well with Annan. Aware of the pressures that he must daily face from Washington, they assume the role of the patient (but responsible), wise (but decisive), prudent (but firm), avuncular counsellor. They can be relied on, they can be turned to.

But a delicious row has broken out about bugging at the UN. It started slowly and has been simmering for a while but has now come wonderfully to a boil. It started months ago when it was learnt that the Americans had asked for British help in monitoring the activities of the six Third World countries on the Security Council who had equivocated about supporting the planned invasion of Iraq. Now the former British Minister of International Development

Cooperation, Clare Short, has enhanced her reputation for untimely indiscretions by stating that Annan's office is bugged and leaving the impression that this is the work of the British intelligence services.

The day after the Short indiscretion, Kofi Annan issued a formal rebuke through his Spokesman. The tone of the statement and the swiftness of the reaction suggested a real anger. Constant American pressure and machination are known, but to find that the trusted interlocutor is, underneath, untrustworthy after all must have been enough to scratch and even scar that serene exterior.

"We have seen today's media reports alleging that the Secretary-General's phone conversations were tapped by British intelligence. We would be disappointed if this were true...

"Such activities would undermine the integrity and confidential nature of diplomatic exchanges. Those who speak to the Secretary-General are entitled to assume that their exchanges are confidential.

"The Secretary-General, therefore, would want this practice stopped, if indeed it exists."

Asked whether bugging would be illegal, the Spokesman presses on:

"It is indeed considered illegal."

A great furore has broken out in the press, particular in Britain, about all this but I find it quite farcical. Those of us working in the building are inclined to shrug it off for it is regarded as almost a badge of honour to be subjected to the dishonourable practice of being bugged, because it shows you have arrived. I'd always assumed Annan's office and boardroom were bugged, and I'd been pleased to think that twice in my career my phone had probably been tapped – during the Reform and Millennium Summit years.

In the cold war days we'd speculate a lot about who were CIA and KGB among the staff from the protagonist countries who turned up to occupy posts in the Secretariat. The Russians and Eastern Europeans were easiest to spot but the CIA types were not too hard to identify either. No Secretary-General had ever, during those cynical days, done other than turn a blind eye to spying activities in the Secretariat. They had limited themselves to making sure that no Soviet bloc personnel, or Beijing passers-by for that matter, ever occupied positions in their inner circle of staff, or were put in charge of important departments, or given sensitive responsibilities. Thus the Russians always headed a Department of Political and Security Council Affairs but there was always also an Office for Special Political Affairs, attached to the SG's Executive Office, where the real political work was done. The Chinese were given the Department of Technical Cooperation for Development but the real development work in the field was done by UNDP and the specialised agencies. The Eastern Europeans got the Department of Conference Services but the real work of providing substantive input into the work of the UN bodies was done by other departments.

My own lack of surprise, or even indignation, is reflected in other comments. It's not only Marrack Goulding who had known about "devices."

"If you take telephone calls there are dozens of governments monitoring," Rolf Ekéus comments.

"You should be flattered that someone is interested in your conversations."

Richard Butler says he was shown copies of his bugged conversations.

"Those who did it would come to me and show me the recordings they had made on others. 'To try and help me do my job of disarming Iraq,' they would say. 'We're just here to help you'."

"I was utterly confident that in my attempts to have private conversations, trying to solve the problems of disarmament in Iraq, I was being listened to by the Americans, British, the French and the Russians. And they also had people on my staff reporting what I was trying to do privately. Do you think that was paranoia? Absolutely not. There was abundant evidence that we were being constantly monitored.

"I was reduced to having to go either to a noisy cafeteria where there was so much noise around, and then whisper in the hope that we wouldn't be overheard, or literally take a walk in the park."

Hans von Sponeck notes that in Baghdad, "The UN had been bugged by everybody – the Iraqis and the other intelligence services, both in the region and overseas."

"Everybody spies on everybody," is the comment of Inocencio Arias, the Spanish Ambassador. "And when there is a big crisis, big countries spy a lot. If your mission is not bugged, then you are really nothing."

"The fact is that this sort of thing goes with the territory. You have to be very naive to be surprised," remarks Munir Akram, the Pakistan Permanent Representative.

Sergei Lavrov, though, reacts with tongue presumably firmly in cheek.

"Never, never," he says. "I don't think you could find even any suspicion that the Secretary-General's office was bugged by the Russian intelligence service."

The fuss created first by Short's comment and, next, by his Spokesman's rebuke, apparently discomforted Annan. Short herself began to backtrack, indicating that she could not be certain that the transcripts she had seen were actually obtained via bugging. The British indicated that Short may have seen analyses of Annan's views, or transcripts of records of his conversations with them, obtained by methods other than bugging. Suddenly, Annan disappeared.

"Question at Press Conference: The Secretary-General has seemed to have gone into hiding the last day or two, sneaking down back staircases and giving a press conference on Monday but not taking questions. How long is that going to go on... Eventually he's going to have to say something about it.

Spokesman: Well first of all you're right. He did not come in the front door or walk in front of your noses as he went to the Security Council this morning, because he felt that everything we had to say on this subject was said yesterday by me and by other members of the Secretariat..."

A few days later, on entering the building, he allowed himself to be accosted. It had been noticed that he was scheduled to meet the British Ambassador that day and he was queried as to whether the bugging incident would be discussed.

"It's not high on the agenda," he had replied. It was time to move on.

Confirmation of the change of tone was made apparent the day before the Short revelation when his Spokesman had been asked to comment about the allegations of bugging the six Third World missions. The Spokesman was all insouciance.

"Question:...is this a good thing for the security of the Organisation... for one country to be thought of and accused of spying in essence with the help of another country to spy on other members of the Security Council?

Spokesman: These allegations don't concern something that is said to have happened within this building or on our premises. It is something that is alleged to have happened on the premises of governments across the street, across town. And so, it's a matter between those governments who may or may not feel aggrieved and the host country, the United States...

Question: Do you know if the SG intervened in any way in this matter... or was notified of their complaint?

Spokesman: To my knowledge, no..."

"There is a tradition of bugging the office of the SG and also his residence," Boutros Boutros announces.

"From the first day I entered my office they said, 'Beware your office is bugged, your residence is bugged and it is a tradition that the member states that have the technical capacity to bug will do so without hesitation. That would involve members of the Security Council. The perception is that you must know in advance that your office, your residence, your car, your phone, is bugged. When I didn't want to be overheard I went for a walk in my garden."

After Boutros' comments, I lose some of my own insouciance. Boutros may have his own reasons to malign the great powers and the US in particular, but the cruelty of the situation is that he must have had to proceed on the assumption that he was being permanently bugged. And who did they, he and Annan, have to sweep their offices and residences for bugs? The UN administrative and security services managed and staffed overwhelmingly by Americans? A New York security firm? Does Kofi Annan have to go through every day wondering if his office is bugged, his car, the study in his house, his dining room, his bedroom for God's sake?

On leaving Hunte's office, I make my last obeisance by shouting at the plate glass wall that abuts the river and gives clear access to the unidirectional microphones no doubt surreptiously located on the other bank:

"AND MAY GOD BLESS THE UNITED STATES OF AMERICA FOREVER."

33
MAKING IT WORK TO SERVE THEIR ENDS

The Pro-Consul's (retired) **pronunciamento** *– Lakhdar Brahimi – Ayatollah Ali al-Sistani*

Sunday, 29 February–Tuesday, 2 March 2004

The Pro-Consul (retired) can always be relied upon to get to the point without prevarication.

"Make it [the UN] work with us to serve our ends."

The Pro-Consul's appreciation is delivered on a Sunday morning talk show in the course of a conversation about the UN's role in Haiti and Iraq. This unabashed analysis of the UN's purpose in the twenty-first century comes not from the armchair warriors in the White House, or the right-wing think tanks of the Heritage Foundation and the American Enterprise Institute, but from a former US Ambassador to the UN, a putative Secretary of State in a Democratic Administration, and a vociferous admirer of Kofi Annan – "The best Secretary-General of all time," in his expressed view.

Lakhdar Brahimi

The United States had now determined that it was time to make the UN work with it to serve its ends in Iraq. The chief server had been identified in the person of Lakhdar Brahimi as the natural successor to De Mello. Brahimi decried any such ambition letting it be known that, at seventy, he was "too old." Annan announced that he was appointing him his, "Special Adviser for Conflict Situations." Whatever Brahimi's real intentions were, he was destined for Iraq.

Tempted by Annan, he was invited to Washington to be wooed by Condi, courted by Cole-in and exposed to Dubya's boisterous charm.

I'd first met Brahimi in 1991 when, serving as its Secretary, I'd taken the lead in organising the first meeting in decades of the Economic and Social Council at the ministerial level. Then the Foreign Minister of Algeria, he had presided over the meeting. He was clearly very bright, worldly and sophisticated but, most strikingly, carried himself with an easy dignity that was compelling. I'd liked him enormously.

I'd met him again the following year when I had served as Secretary and he as Rapporteur of the UN Conference on Environment and Development – the "Earth Summit." After that, I'd met him casually over the years but had only seriously renewed acquaintance in the summer of 1999 when I'd organised the Arab regional meeting in preparation for the Millennium Summit. I'd invited Brahimi to be a panellist and found my previous impressions confirmed. Regarding Iraq, I could not ascribe petty reasons to his readiness to consider coming on board. Perhaps, as an Arab, he felt a sense of overriding duty, or as someone who had gained public acclaim for his missions on behalf of the UN in recent years, he had come to believe in the indispensability of the UN. Perhaps he simply liked to keep busy, to be involved in political life.

But in politics there is only one valid test and that is the one set by Groucho Marx when he'd asked: "Who do you believe – me, or the evidence of your own eyes?"

On the weekend of the 7 February, the United Nations returned to Iraq. The main part of the team had left from New York and had no knowledge of Brahimi's involvement, as their leader, until he joined them en route. Brahimi had let it be known that if word of his participation leaked in advance he would withdraw. On Tuesday, 10 February, former regime employees (or maybe fedayeen, Osamists, al-Qaedists, rumpists, dead enders, Iranians, Syrians, Chechnyans, Uzbeks, Muslims) decided to make a point: a car bomb destroyed a police station south of Baghdad killing 50 and wounding some 150. The next day, as an exclamation mark, a suicide car bomber exploded at an Iraqi recruitment centre in Baghdad killing another 50.

Ayatollah Ali al-Sistani

The UN had been summoned to Baghdad by the meddlesome Ayatollah who had refused to accept Annan's fatwa from New York that elections could not be held before the handover date of 30 June. Sistani's opposition had put paid to the plan for guided democracy through caucus "elections" so the US was left with two immediate concerns. The first was to defeat any thought of direct elections for it would be insupportable to have a Shiite government in place in Iraq or, at any rate, in place before the American elections in November 2004. The second was to confirm the return of "sovereignty" to Iraq by the advertised date of 30 June, again geared to the November elections, in order to show that progress was being made and disengagement from Iraq was well in train.

The UN team spent ten days in Iraq. Brahimi travelled to Najaf to meet Sistani in his stronghold, and conferred with the Governing Council and the CPA. Upon his return, he announced that elections would not be possible before the following year but that the handover date of 30 June should be maintained.

Make it work with us to serve our ends.

34
COMING HOME TO ROOST

Oil-for-food – Ruling out a third term – Rwanda persistent
– A question of accountability

———◦———

"Bad ting neva got owner."

West Indian proverb

———◦———

Oil-for-food

Monday, 8 March

The undermining of the years-long effort to win support for the Organisation in the United States is well underway. The United Nations, and Kofi Annan himself, has become engulfed in the biggest public controversy of his tenure.

The trouble began a month ago when the *Wall Street Journal* reported that my friend Benon's name was to be found amongst a list of names uncovered in the Iraq Oil Ministry purportedly as receiving oil allocations from Saddam Hussein, which could be sold; in other words, that Benon had accepted bribes. The matter has now taken on a broader dimension with credible evidence emerging that Iraq had for years run a "kickback" scheme that may have siphoned off as much as $5 billion from "oil-for-food" proceeds. The UN is being accused of ignoring the evidence of corruption or, at a minimum, treating it lightly. The scandal has taken on an even more personal dimension for Annan as it has been revealed that Annan's son Kojo had worked for a Swiss-based company called Cotecna that the UN had employed in 1999 to inspect the entry of goods into Iraq secured under the "oil-for-food" programme. Cotecna took over from Lloyd's Register on the basis of a lower bid.

William Safire of the *New York Times* has dubbed the affair, "Kofigate."

It is preposterous to suggest that Kofi or Benon have been engaged in financial improprieties of any sort.

Thursday, 18 March

The UN has been formally invited back to Iraq to advise on the establishment of a successor government to the Governing Council and on the organisation of elections.

The invitation took a little doing. Brahimi had angered many Iraqi factions by his advocacy of "sovereignty first, elections after", and had also come under attack in Shiite quarters for the impertinence of being a Sunni. The invitation letter was written only after Bremer had virtually locked the members of the Council in a room for four hours in order to obtain their compliance. This pressure in favour of Brahimi by the US does little to establish Brahimi as an independent force to be trusted.

Friday, 19 March

The *Wall Street Journal* is not letting up. In a series of articles, the UN has been excoriated.

> "The Cash-for Saddam Programme" (8 March)
> "The Oil-for-Food Scandal" (11 March)
> "Rely on the UN? Are You Kidding" (16 March)
> "Oil for Scandal" (18 March)

The SG has announced that he will ask OIOS to examine the administration of the programme and any UN role in the alleged corruption. Other newspapers have now joined in the hunt.

"UN caves in on inquiry into its oil-for-food 'scandal'; Officials deny pocketing huge sums through Saddam's 'voucher' system" (*Sunday Telegraph*)

"UN considers probe into oil-for-food programme" (*Financial Times*)

"Corruption charges betray Iraq's ambivalence towards UN: Oil-for-food scandal" (*National Post*, Canada)

"Kofi probes Saddam oil 'Bribes' for UN" (*New York Post*)

"UN probes oil-for-food corruption: Programme's ex-chief under investigation" (*Ottawa Citizen*)

"Scandal at the UN" (William Safire, *NY Times*)

"Kickback probe targets chief of UN program" (*Washington Times*)

"GAO: Iraq Oil Program Profits Understated; Investigation Finds $10.1 Billion Earned Illegally Under Hussein's Government" (*Washington Post*)

"UN Program Lost More to Hussein GAO Raises Value of Assets Stolen to $10.1 Billion from Oil-for-Food Plan" (*Wall Street Journal*)

"Hussein's Fund Thefts higher Than Estimated" (*Los Angeles Times*)

"UN probing Saddam's 'foreign bribe' cases" (*The Pioneer*, New Delhi)

Rwanda persistent

Friday, 26 March

Ten years after the genocide in Rwanda and five years after he had limited himself to expressing only collective remorse on behalf of the international community for the failure to act to prevent the slaughter, Kofi Annan acknowledges a degree of personal responsibility for the institutional inertia that permitted the killings to occur.

"The international community is guilty of sins of omission," he says on Friday at a Memorial Conference on the Rwanda genocide organised at the UN by the governments of Canada and Rwanda.

"I myself, as head of the UN's peacekeeping department at the time, pressed dozens of countries for troops. I believed at the time that I was doing my best. *But I realised after the genocide that there was more that I could and should have done to sound the alarm and rally support.* This painful memory, along with that of Bosnia and Herzegovina, has influenced much of my thinking, and many of my actions as Secretary-General."

I'm reminded of that day I had met with him in his office, the day before the Carlsson report on Rwanda came out. He was in a mood then, and had travelled to a place, that I had never witnessed in him before or since. He had gone beyond his usual calm to a sanctuary of morbid and watchful stillness. He had been glad to see me that day, glad to welcome me to his armoury.

It has taken many years for him to bring himself to utter these words of personal regret and self-admonition. Previously, he had been defensive, and even cavalier.

"It's an old story," he had said in May 1998 in response to a *New Yorker* article in which it was charged that he had ordered peacekeepers in Rwanda not to intervene after he, as the then head of UN peacekeeping, had been alerted to the pending onslaught.

"The failure to prevent the 1994 genocide was local, national and international. The fundamental failure was the lack of political will, not the lack of information," he added.

241

This was not a view held by the Rwandans, and they could not have been pleased that he had voiced it immediately prior to a visit he was about to make to their country, which they would have expected to be a pilgrimage of reconciliation and atonement. In a speech to the Rwandan Parliament on 7 May he acknowledged that, "The world failed Rwanda," but, in that lecturing tone that he and his speechwriters easily slip into when speaking of Third World problems or addressing Third World audiences, he could not resist the rebuke and the historical correction.

"It was a horror that came from within," he decided to remind them. And, "Evil in Rwanda was not aimed only at Tutsis. It was aimed at anyone who would stand up or speak out against the murder. Let us remember therefore that when the killers began they also sought out Hutus now described as 'moderate.'"

Anticipating undiluted contrition, the Tutsis were instead offered a balanced perspective. They reacted predictably. The President, Vice-President, and Prime Minister declined to attend a dinner they themselves were hosting in his honour. A Presidential spokesman described the speech as, "arrogant." Arriving at a technical college on the outskirts of Kigali to talk to a group of survivors of the genocide, he found that no one was there to meet him.

In September 2001, he tried again. By this time the Rwandans were no longer the pitied survivors but the backers of a new government in the Congo that they had helped install by force of arms. The world was concerned about the Congo because the Congo was rich and strategic and Rwanda now held the key. President Kagame demonstrated Rwanda's recently-acquired self-confidence when he thanked Annan for his, "timely visit which is an embrace for the Rwandan government in its tireless efforts in seeing that there is peace and stability in the region."

But the legacy of Rwanda remained, for on 7 April the world will bear witness to the Rwandan neglect when the "International Day of Reflection on the 1994 Genocide in Rwanda" is observed though not as a result of a UN initiative but upon the recommendation of the African Union.

Others have already preceded him with more fulsome expressions of remorse.

"I failed in Rwanda... It is a failure that I was not able to convince the members of the Security Council to intervene, and it is another failure that I was not able to understand from the beginning the importance of what was going on. So we have a double failure... It took me weeks before suddenly we discovered that it was genocide. So this is another kind of failure..." So Boutros-Ghali.

"I will feel guilt for the rest of my life, I understand that people think it's irrational, but I can't sit here and say I did everything I could, and I still ended up smothered in bodies... I was the UN commander out there and I failed." So General Dallaire, the UN commander of the peacekeeping force in Rwanda.

Bill Clinton had given his own version of responsibility on a visit to Rwanda in March 1998 – or rather the airport in Kigali the capital from whence he did not care, or dare, to tread. It was billed as the "Clinton apology." It was hardly that.

"The international community, together with nations in Africa, must bear its share of responsibility for this tragedy, as well. We did not act quickly enough after the killing began. We should not have allowed the refugee camps to become safe haven for the killers. We did not immediately call these crimes by their rightful name: genocide," he said.

"It may seem strange to you here," he continued, "especially the many of you who lost members of your family, but all over the world there were people like me sitting in offices, day after day after day, who did not fully appreciate [pause] the depth [pause] and the speed [pause] with which you were being engulfed by this unimaginable terror."

Beginning 8 April 1994, and regularly for days thereafter, the *New York Times* and the *Washington Post* ran extensive articles about the terror which Clinton, famed for his omnivorous reading, would seem to have missed. He must have missed too information from his own State Department letting him know that between 9–10 April 250 Americans, including his diplomats from his Embassy in

Kigali, were being evacuated from Rwanda by five land convoys. His attention had also apparently not been drawn to the despatch of US Marines to neighbouring Burundi (where they stayed.) Nor could he have been aware that his Permanent Representative to the United Nations, Madeleine Albright, had demanded that all UN peacekeeping troops should be withdrawn forthwith from Rwanda, a policy position she must have arrived at unilaterally. And at the UN, despite his detailed reporting to DPKO, General Dallaire was receiving instructions not to intervene or, if he felt he must, to do so only on behalf of the western expatriates. And the killings in Rwanda went on for three months.

In an interview with *Frontline* on 17 February 2004, Kofi Annan was asked:

"The warning fax that came in from General Dallaire did you see it? What was your response?"

He replied:

"I think the fax came in, and General Dallaire had also been in touch on the phone with General Baril [in the U.N's DPKO]. In fact, [Dallaire] had sent other messages, where sometimes he questioned that, 'Somebody came and gave me this information. I don't know how sincere it is, whether I am being manipulated or not,' because intelligence can be used to manipulate you; and knowing also the situation in the Security Council, that we were discussing this in the Council... So the idea was to really, first of all, act very quickly. *The Assistant Secretary-General [Iqbal Riza] was dealing with that,* and I had my hands full at that time also with Yugoslavia. We had Yugoslavia, and we had Rwanda..."

"There was a void of leadership in New York," General Dallaire writes in his book, "Shake Hands with the Devil."

"We had sent a deluge of paper and received nothing in return;

no supplies, no reinforcements, no decisions."

And no taking of personal responsibility. And no resignations.

A question of accountability

Tuesday, 30 March

The report of the Accountability Panel (SIAP), which had been established to follow up the Ahtisaari Report, was released yesterday. The UN Security Coordinator and the Designated (Security) Official in Baghdad, who had already been publicly identified as the likely miscreants, have had their provisional sentences confirmed. The Security Coordinator has been asked to resign and the Designated Official demoted in rank.

The sins of the sinners are many. The Security Coordinator put forward a flawed security plan and the Designated Official went along with it. Fréchette's group endorsed it, but they were misled. They get a slap on the wrist, with a letter from the SG chiding them for lacking "due care and diligence in the manner in which they dealt with the circumstances of the return to Baghdad." Louise gets a little slap too with a letter from the SG expressing his disappointment and regret with regard to the failures identified by the Panel which are attributable to the Group. It is announced that Louise had tendered her resignation to the SG but he has declined to accept it, taking into account the collective nature of the failures attributable to the group as a whole.

As for Annan, he is said to have acted faultlessly.

"Having approved a proposal put forward by the Designated Official which was endorsed by the Group, and on which there were no reservations expressed by the UN Security Coordinator, the Secretary-General acted in a proper manner," the report concludes. Or, as his Spokesman puts it, "The Secretary-General took the decision to send staff back to Iraq last summer on the basis of the recommendations of his most senior officials."

It is all the fault of the Designated Official.

"The proposal to return to Baghdad originated with the Office of the Humanitarian Coordinator/Designated Official," the report confides.

What a siren that Lopes da Silva is, luring the passive Secretary-General, and his disinterested Deputy Secretary-General, and the indifferent heads of the UN agencies, the British head of UNDP, and the American head of UNICEF, and the American head of WFP, the three major agencies involved, all lured unsuspectingly by Ramiro Lopes da Silva back to Iraq.

The hierarchical nature of the judgements is wonderfully drawn. The SG is absolved. Fréchette and the heads of the UN agencies are semi-absolved. The Designated Official is downgraded. The Security Coordinator is dismissed. But the full fury of the report is not directed at any of these, even the dismissed and the downgraded. The bureaucratic order must be observed. So the most censorious language is reserved for those lowest down the ladder – the Chief Administrative Officer and the Building Manager are charged with displaying, "profound lack of responsibility and ineptitude... Their combined response indicates a lethargy bordering on gross negligence..." They are to be charged with misconduct and disciplinary procedures initiated against them.

Kofi Annan distances himself from the events.

"The Secretary-General regrets the failure identified by the Panel and expresses his determination to take all corrective measures, within his authority, to enhance the safety and security of all UN staff."

As his Spokesman has it, referring to the Security Coordinator, "So, the buck stops there."

35

A CACOPHONY OF CATASTROPHES

*The protest of the sixty – Reflecting on Rwanda – The
Bees of Baghdad – Accusing headlines – Anticipatory
genuflection – A Cyprus stumble – The Great Brahimi –
Ultimate responsibility – Learning to vote right –
A Hollywood production*

The protest of the sixty

Monday, 5 April

[The following letter was sent today to the Secretary-General
by sixty staff members of the Departments of Political Affairs,
Peacekeeping Operations, the Offices for the Coordination of
Humanitarian Assistance and the Security Coordinator.]

New York, 5 April 2004

Dear Secretary-General,
We, the undersigned staff members of the United Nations
Secretariat, are writing to express our concern at your
response to the investigation into accountability for the
tragic events of 19 August 2003...

From the very outset, the parameters for the UN's
proposed engagement in Iraq were set by you and by the
Steering Group on Iraq (SGI). These parameters were shaped
by your early decision that the UN should play a political
role in the aftermath of the invasion. Moreover, following
the adoption of Security Council resolution 1483 (2003),

the role played by you and other senior managers in New York in encouraging senior officials in Iraq to maintain and increase the UN's operational presence in order to fulfil the mandate significantly affected the management of the security situation in Iraq. ....We believe the full extent of the exceptional internal and external political pressure, and its adverse impact on UN decision-making on the ground in Iraq and at Headquarters, has not been properly taken into account.

Second, in light of the above, we are disappointed by your lack of acknowledgement of your personal responsibility in this matter:

You were the official ultimately responsible for the key decisions affecting the UN's deployment and posture in Iraq, and were intimately involved in all aspects of the crisis... You are ultimately responsible for the security of UN staff. We believe that implying... that you bear no such responsibility because you were poorly advised, is disingenuous. It is entirely reasonable that the staff of the UN should look to you to take responsibility for your decisions in relation to Iraq.

We believe that the Security Coordinator and the Designated Official (DO) have been forced to bear a disproportionate amount of responsibility for the tragedy in Iraq. In addition, few if any of the failures or omissions specifically attributed by the Accountability Report to these two officials would have affected the fact that the UN was targeted in this unprecedented manner.

Third, we believe that you have failed to apply fundamental principles of fairness and due process in the case of the Field Security Coordination Officer (FSCO) and of the two senior managers concerned:

By seeking the resignation of the two senior officials and reassigning the FSCO without any written notification of the charges against them, their right to know the basis of the disciplinary action taken against them and to defend their actions was denied. To our knowledge, none of them has been provided with a full copy of the ... report. The Staff Rules clearly outline the rights of individual staff members in this regard.

Fourth, the actions you have taken in response to the Accountability Report are very likely to severely restrict the UN's ability to carry out its humanitarian and peacekeeping mandates in the future:

By disregarding the wider context, including the political pressures from within the Organisation as well as those from outside, and by placing excessive emphasis on individual responsibility over and above the United Nations system's shared responsibility for security, we fear that [officials in charge] may adopt an overly risk-averse posture simply to avoid a similar sanction.

In conclusion, we feel that your Spokesman's statement on 29 March 2004 was incomplete, and that a review of your decisions following the Accountability Report's release is appropriate.

Therefore:
We ask you to state to the staff of the United Nations that you, as our Secretary-General, take responsibility for your decisions in Iraq as well as for the collective failure of the system that you head to protect its staff. In times of crisis, the staff expects you to provide leadership.

We urge you to review your acceptance of the resignations of Mr. Tun Myat and Mr. Ramiro Lopes da Silva and the absence of due process afforded to them.

We ask you to pursue vigorously the issue of the role and responsibility of the CPA, as the Occupying Power in Iraq, in providing security to UN premises and staff, and in bringing to justice those who conspired to murder our colleagues.
Yours sincerely,
(Signed)

Tuesday, 6 April

The protest of the sixty is not the only manifestation of discontent. The Staff Union has issued its own condemnation entitled, "Where is accountability? The Accountability Report (SIAP) and Secretary-General's response falls far short in holding senior officials accountable." The release goes on to claim that, "The report, as well as the response, is selective in who is accountable and the extent to which they are culpable." It concludes: "These latest developments do not go far enough to solve the real problem facing the United Nations – the accountability of senior officials." [30/3/04]

Reflecting on Rwanda

Wednesday, 7 April

The "International Day of Reflection" on the tragedy in Rwanda is to be observed by the General Assembly this morning and Hunte is sitting at his place on the podium looking around. The seat to his right, due to be occupied by the Secretary-General, is empty and Hunte is getting restless.

Hunte has done his best to set a standard of punctuality for the Assembly since assuming office. Conscious of the habitual deriding of the UN as a place where meetings never begin on time, he arrives early and starts meetings promptly.

The meeting was supposed to start at 10 a.m. and it is already 10.15 a.m. and now Louise turns up and slips into the chair reserved for the Secretary-General. People look at one another and begin to whisper as it becomes apparent that Kofi Annan is not about to appear. Hunte bangs the gavel and the sad ceremony begins. At 10.30 a.m. Iqbal Riza slips in unobtrusively and takes a seat off to the side, just in front of me.

The International Day is, naturally, also being observed in Rwanda. A massive ceremony is held in the stadium in Kigali and Belgium stolidly sends its Foreign Minister to attend. President

Kagame uses the occasion to launch a violent attack on the French, who he accuses of having armed the Hutu slaughterers. The Foreign Minister of Rwanda is present for the ceremony in the General Assembly Hall, and a repetition of the public scolding Annan had received six years ago in the Rwanda Parliament during his visit of reconciliation is something that the Secretary-General must have decided he could not risk. Instead, he is in Geneva where he addresses the Commission on Human Rights and launches a programme to guard against genocide in the future, the centrepiece of which is the appointment of a Special Adviser on Genocide, and warns about the impending tragedy in Darfur.

Afterwards I decide to have a look at the speech he delivered in Geneva. I do so tentatively, hopefully, timorously, fervently, despairingly, treacherously and, as it turns out, presciently.

In the speech in New York, voiced at the Canadian-Rwandan remembrance, a degree of personal responsibility had, ten years later, been finally acknowledged:

> "I myself, as head of the UN's peacekeeping department at the time, pressed dozens of countries for troops. I believed at the time that I was doing my best. *But I realised after the genocide that there was more that I could and should have done to sound the alarm and rally support.*"

Today he says:

> "First we must acknowledge our responsibility for not having done more to prevent or stop the genocide.
>
> *Neither the United Nations Secretariat, nor the Security Council, nor Member States in general, nor the international media, paid enough attention to the gathering signs of disaster. Still less did we take timely action.*
>
> When we recall such events and ask 'why did no one intervene?' we should address the question not only to the United Nations, or even to its Member States. *No one can*

claim ignorance. All who were playing any part in world affairs at that time should ask, 'what more could I have done? How would I react next time – and what am I doing <u>now</u> to make it less likely there will <u>be</u> a next time?'...."

So it is a matter of collective guilt, in fact we have now arrived at *universal guilt*; for the media is sucked in, as well as everyone else – "no one can claim ignorance."

[In his book "Interventions", Kofi Annan avoided relitigating the question of his personal responsibility. He did not avoid the subject of responsibility altogether though commenting that, "The world knew the scale of the killing in Rwanda, and *yet we could not get anyone, from governments across the world, to do anything seriously to help*". He also wrote, "The Security Council turned its back [on Rwanda]...".]

Louise explains in her speech to the Assembly that the SG had thought it more fitting for him to speak on the subject to the body charged with protecting human rights than to be here, in his house. He could also have gone to the remembrance in Kigali, one imagines, but he was wise not to do so, as Kagame would have flailed him as he flailed the French.

Louise lets us know that the best thing we can all now do in tribute to the massacred Rwandans is to support the SG's new programme.

The Bees of Baghdad

Brahimi and his team have slipped back into Baghdad. They are holding talks with the CPA, members of the Governing Council, NGOs and others.

Robert Blackwill, Deputy Assistant to the President, Coordinator for Strategic Planning for the National Security Advisor and the Iraqi expert on Bush's National Security Council, has also slipped into Iraq, as he invariably does when Brahimi is there. It is the concert of the three "Bs" – Blackwill, Bremer, and Brahimi. One sits on Brahimi's right; one sits on his left. But who's the Bumblebee?

Some dozen cities and towns in Iraq are places of carnage as "thugs" and "former regime elements" assault the occupiers. Twelve foreigners have been kidnapped.

Accusing headlines

Thursday, 8 April

The unrelenting barrage of unfavourable publicity that the oil-for-food affair has produced continues without a pause.

"UN knew of kickbacks in Iraq's oil-for-food programme: Documents show how politics and caution at the UN enabled Iraq to exact kickbacks long after tales of corruption began to circulate" (*Financial Times*)

"Shams, scams and Kofi Annan" (*New Zealand Herald*)

"Follow-up to Kofigate" (William Safire in the *NY Times*)

"UN Chiefs probed in giant Iraq oil scam" (*Sunday Times*, London)

"Get to heart of UN role in Iraq Oil-for-Food scandal" (*Newsday*, New York)

"Oil-for-Palaces" (*New York Post*)

"Saddam's UN Financiers" (*Wall Street Journal*)

April is the cruellest month...

Anticipatory genuflection

Friday, 9 April

"She'll be right down."

Louise has been summoned to his office by an angry Hunte to explain why the UN Secretariat is acting demonstrably in the interests of the great powers. The SG is away and she is in charge. If he had been here, I think Hunte is furious enough to have attempted to summon him. (The 38th Floor won't like this. They'll think I set it up to humiliate Louise, which is not the case. Another colleague had demanded her presence. I don't particularly mind annoying them but I'd much prefer to do so wittingly.)

A few days ago, we had discussed preparations for future meetings on Security Council reform with the Secretariat officials working with us. They were from the US, the UK and China. We had asked them to provide a historical record on the exercise of the veto – by whom, when and in what circumstances.

"We are not allowed to provide that information," we had been told.

"But it's public information!"

"It's too sensitive. Even when delegations contact us to ask for information on when the veto has been used on particular issues, we refer them to the Library."

"But the veto is not cast surreptitiously. People raise their hands in front of the TV cameras!"

"It can't be done. Perhaps you could consult the internet. Anyway, we don't keep that information."

"We are asking you. It is your job to provide authoritative information. Or does the Secretariat now have a veto too?"

"We are not allowed to provide it."

The next day we were visited by a more senior Secretariat delegation, of similar composition, led by another American.

"We don't provide such information. But here is data down-loaded from a website. Perhaps, you could prepare something on this basis," they said nudging a document in my direction.

"The veto is not cast in camera," I reply, nudging the document back. "You have no reason not to provide the information."

"It is politically sensitive," they continue to insist.

"This is despicable," says Hunte, ending the meeting.

Upon arrival, Louise advises that this is the first she has heard of the controversy. She is not sure what the problem can be. But the information is sensitive; it will show that in recent years the veto has been cast almost exclusively by the US on Middle East issues. That would make for a politically divisive discussion.

"But that is our responsibility to decide, not the Secretariat's. This cannot be said to be secret information."

She will look into it, although it is already nearly 6 p.m. and she is leaving for Canada for the Easter weekend, and anyway this is a matter for Riza to deal with, but she will brief him fully.

Louise's bureaucratic skills are undiminished.

Even I, who have long decried the influence of the great powers, most particularly the US and the UK, on the UN, am astonished. The Secretariat is so cowed that it is unwilling to provide basic data on public actions in the most watched area of the UN's work. Moreover, they have gone as far as to claim that they do not even maintain such records for their own purposes.

We inconsiderately publicised the Secretariat's reluctance and they were obliged to reassess. Yesterday, a former colleague from the Secretariat turned up and gave me, with a conspiratorial air, a document emblazoned with the caution, "NOT AN OFFICIAL DOCUMENT"; this, I was told, contained the secret data. Interestingly, it contained more than that since it listed all negative votes by both permanent and non-permanent members on occasions when the veto had been cast, which usefully served to bury the requested information.

I doubt whether the Secretariat has acted on specific instructions from the US or the UK or any of the other great powers. They are acting from an acquired orientation, which teaches that great powers cannot be offended.

In September 1960 Nikita Khrushchev came to the United Nations determined to undermine Dag Hammarskjöld. He called for his resignation. Hammarskjöld replied:

"Use whatever words you like, independence, impartiality, objectivity – they all describe essential aspects of what, without exception, must be the attitude of the Secretary-General.

"Such an attitude," he went on, "may at any stage become an obstacle for those who work for certain political aims which would be better achieved if the Secretary-General compromised with this attitude. But if he did, how gravely he would then betray the trust of all those for whom the strict maintenance of such an attitude is their best protection in the world-wide fight for power and influence."

His speech was greeted by an ovation.

A Cyprus stumble

Sunday, 25 April

The UN's proposals for the reunification of Cyprus have been rejected by the Greek Cypriot side in a nationwide referendum.

As it happened, I knew a lot about Cyprus and its dramas. I'd been a member of the Guyana Mission, the Deputy Permanent Representative, when the Turks invaded Cyprus exactly thirty years ago. For Guyana, with our still innocent perception of international affairs, the issue required no debate – Turkey had violated international law by invading Cyprus and occupying the Northern region where the Turkish Cypriots were concentrated.

We were prepared to admit to some complicating factors such as the *coup d'état* in Athens which had brought a junta to power and the right-wing uprising in Nicosia that had driven Archbishop Makarios off the island and temporarily into exile. But, for us, none of these factors outweighed the essential principles that were the pillars on which we thought the UN stood – non-interference in the internal affairs of states and respect for state sovereignty.

A group of five non-aligned countries were selected to craft a resolution suitable for the circumstance; Guyana was a member. We took the lead and prepared a short text demanding Turkey's withdrawal. In parallel we met covertly with Makarios and Kyprianou, being smuggled late at night into hotel suites, for although the Greek Cypriots did not determine our position, they certainly benefited from it.

We soon learnt the reality of religious and ethnic politics. Algeria and Yugoslavia were both members of the "Group of Five" and were more influenced by their Muslim affiliations than by Turkey's act of aggression. The resolution that emerged from the Group, and which was adopted overwhelmingly by the General Assembly, balanced respect for non-interference with appreciation of the Turkish Cypriots' minority status. When we joined the Security Council the following year we found that it was not possible to move the Council to act decisively on Cyprus. A UN peacekeeping force was authorised to keep the communities apart, and thereafter began a thirty-year process of intermittent negotiations on Cyprus.

Cyprus represented a convergence of themes that acquired greater resonance as the years passed. Strategically placed in the middle of the Mediterranean, Britain had retained a base there and had no intention of surrendering it as tensions in the Middle East showed no signs of abating. Greece and Turkey were wrapped in a long, internecine history of blood as traditionally befits neighbours with proud, imperial pasts, memories of occupation and distinct religious traditions. But the resonance in this case went even deeper, reaching back to Greece's position as the origin of Western democratic traditions and the inspirer of Western youth with the Homeric epics, and Turkey as the home of the Ottoman Empire, the place of the last Caliphate, and forever the invader of Christian Europe. Cyprus was the unfortunate depository of the narrative of division separating East and West.

The lengthy hiatus in the Cyprus negotiation had largely been the fault of the Turks. Under the scrutiny of the Turkish army, no Turkish government had been prepared to risk making concessions to Greece or to appear to view with less than acclaim the martial feat that the 1974 invasion represented. The Turkish Cypriot leader, Rauf Denktash, proved to be an intransigent foe of reconciliation preferring to press for independence or complete autonomy within a unitary state in name only.

After "9/11," solidifying Turkey in the NATO alliance became an imperative for the West. The two Mediterranean islands of Cyprus and Malta, that at one time had proved to be irritants, needed to be admitted to the European Union to avert any possibility of their return to "questionable" alliances, given their strategic position. The admission date for Cyprus was to be 1 May and this deadline came to represent a means of forcing, at last, a Cypriot reconciliation which would, in turn, ease relations between Greece and Turkey and set the stage for Turkey's own eventual admission to the EU.

Combined US, EU and UN pressure achieved a scenario in which Kofi Annan would conduct negotiations first with the two Cypriot entities. If, as expected, this proved to be unsuccessful, Turkey and Greece would be asked to join. If an agreement could still not be reached, Annan would convene a meeting of all the parties to offer a solution. In the event that his solution proved unacceptable, he was given the authority to impose one, which would then be submitted to the two parties for separate referenda. The Annan settlement would only be valid if both sides voted in its favour.

The deal Kofi Annan presented was deemed unsatisfactory by the Turks. He then amended it, to produce a conclusion palatable to them. It effectively left Cyprus as a divided island of two communities, with a weak central government, minor border adjustments involving Turkish concessions, a limited return of Greek Cypriot land, the legitimisation of the presence of mainland Turks who had emigrated since 1974 and the continued presence of Turkish troops on the island. The Turkish side hailed the agreement; the Greek Cypriots felt betrayed. Thirty years of Turkish intransigence had worn down the negotiators – acquisition of territory by force was being legitimised by the UN, prompted by Washington and Brussels, and the EU was ready to abandon a principle tenet of its existence namely freedom of movement for all EU citizens. Fear of Turkish waywardness had overwhelmed adherence to fundamental international principles of interstate behaviour.

Turkey and the Turkish Cypriots lauded the agreement. Greece guardedly went along but the Greek Cypriot Prime Minister opposed it. In the run-up to the referendum, and with the realisation that the Greek Cypriots were set to reject it, Annan unexpectedly sought help from the Security Council by urging that a resolution be passed that would extend the prospect of security guarantees to Cyprus. Russia vetoed the resolution, arguing that it constituted an unacceptable attempt to influence the outcome of the referendum. More likely, Russia felt that it had no incentive to assist NATO and the EU, both of which had moved without compunction to advance, militarily and politically to Russia's southern boundaries, in order to secure the West's northern flank.

The Turkish Cypriots voted for the Secretary-General's plan with a two to one majority; the Greek Cypriots turned it down overwhelmingly by three to one.

Monday, 26 April

Hunte was in a meeting with the Secretary-General this morning. He remarked afterwards that the SG's speech was ordinary. But it is his other remark that disturbed me.

"He looked..." He had paused, searching for a word.

"He looked... dishevelled."

This I found hard to accept. He had become known for the elegance of his dress, suits of sombre colours, with a touch of the dandy in the fine quality of his shirts, and the subtle richness of his ties, always perfectly turned out. I hated the thought of him looking dishevelled.

Tuesday, 27 April

I'm standing in the corridor, outside our offices, when the door leading from the Economic and Social Council Chamber opens and Kofi Annan strides out. We exchange glances. He changes direction, and comes towards me.

"Miles, how are you?" he says, holding out his hand.

I'm carrying papers in my right hand, and struggle to transfer them to my left. He waits patiently, with his hand held out.

"Fine, SG. How are you?"

"You're looking well. And say hello to L and 'The Princess'," he remarks with a smile, before walking away.

And he himself is looking well. A little tired perhaps, but not dishevelled at all. I find I'm glad of that.

Wednesday, 28 April

"Congress to investigate claims of Saddam's Oil-for-Food bribery" (*The Independent,* London)

"UN officials took oil bribes from Saddam" (*The Times*, London)

"UN officials 'covered up Saddam theft of billions in aid for Iraqis'" (*The Daily Telegraph*, London)

"Probe turns to $1 billion collected by the UN" (*The Washington Times*)

"UN moment of truth" (*The Washington Post*)

"Hussein Allegedly Made Payoffs for Support in UN" (*The Wall Street Journal*)

"Food for scandal" (Editorial, *The Times*, London)

"Senior UN officials stole from oil-for-food program: report" (Agence France-Presse)

"UN big still denies oil rig: Annan" (*New York Post*)

"Seduced by Saddam" (Op-Ed, *New York Post*)

"The UN must investigate the scandals of its Food-for-Oil Programme in Iraq" (Editorial, *The Independent*, London)

"The UN has to come clean" (*The Los Angeles Times*)

"UN apologists remain silent on oil scandal" (*The Australian*)

"Oil for terror" (*The Wall Street Journal*)

The Great Brahimi

Thursday, 29 April

Lakhdar Brahimi has returned to New York and briefed the Security Council on the UN's plans for Iraq. An Interim Government is to be established by the handover date of 30 June to be followed by a national conference to be convened shortly thereafter which would select a consultative body to advise the Interim Government. National elections would be arranged for January 2005.

The US is currently giving the impression that Brahimi will determine the political future of Iraq. Asked at a Press Conference on 13 April, "Who will you be handing the Iraqi government over to on June 30th?" Bush replies:

"We will find that out soon. That's what Mr. Brahimi is doing; he's figuring out the nature of the entity we'll be handing sovereignty over to."

The understanding is that the UN will select the Interim Government in consultation with the CPA and the Governing Council. In clarifying the process, Ahmad Fawzi, Brahimi's Spokesman says, "The UN will make the final selection."

The UN is being lauded around the world for its positive role in

Iraq and for its taming of the Shrew. Happiness and hubris abound.

Brahimi has himself announced that he wants a government of "technocrats." He expresses his disinclination to have Governing Council members serving in the Interim Government.

"My personal view at the moment is that people who have political parties and are leaders should get ready to win the election and stay out of the Interim Government."

Brahimi is being hailed as, "The Great Brahimi," who is said to be exercising pro-consular power. He is seen on television in Iraq wearing the modified Mao tunics that were the badge of revolutionary honour in the 1970s. He has, additionally, began to act as a man of the 70s. In television interviews he has described Israel as, "the big poison in the region." He has also attacked the US for its heavy-handed tactics in Iraq.

"When you surround a city, you bomb the city, when people cannot go to the hospital, what name do you have for that? If you have enemies there, this is exactly what they want you to do, to alienate people so that more people support them rather than you."

Washington does not criticise Brahimi for his comments; Kofi Annan does not take him to task. The Great Brahimi has been given a lot of rope; the question is, when will it be withdrawn? For "The Lord giveth and the Lord taketh away."

Administration officials have told the US Congress that the sovereignty to be handed over will be "limited." Or as Cole-in, standing in for "The Lord," puts it:

"It's sovereignty but (some) of that sovereignty they are going to allow us to exercise on their behalf and with their permission."

Ultimate responsibility

Friday, 30 April

The Secretary-General has issued two open letters responding to staff concerns about the results of, and his response to, the inquiries into the Baghdad bombing.

The first is a circular letter to all staff, dated 19 April. The Staff Council had called on the senior management of the Organisation to take responsibility for the actions that had led to the Baghdad tragedy. His reply needed to be a simple one in which he acknowledged the responsibility of the senior management of the Organisation, including himself as its leader, for the policy and planning decisions that had contributed to the Baghdad outcome.

He writes:

> "Dear Colleagues,
> Many of you have expressed concern over the measures taken following the findings of... the Iraq Accountability Panel... These decisions were among the most difficult I have had to take as Chief Administrative Officer of the Organisation. *I had to impose severe penalties on valued colleagues and friends who were found individually accountable, even while knowing that as Secretary-General, I bear the ultimate responsibility for the security of United Nations staff.*"

The second is a reply to the disaffected sixty. They had asked him to do the following:

> "We ask you to state to the staff of the United Nations that you, as our Secretary-General, take responsibility for your decisions in Iraq as well as for the collective failure of the system that you head to protect its staff. In times of crisis, the staff expects you to provide leadership."

The sixty had taken a perilous path. Many of them would have worked under him, and some beside him, in his years at the Peacekeeping Department. Most would have come to view him with admiration, a man risen from the ranks, who had become an eminent world figure. They had risked a great deal professionally by speaking out so frankly.

He writes:

> "I read in your letter a deep commitment from all of you to the United Nations as an Organisation, and to the people we serve all over the world. I value that greatly and in return I pledge to you that concrete actions will be taken to improve our security system and practices..."

The Secretary-General will take institutional responsibility and *ultimate* responsibility but avoids applying the criterion of *"individual accountability"* to himself that had resulted in his dismissal of a number of his colleagues.

Thursday, 6 May

Lakhdar Brahimi has returned to Iraq. Robert Blackwill has returned too.

Learning to vote right

Friday, 7 May

The Cypriot referenda had been described as a democratic process. It now emerges that there was a right vote and a wrong vote, and the Greek Cypriots have got it wrong

The full fury of the EU and the US have been vented on them due to their impudence in freely exercising their right to dissent. The yelp of Euro-American protest could be expected although the way the upset was conveyed bordered on the petulant. Kofi Annan, on the other hand, might have been expected to confine himself, as Secretary-General, to expressing disappointment while committing to resume negotiations when the time seemed right.

But the nature of Kofi Annan's reaction is unusual for him. He indicates his displeasure at the Greek Cypriots and their Prime Minister in press comments and in a report to the Security Council.

In a statement on 28 April 2004 he says: "The vote by the Greek Cypriots to reject my proposals last Saturday was of course a great disappointment... I salute the Turkish Cypriots for their courageous vote in favour of the proposals. *We must all do our best to see that they are not penalised for the way the vote went in the other part of the island"*. But then the result of the referenda must, indeed, have come as a great disappointment when a timely triumph seemed within reach. In any case, he had concluded that it was not his plan that was faulty; the blame lay with the Greeks for rejecting it.

A Hollywood production

Thursday, 3 June

And the Lord taketh away.....

Ayad Allawi, a member of the Governing Council, is to be the Prime Minister of the new "Interim" government. This was announced earlier this week in Baghdad. It wasn't announced by "The Great Brahimi" though, or by the Secretary-General of the United Nations. It was announced by the Governing Council and promptly lauded by "The Great Bremer" who can be seen on television squiring Allawi to press conferences. Bremer is "the Bumblebee."

Allawi is head of something called the Iraqi National Accord, an exile group based in London. Whereas other exile groups were funded by the Pentagon, Allawi's group was known to be funded by the CIA and understood to have close ties to Britain's MI6.

The day before the announcement Ahmad Fawzi says:

"The Governing Council is not going to appoint itself, it's not going to clone itself."

Five Governing Council members have been appointed to the eight senior posts in the Interim Government.

Soon after his return to Iraq, Brahimi was told that his plan for a "technocrat" government was not viable. Governing Council members would have to serve. Soon after he let it be known that his choice for Prime Minister was Hussain al-Shahristani, a nuclear scientist unaffiliated to any political party; he was advised that his choice was unacceptable. Soon after he indicated that his choice for President was Adnan Patachi, a former, senior Iraqi diplomat; soon after Patachi asked that his name be removed from contention.

An anonymous US official says that while Washington had been interested in Mr. Brahimi's advice, that "doesn't necessarily mean that whatever Brahimi said we would automatically endorse."

Ghazi al-Yawar, a member of the Governing Council, has been appointed President. Thirteen of the thirty-three Cabinet posts are to be held by either former Governing Council or cabinet members.

Ahmad Fawzi says:

"It would be absurd to think you could run a country without politicians backed by political parties."

Brahimi says:

"You know, sometimes people think I am a free agent out here, that I have a free hand to do whatever I want."

The Arab press says, "Brahimi may not have been a free agent but he does have free speech."

Condi says:

"I can tell you firmly and without contradiction, this is a terrific list, a really good government, and we are very pleased with the names that have emerged. These are not American puppets."

Kofi Annan says:

"I think we all have to recognise that the process wasn't perfect and it was a difficult environment. And I think, given the circumstances, I believe Mr. Brahimi did as best he could."

Ahmad Fawzi says:

"Brahimi never promised a government of angels."

Today, in his humiliation, Brahimi is reported to have derided Bremer as "the dictator of Iraq," a characteristic that he had evidently failed previously to discern although the "Bumblebee's" role in Iraq had not seemed in doubt.

Annan and Brahimi have served as the advance guard, the foot soldiers that clear the path and draw fire for those in command.

Their thinking it could be otherwise is the only real surprise.

"He has the money. He has the signature," Brahimi says of Bremer, speaking as if in tongues.

"I will not say who was my first choice, and who was not my first choice... I will remind you that the Americans are governing this country," he added.

Saadoun al-Dulaimi, the head of a Baghdad research organisation and polling center, said he spoke with Brahimi last week and that the diplomat was discouraged.

"He was very disappointed, very frustrated," al-Dulaimi said.

"I asked him why he didn't say that publicly (and) he said, 'I am the UN envoy to Iraq, how can I admit to failure?'"

Assessing the experience at an internal Secretariat meeting upon his return to Headquarters, Ahmad ("The UN will make the final selection") Fawzi is reported to have said: "It was a Hollywood production."

Make it work with us to serve our ends.

36
CONTINUING CATASTROPHES

"Lewd" Lubbers – Emergency sex – Integrity in doubt – The attacks on Dileep Nair – The exoneration of Lubbers – My friend Benon – Containing a scandal

———— ‹○› ————

"I was here but I disappear."

Ivanhoe "Ivan" Martin

The Harder they Come

———— ‹○› ————

"Lewd" Lubbers

Wednesday, 9 June

The UN High Commissioner for Refugees, Ruud Lubbers, is being investigated on the charge of sexually molesting one of his female staff members. Specifically, he is reportedly accused of "grabbing her behind." Lubbers has denied the allegation.

Following the initial complaint, it is reported that four other women have come forward with charges. Meanwhile, Lubbers' wife has let it be known that he just likes to put his arm around women.

Once the matter came to light, Ruud Lubbers immediately became, "Rude" Lubbers but that quickly morphed, more incisively, into "Lewd" Lubbers.

Lubbers is a former Dutch Prime Minister and Holland is a strong supporter of the UN in both political and financial terms. He is being investigated by the OIOS. Let us see what we shall see.

Emergency sex

Thursday, 10 June

Two serving UN staff members (Heidi Postlewait and Dr. Andrew Thomson) and one former staff member (Kenneth Cain) have written a book about their experiences in taking part in UN peacekeeping operations. The book is called, "Emergency Sex and Other Desperate Measures: A True Story from Hell on Earth."

The book describes their experiences in Cambodia, Somalia, Haiti, Rwanda, Liberia and Bosnia. It recounts sex parties, drug-taking, rape of the local population, financial irregularities, kickbacks and sexual harassment. The reporting of these episodes has created a stir.

The UN rules on publishing are clear – while working at the UN permission must be sought before anything is published. Once you leave, there are no continuing restrictions, save for prudence on the part of those interested in re-employment. Disciplinary measures, including dismissal, can, therefore, be taken against the two serving staff members but the media would thence only criticise the UN severely and suggest that a cover-up is underway.

Apart from the sensationalism, the book's serious purpose is to decry the deaths of civilians that took place in situations where the UN had been sent as a protector, Bosnia and Rwanda being the prominent examples. There is, additionally, harsh criticism of UN senior staff for incompetence in respect of their substantive, and indifference with regard to their moral responsibilities in peacekeeping missions.

There are, inevitably, more headlines:

"UN threatens authors of 'racy' expose" (*The Daily Telegraph*)

"UN missions painted as booze-soaked orgies" (*The Washington Times*)

"Tale of sex, drugs and corruption riles UN" (*The Times*)

"Book reveals scandal-ridden UN" (*CNN*)

"UN beset by sex, drugs, book says: Peacekeeping missions marred by corruption and incompetence" (*National Post*, Toronto)

"When Peacekeeping turns to despair" (*UN Wire*)

"Sex in drugs and hell" (*Salon*)

"UN-flattering" (*The Daily News*)

"Emergency sex authors fear firing, blast UN" (*NewsMax.Com*)

Integrity in doubt

Saturday, 12 June

The lead comment by the *Financial Times* sums it up well: "United Nations staff are dissatisfied with procedures to deal with corruption within the Organisation and fear reprisals if they report offences, an internal UN report has found."

The report is entitled, "United Nations Organisational Integrity Survey" and was commissioned by the Office of Internal Oversight Services (OIOS), the UN's equivalent of an Inspector-General. (Well not quite an "Inspector-General" which is, in other organisations, a completely independent institution charged with investigating corruption, misconduct and misadministration. The US proposed the establishment of such a body in Boutros' time but could only get a semi-independent group, set up within the Executive Office of the Secretary-General, whose reports go to him. It was agreed, as a compromise, that the Inspector-General would be appointed for a five-year term with no possibility of renewal, an arrangement which was designed to allow for freedom of action.)

The survey was sent to all UN staff around the world, a "population" of 18,035 employees. 6,086 responded, a 33% response rate that, according to the report, "is sufficient for results to be generalisable (sic) to the overall UN population and among the highest participation rates of any large-scale employee survey conducted by or for the United Nations."

The survey results indicate that:

The staff have little confidence that "senior leaders place their values and ethics ahead of their personal interests, aspirations or prior relationships";

"Political pressure shapes the meeting of justice under the guidelines of professional conduct and people of the same cultural background favour their own";

"Staff members feel unprotected from reprisals for reporting violations of the codes of conduct";

"Staff seem to wonder: Who can (or should) be held accountable if leaders and supervisors are not?"

"Personnel disciplinary actions are rare and focussed on staff" [rather than senior managers];

"The UN's culture and organisation is hierarchical and too much like a class system composed of have and have-nots."

The consulting firm of Deloitte Consulting LLP prepared the report. In return for participation, staff were promised anonymity for their responses and that the full results of the survey would be published.

Thursday, 17 June

The results of the Integrity Survey have received wide dissemination in the media worldwide.

"UN STAFF FEAR WHISTLEBLOWERS WILL SUFFER INTERNAL REPRISALS" – *The Independent*

"UN STUDY FINDS WORKERS UNEASY ABOUT REPORTING CORRUPTION" – *The New York Times*

"UN STAFF OUTRAGE" – *New York Post*

"UN WORKERS SKEPTICAL OF ITS INTEGRITY" – *The New York Sun*

"THE PROBLEM WITH THE SECRETARIAT" – *The Wall Street Journal*

"UN STAFF UNHAPPY AT SYSTEM TO DEAL WITH CORRUPTION" – *Financial Times*

"HONESTY DOESN'T PAY AT UN, STAFF SAY IN SURVEY: WHISTLE-BLOWERS FIND THEMSELVES PASSED OVER FOR PROMOTIONS" – *National Post*

"TEAR DOWN THIS UN STONEWALL" – William Safire, *The New York Times*

The attacks on Dileep Nair

The head of our "Inspectorate-General" (the OIOS), Dileep Nair of Singapore, who was responsible for initiating and conducting the Integrity Survey, has himself been accused of misconduct, financial irregularities and sexual harassment. The accusation of misconduct came in a resolution adopted by the Staff Council in which it expressed concern that "recent personnel decisions made by [Nair] have violated the rights of staff members within OIOS ..." The more scandalous accusations of corruption, bias and nepotism come by way of an anonymous letter, written on OIOS letterhead, distributed widely to all Ambassadors, heads of departments and poor Mrs. Nair. Annan has written to Nair asking him to respond. Nair is at home ill but publicly denies the charges. This story is also widely reported.

"UN INVESTIGATES CLAIMS OF SEXUAL MISCONDUCT" – *Ottawa Citizen*

"UN PROBER IN GRAFT SCANDAL" – *New York Post*

"THE BIG STORY: The investigation of impropriety in the UN oil for food program appears to have unleashed more allegations of wrongdoing at the UN" – *Fox News*

June too can be a cruel month.

The exoneration of Lubbers

Wednesday, 7 July

"Lewd" Lubbers has written to his accuser suggesting that she drop her complaint against him and return to the fold, following which all will be forgiven. He's also emailed a message to his staff (28 May) acknowledging that he is under investigation and complaining that the investigation has been expanded.

In the message to the staff he said, "I made what I consider, and I still consider to be, a friendly gesture." He "would have refrained," he concludes, if he thought it would have been taken amiss.

"I'm really sorry for that."

The man may not be a molester but he is undoubtedly a bit of a fool.

Thursday, 15 July

"Lewd" Lubbers has been exonerated. Today's announcement states:

"SEXUAL HARASSMENT COMPLAINT AGAINST LUBBERS CANNOT BE SUSTAINED

Secretary-General Kofi Annan has thoroughly reviewed the report of the Office of Investigative Services regarding the investigation into the complaint of sexual harassment brought by a staff member against the High Commissioner for Refugees Ruud Lubbers. He also carefully considered Mr. Lubbers' response to the report of that investigation.

The Secretary-General found that the complaint against Mr. Lubbers cannot be sustained by the evidence. However, he has written to Mr. Lubbers conveying his concerns and has sent his Under-Secretary-General for Management, Catherine Bertini, to Geneva to consult with the High Commissioner and his senior managers, as well as with the staff, to help them rebuild trust and confidence.

He has also written a letter to all members of the High Commissioner's staff.

The Secretary-General now considers this matter closed."

The press does not share this view.

"Asked whether the complaint had been found to be false, and whether the Secretary-General had been looking for corroboration, the Spokesman said that the Secretary-General's decision was based on the facts as he received them, and the allegations could not be sustained by the evidence.

Asked about what the concerns were that the Secretary-General had expressed to the High Commissioner, the Spokesman said the concerns were conveyed in a letter to

Lubbers that will not be made public.

Asked whether Lubbers had offered to resign, he responded that he was unaware of any such offer.

Asked why the text of the investigation would not be made public, he said that they are not made public as a matter of due procedure.

In response to a question about why the Secretary-General was sending Bertini to Geneva, the Spokesman said that this has been a long and protracted process, and UNHCR staff had been affected. It is important for Bertini to sit down with Lubbers and his managers and staff, listen to their concerns and work with them, so that the agency can move forward."

It is a strained announcement, not saying what the investigation revealed, only reporting what Annan has decided to do: "The Spokesman said that the Secretary-General's decision was based on the facts as he received them, and the allegations could not be sustained by the evidence."

This has not been handled well with the denouement overcooked. No longer "Lewd" Lubbers, but not exactly "Innocent" Lubbers, more like "Not Proven" Lubbers, he gets a letter from the SG expressing "concerns," a letter that is not released. The haughty, "The Secretary-General now considers this matter closed," but Bertini is to hurry to Geneva to immediately consult with Lubbers, his senior managers and staff? Hardly a convincing process, or a ringing endorsement of the accused, more than a hint of unhappiness of an undisclosed nature, giving rise to the supposition that the OIOS report is unfavourable to Lubbers, which is in itself unfair to him, or that Lubbers' frantic moves to bolster his position are felt to be inappropriate. How tenable can Lubbers' position now be?

The report should have been released publicly or, at minimum, an executive summary provided. The awkwardness of having an Inspectorate-General that is, in reality, not an independent entity but a part of the SG's Executive Office and, thus, ultimately subject to his determinations, is highlighted by this outcome. It is particularly unfortunate to have Lubbers investigated at this time by an office whose head is himself currently under investigation for accusations involving sexual behaviour.

Whatever the truth of the matter, the outcome will be treated with cynicism, especially by the staff. Coming so soon after the Integrity Survey, with the devastating finding that "whistleblowers" are not a welcome breed, it will feed into the suspicion that the powerful have a distinct advantage in these cases. It also, classically, will give the appearance of conforming to the belief of sexually harassed women that it is difficult for them to have their accusations sustained.

Lubbers has fought to keep his job. As a former Dutch Prime Minister, he has the support of his government, whose Prime Minister called Annan in June about the case. The Netherlands is serving currently as President of the European Union, a position of considerable political influence. The Netherlands is one of only three countries that have attained the target of contributing 0.7% of GDP to development assistance. It is a substantial donor to UN voluntary programmes.

My friend Benon

Benon had been away from New York on pre-retirement leave when the story broke about the reputed bribes. Not one to go quietly into that good night, since his return he has let it be known that he took no actions that had not been authorised by Annan.

"They'd better be careful", he says at one of our "Boys" lunches. "If the wall falls down, they'd better be sure it falls on the right side."

Benon explains how he had issued his own subpoena.

"They said that they didn't have subpoena power so I said, 'Here; look at all my files.' Then they came in and took all my personal things, my photos of forty years at the UN, my wedding pictures, family pictures. I said, 'Can't you look at those and give them back?' but I haven't heard from them."

He continues: "People told me to get a lawyer but I didn't think it was necessary until recently. Then I told them, if I got one, the UN should pay. They said the SG would have to approve it. I haven't had an answer. 'The SG is very busy,' they say."

"I've learnt who my friends are," Benon says. "I'm prepared to be a septic system," he continues, "but even a septic system has its limits and can explode."

Containing a scandal

Friday, 16 July

"UN Official Stymied Investigation" (*The Wall Street Journal*)

"UN Big Eyed In Cover-up" (*The New York Post*)

"The biggest scandal ever?" (*The Economist*, UK)

"Oil for favors at the UN?" (*The Japan Times*)

"The scam that financed Saddam" (*Chicago Tribune*)

"Massive Fraud Uncovered in UN's Oil-for-Food Program" (*Fox News*)

"Kofi's Coverup" (*The Wall Street Journal*)

"Don't trust the UN to run Iraq" (*Ottawa Citizen*)

"Kofi Annan's son faces probe in UN oil scandal" (*Sunday Times*, London)

"Oil-for-food probe looks at UNstaff" (*The Atlanta Journal-Constitution*)

"The Great Cash Cow" (William Safire, *The New York Times*)

"Oil for Hussein" (*The San Francisco Chronicle*)

"Investigators crawl over Iraq's oil billions: No fewer than 10 probes are trying to find out if proceeds from oil sales have been wasted or stolen" (*Financial Times*, UK)

"Weasels blocked US probe of UN oil scam" (*New York Post*)

"The UN Asylum" (Oliver North in *The Washington Times*)

It turns out that the UN has very few supporters in the two countries that we have relied on and it is the newspapers of these countries which are the ones running with the "scandal." Richard Holbrooke, to his great credit, chooses this moment to write an Op-Ed piece for *Time* lauding Annan – "Kofi Annan – Problem solver." John Ruggie has been faithful too, appearing before a Congressional Committee to defend the UN. Tom Lantos [California Congressman] writes an Op-Ed article for the *Washington Post* entitled "Investigate, Don't Incapacitate," in which he decries the rush to judgement. But the political leaders in the US and the UK maintain their silence, and the assault comes not only from predictable conservative quarters but also from the mainstream media.

Recognising that scrutiny by his investigative house organ, the OIOS will not suffice, the SG sets up an independent investigative panel headed by Paul Volcker and sensibly obtains a Security Council endorsement for the initiative. Despite complaints by his opponents that the panel can hardly be independent as it is set up, and its members appointed, by him, is financed by the UN and lacks subpoena power, this action serves to quiet the onslaught. The SG himself holds press conferences and gives interviews in which he vigorously defends himself, his investigation, his son and the benefits of the oil-for-peace programme. Shashi [now Under-Secretary-General for Communications and Public Information] and Mortimer [now Director of Communications on the 38th Floor], manage to get defending letters into the columns of *The Times*, the *Ottawa Citizen*, *The New York Times*, the *San Francisco Chronicle*, and the *New York Post*. *The Wall Street Journal* prints a letter from William Luers, the President of the UNA of the US, attacking the *Post*'s reporting.

And Paul Volcker publishes an article in *The Wall Street Journal* explaining what his enquiry is about.

The counter-attack has had to come mainly from Kofi Annan and his staff; the political institutions of the United States and Great Britain, the countries that have been his persistent supporters, leave him to fend for himself. Iraq is now a pestilence that overwhelms, and a UN which can be made to appear to have succoured Saddam is the same UN that failed to authorise an invasion of that country. The equation in the minds of the UN haters, quiescent for so long, is clear.

The imputations against Kofi and his son are flimsy and unconvincing. Benon's name on a list prepared by the same Iraqis derided by the same UN attackers as congenital liars, should not have been enough to have set off the ferment. But the capacity of Iraq to doom all outsiders who venture there is real, as the historical list of the damaged confirms. Saddam's graveyard has room for many more.

The scandals are seemingly endless, many self-inflicted, but some simply the inevitable eruptions that accompany the process of governance. But taken together they are devastating for the reputation of the UN and the morale of the staff.

Mais où sont les neiges d'antan?

37
FASHIONING A LEGACY

Into opposition – Adjusting history on Iraq – Drawing a line
– Saving Darfur

Into opposition

Sunday, 18 July

The onset of spring has signaled a general toughening of the Secretary-General's tone towards those he had previously handled with care.

This toughening was confirmed on 10 June when Annan delivered the Harvard Commencement address. He said:

> "It is in the interest of every country to have international rules and to abide by them. And such a system can only work if, in devising and applying the rules, the legitimate interests of all countries are accommodated, and decisions are reached collectively. That is the essence of multilateralism, and the founding principle of the United Nations."

It is a straightforward criticism of the path being followed by the Bush administration.

"All great American leaders have understood this. That is one of the things that make this country such a unique world power. America feels the need to frame its policies, and exercise its leadership, not just in the light of its own particular interests, but also with an eye to international interests, and universal principles."

At a time when Bush is travelling the country on his re-election campaign, pledging to act only in the interests of the United States, this is a direct attack on him. It is amazingly frank; by the SG's criterion, George W is obviously not one of those "great American leaders."

"American leaders have generally recognised that other states, big and small, prefer to cooperate on the great issues of peace and security through multilateral institutions such as the United Nations, which give legitimacy to such cooperation.

They have accepted that others with a different view on a specific issue may, on occasion, be right. They have understood that true leadership is ultimately based on common values and a shared view of the future.

Over sixty years, whenever this approach has been applied consistently, it has proved a winning formula."

It could not be starker. Kofi Annan has taken on the Bush approach to the world, and the UN in particular, and found fault with every bit of that approach.

The SG goes on to talk about Iraq and the crisis that arose in the UN last year over it. He refers to his panel which he hopes will render sound advice. But the heart of the speech has been his declaration of independence, in leaf now for some time, but come to full flower today.

It has been an awful period, the last ten months, beginning with the deaths in Baghdad of his staff and followed by one controversy and unfavourable headline after another. He had dodged and weaved over Iraq, striving to maintain a position "anchored in reality" against a background of international opposition to the actions of the US and the UK. Unwilling to have the UN keep out completely, he had continued to dip his toes into the Iraqi quicksand, caught between the "victors" who sought to bring him in on their terms and the opponents of the war who promoted greater post-conflict UN involvement as a convenient, even cynical, way to escape the burden of continued, outright criticism. His most recent "dip" has been to send fifteen UN election advisers to Baghdad to assist in preparations for the scheduled January 2005 elections. The advisers live and work in the fortified "Green Zone" under American military protection.

Adjusting history on Iraq

As part of the repositioning, his media meisters have been quietly portraying him to the UN press corps as having consistently opposed the war in Iraq. This effort has gained few adherents save for the *NY Times* UN correspondent, who has begun to refer to Annan's "well-known opposition to the war." This is, of course, fiction. If he had been against the war, it would have been a famous dissent, well-fixed in the public mind.

To have come out against the war meant angering his powerful patrons, the US and the UK. To support it would paint him as their toady. To fail to indicate concern would risk alienating the institutions of civil society whose regard he treasured as well as the majority of UN Member States that reviled the adventure. So he had hewn to a middle course of not objecting, yet not supporting, with the occasional dropped whisper of disquiet.

In a television interview on 2 April 2003, to which he had imprudently assented, he had been given a chance to say that the war was wrong. He could only resort to despairing ambiguity.

"Question: Would you say that this war is a legitimate one? Does it have the cover of legitimacy from your Organisation?

SG: Obviously, it is not a UN-sanctioned war. The Council did not endorse this war, and I think that was clear.

Question: Therefore, because you are saying that the Council did not endorse this war, would you condemn it?

SG: And that is why the legitimacy of this action has been questioned, and widely questioned, and I myself have raised questions about it. I have raised questions about the legitimacy and whether it was in conformity with the Charter.

Question: But does that mean that you do condemn it or not?

SG: I think, in my statement in the Council I made it quite clear that we would have preferred that it should be done peacefully and that we wouldn't have had to go through what we are going through. I have never justified nor supported this war."

But neither had he opposed or condemned it.

Drawing a line

On Thursday 17 June, in an as clear and unequivocal statement as he has ever made, and consistent with his new, sharper tone, Kofi Annan expresses his opposition to the continued exemption of US citizens from the jurisdiction of the International Criminal Court.

"I think it would be unfortunate for one to press for such an exemption, given the prisoner abuse in Iraq," Annan told reporters as he arrived for work.

"I think in this circumstance it would be unwise to press for an exemption and it would be even more unwise on the part of the Security Council to grant it," he stressed.

"It would discredit the Council and the United Nations that stands for rule of law and the primacy of rule of law," Annan added. "I don't think it should be encouraged by the Council."   The ICC had come into being on 1 July 2002. For the first time in history, a court was set up with universal jurisdiction over genocide, crimes against humanity and war crimes. Established by Treaty, the Court could, nonetheless, in certain circumstances, try citizens of states that were not party to the Treaty. Clinton, as one of his last acts as President, had committed the US, by signature, to the Treaty but had not sought to have it ratified. Bush, as one of his first acts as President, had withdrawn the US from the Clinton adherence.

In order to ensure that no US citizen would appear before the Court, the US proceeded on two paths. It persuaded, or obliged, a large number of countries that had ratified the Treaty to enter into bilateral agreements pledging never to submit US citizens to trial before the Court for any acts committed on their territories. To close the last loophole, it had in 2002 and 2003, insisted that the Security Council pass a resolution that gave US troops a one-year, world-wide exemption from prosecution. To help encourage the waverers, the US let it be known that without the exemption all US troops would be withdrawn from UN peacekeeping operations, a loss that would mainly affect the Kosovo operation.

By Thursday 24 June, Kofi Annan's intervention had proved to be decisive. The US announced that it would not insist on an exemption from the jurisdiction of the ICC. Of course Washington may have come to realise that it did not really need the exemption. Of the ninety-four countries that have ratified the Treaty, eighty-nine have entered into bilateral agreements to protect US troops from prosecution. Another ninety odd countries have not signed the agreement at all. Still, the Secretary-General's statement, in its clarity and its substance, is to be applauded.

Saving Darfur

And on Darfur, the Secretary-General has maintained his focus. It is now estimated that some 50,000 Sudanese have perished and as many as a million more may be at risk.

Initially, Annan had drawn attention to the situation there in order to galvanise the world's attention. He had chosen the International Day of Remembrance of the 1994 Genocide in Rwanda to launch his appeal. Since that day, he has been resolute in maintaining the focus on Darfur. He has ensured that the UN's humanitarian agencies made Darfur a priority, paid a visit to Sudan and visited the region to witness the suffering for himself, put pressure on the Sudanese Government to change its policies and forced the Security Council to act. He could not have handled the matter better and it is part of the tougher approach on a range of issues that has recently emerged.

So he has taken on the Bush administration on the role of the United Nations; repositioned himself on Iraq; spoken out resolutely against the exemption from the jurisdiction of the ICC for US troops; and, remembering Rwanda, acted resolutely on Darfur. He is concentrating on his legacy; he is demonstrating independence; he is preparing his departure.

38
A KIND OF ACCEPTANCE

His Life – A suitable ending – The Little One – Watch your back, Mister, watch your back

His Life

Monday, 19 July

Bill Clinton has published his autobiography. It is called, "My Life".

There are 957 pages of his life; with the index it runs to over 1,000 pages.

From mid-April 1996 the Clinton administration waged a cruel campaign to remove Boutros-Ghali from office. The undermining of Boutros was well reported in the media, and the concluding Security Council discussion, highlighted by the immovable US opposition, dominated international news from mid-November, when the US cast its first veto against Boutros-Ghali, to mid-December, when Kofi Annan was elected.

The installation of Kofi Annan is covered in a few lines, amounting to barely half a page, in the thousand pages of "My Life".

> "There were several interesting developments in foreign policy in December. On the thirteenth, the UN Security Council, with the strong support of the United States, selected a new Secretary-General, Kofi Annan of Ghana... Madeleine Albright thought he was an exceptional leader and had urged me to support him, as had Warren Christopher, Tony Lake, and Dick Holbrooke."

No mention is made of Boutros-Ghali's desire to have a second term, of the relentless US opposition, of the lengthy Security Council consideration, of the many calls to Bill from heads on Boutros' behalf, of the US veto of Boutros' re-election, or the not unimportant fact that Kofi Annan was not simply supported by Clinton but was the sole American candidate.

It was a near-immaculate conception, with which Bill had little or nothing to do.

A suitable ending

Tuesday, 20 July

My wife and I are waiting for the elevator on the second floor when the doors open and Kofi Annan steps out, accompanied by his bodyguard. He is beautifully dressed, and looking spry. He'll survive all this, I think. Plinthdom will be his.

I'm looking dishevelled, with my shirtsleeves rolled up, jacket over arm, collar unbuttoned, and tie askew.

"Miles, how are you?" and, to my wife, "How are you?"

I'm disordered again, even more so than at the last chance meeting, coat and keys and papers in my right hand, which I again have to transfer to my left before shaking his. L and he shake hands too, which is disconcerting for previously they would have embraced, but now, with his exquisite sense of time and place, he knows better than to so presume.

Behind me stretches the corridor, with its flags of the Member States, that marks the way to the General Assembly Hall. To my right begins the pathway that leads to the Economic and Social and Security Council Chambers. To my left, a few, short steps lead to the Delegates' Lounge, that hub of UN life. These rooms have been my world for over thirty years, and in front of me is Kofi Annan, who I've known for almost all that time, and who has been such an overwhelming influence on me for much of the last decade.

How hard it is to see him whole this midsummer evening, with the spokes of my past arrayed around me, and the memory of shared meals, and of cigars exchanged, and of talking late into the evening, and the dinner with close friends we both attended two nights before his election.

In "The Middle Passage", V.S. Naipaul writes, "I had been travelling around [the West Indies] for seven months. I was getting tired...There was nothing new to record... Every day I saw the same things... and every day I heard the same circular arguments... The situation required not a leader but a society which understood itself and had purpose and direction."

I had made my own journey in and around the society of the United Nations, in the service of a greying ideal. Now, I too was tired. I had gotten tired working for four Secretaries-General and, most recently, for a fifth. Content to return to the life of the delegate, where I had begun my apprenticeship, and had spent the first ten years of my career, I'd not remembered, or had chosen to forget, how selfish that world was, with each country torturously pursuing its own narrow interests, while masking its intentions behind cocktail-party smiles. For how many States had in mind the interests of the United Nations, or of the international community as a whole, or, God help us, the interests of those generations still facing the scourge of war that we were pledged to save? And I'd forgotten that in this place self-promotion is a virtue, the trickster is king, and political success is the only standard of achievement.

———◇———

Scattered droppings soil; accumulated droppings bury. As the scales fell from my eyes, they littered my shoulders and stuck to my skin. I felt soiled by the unveiling, and soiled by my own trawling. For was I not imposing on the United Nations my own disillusionments, weighing the institution down with my own failures, as much as its own? And was Kofi Annan not merely a man of his times, the man for these UN times, patient, tenacious and ever-optimistic, diplomat supreme, subtle and watchful, choosing his moments, avoiding sentimentality, valuing loyalty, shifting ground, skirting moral choices, all in the interests of shoring up his battered domain? And was this so unworthy of him when states behaved as they did, and when, without the United Nations, the world would be even worse off, left unguarded against the rampant intrusions of the powerful?

The Little One

He walks away, then stops and turns, poised to draw on his gift, his wonderful memory allied to that marvellous human touch, that no matter how practised, seems so gracious, so unforced. But he's struggling, trying to remember. I silently urge him on, willing him to conjure the words; it's "The Princess," I try to signal telepathically to him, your name for her is "The Princess."

"And how's 'The Little One'"?

"She's fine, SG; she's fine."

Watch your back, Mister, watch your back

Monday, 13 September

This is Hunte's last day as President and he receives warm and appreciative applause as he closes the 58th Session of the General Assembly. It is also my last day.

I'm walking away from the General Assembly Hall when I hear a voice behind me warning: "Watch your back, watch your back."

I have no idea what the voice is referring to; I continue on my way.

I feel a nudge.

"Watch your back, Mr. Stoby, watch your back," the voice insists.

Of course, I think, this is Caribbean-speak; it's a Jamaican security guard who knows me, and he's clearing a path.

"Watch your back, Mr. Stoby."

I watch it, and step aside. I look behind me.

"Hello, Miles."

"Hello, SG."

He walks away attended.

Not me, SG; I'm out of it. I don't have to watch my back any more. But you are treading water now, as the scandals accumulate, and the piranhas are let loose.

Watch your back.

PART SIX:
THE TRAVAILS OF THE
SECRETARY-GENERAL

"What is important is not what happens to us, but how we respond to what happens to us."

Jean-Paul Sartre

"I do not wish to be moved, but growing
    where I was growing,
There more truly to grow, to live where
    as yet I had languished
I do not like being moved: for the will is
    excited; and action
Is a most dangerous thing..."

Amours de Voyage

Arthur Hugh Clough

With the ending of my attachment to the Office of the President of the General Assembly, I assumed that I and the United Nations were done with one another and I was not distraught at the prospect. Somewhat to my surprise, I learnt some months later that I was to be appointed Ambassador and Permanent Observer of the Caribbean Community to the United Nations (CARICOM.) (The Permanent Observer aspect came by decision of the Secretary-General of CARICOM. The Ambassadorial title came par grace of my own Government which, in conferring it, thoughtfully pointed out that there would be "no emoluments or expectation thereof".) I would thus be returning to work with my own people, in a Caribbean setting, as I had been doing for the last year. It also meant that I would still be inhabiting the corridors of our glass house at least to the end of the Secretary-General's tenure.

My appointment meant that I would have to meet with Kofi Annan to present my credentials. So, on the appointed day, I arrived on the 38th Floor to be escorted into his office by UN Guards in ceremonial uniform, where he awaited me accompanied by two senior officials whose purpose was to make a record of the meeting.

I could not then help but recall the many years of our acquaintanceship. At the time I went to work for him we had been friends but never intimates. Ours was one of those casual, long-time bureaucratic relationships, arising from occasional official dealings, of knowing some of the same people, which led to a silent acknowledgement that we liked each other. But he had a talent for drawing you in, for making you feel that the relationship was more meaningful than you yourself might have thought it to be. He had, moreover, immense charm, which he deployed as a potent force, instrumental in achieving results without apparent effort. It was his special gift.

I felt that we had become closer during that freshly-budding period of his tenure. In those first, sparkling months we had met frequently, both privately and in groups. I treasured his openness and sense of humour and I'd found it easy to send him into deep guffaws of laughter when he would double-up in delight.

At this point I had not seen him for many months and had not met with him in a closed setting for nearly two years. He had since seen his integrity questioned and the esteem with which he had been held in the West, and most particularly in the United States, dented by debilitating attacks, including obviously partisan slanders orchestrated by dedicated enemies of the Organisation. But I saw no change in him, a little greyer of hair perhaps, but as demonstrably gracious, charming, kind and composed as I had ever known him to be. He had welcomed me with seeming pleasure, congratulated me on my appointment and offered that I still had much to contribute to the United Nations. Soon he dismissed his staff, telling them that he wished to have a quiet word with me, at which point I had suggested that the worst seemed to be over, and that he appeared to have managed to survive the sustained assaults. A look of intertwined anguish and anger had flashed from his eyes and he had talked to me about the unfairness of it all. I was happy that day to reconnect with him, I was glad to share together a companionable moment once again. In farewell he asked to be remembered to L and the "Princess".

As the months passed it became increasingly difficult to affect the studied detachment that I had sought to display. With the political storm-clouds gathering around the United Nations, it was apparent that the ideological enemies of the Organisation were intent on diminishing its influence to the extent of placing it on the sidelines of world affairs. Despite all my sometimes questioning of, and doubts about, his actions, it seemed evident to me that, at this hazardous time, Kofi Annan remained best placed to take the lead in securing the United Nations. For he had, after all, accumulated numerous substantive achievements during the course of his tenure. For a goodly period of his Secretary-Generalship these were occurring with frequency and in abundance. He can be credited with restoring the damaged relationship with the United States; contributing decisively to the resolution of the arrears crisis; launching waves of reform that helped prepare the United Nations for the twenty-first century;

attracting Ted Turner's billion dollar donation to the UN; calling for and successfully orchestrating the Millennium Summit and the adoption of the Millennium Development Goals; supporting the establishment of the International Criminal Court and defending its independence; advocating the establishment of a Global Fund on Aids and Health; proceeding resolutely to address the turmoil in Darfur; presiding over seventeen new peacekeeping operations; acting firmly and swiftly to support recovery from the effects of the tsunami in the Pacific; and, overall, providing for a long time an image of a gracious, dignified, accessible and responsive United Nations. And this record was exemplified in the awardence of the Nobel Peace Prize.

When I returned to the Executive Office in 1999 I found that the annual award of the Peace Prize had become a time of expectant waiting. But it was not until October 2001, after his re-election, that the waiting was rewarded. He was cited for his advocacy of human rights, the struggle against HIV/AIDS, bringing new life to the UN, making the most of its scarce resources and advocating humanitarian intervention. It was a long list and there was reason for that. For Kofi Annan's worth as a Secretary-General was due to an accumulation of things, and not one thing. For no one thing stood out.

When Nelson got it, we knew what it was for, and Rabin and Peres and Arafat, and the Landmines campaigners, and Doctors Without Borders, we knew what they had gotten theirs for. But Annan, as ever, remained elusive. He got it because of a feeling that he should get it, that it was the moment to reward him, and the Organisation he headed. It was a pat on the back, an encouraging nod, but if you asked what for, it took some time to explain, for it had all the marks of a cumulative compliment.

Still, he surely deserved it. He had, after all, manufactured the moment. The UN had been in poor shape when he took over. Boutros had alienated many and Annan alienated few. He had helped rescue us from the financial precipice to which we had been pushed by the US, and that was no small thing. He had given the UN an identifiable face, and it was a confident, dignified, and friendly face and that meant a lot. Above all, it had been a triumph as much of style and words as of decisive actions, but that only showed that he had understood well, and adapted well, to a world where perception was also action, which in turn conferred strength.

But his abiding contribution, hinted at in the Nobel commendation, has been the provision of a type of leadership, albeit in carefully selected areas, that no Secretary-General has been able to offer since Dag Hammarskjöld. He realised from the start that the post of Secretary-General was loosely defined in the Charter and this allowed scope to test the limits of his political authority. In this he has been resolute and he had succeeded in frequently usurping the policy role of the General Assembly by establishing, without consultation with the political bodies, a raft of independent commissions and panels to advocate policy directions on peacekeeping, development financing, and civil society.

Now, at this momentous time, I could not avoid recommencing my appreciation of the flow of events, for the stakes could not now be higher for him and, indeed, for his (and my) beloved workplace as well. I could, after all, still observe. But there was no fun to be found anymore in our glass house, no whimsical happenings to relate, no wit to be had in it. With the cracking of the edifice, all the mirth had seeped out.

At the time I could not have anticipated the extent of the near apocalypse to come, nor that the United Nations and its leader were to enter into a period of controversy, turbulence and peril, the sustained like of which had not ever before been experienced by the Organisation.

39
DEALING WITH THE MESSES

An illegal war – The pardoning of Lubbers – The absolution of Nair – A Staff vote of No Confidence in the senior management of the UN – The inconvenient son – Exploiting the defenceless

———◁○▷———

"Pembrooke –
'It is the Count Melun.'

Salisbury –
'Wounded to death'."

King John Act 5, Scene 4

William Shakespeare

———◁○▷———

An illegal war

September, 2004

On Thursday, 16 September 2004, Kofi Annan subjected himself to an interview with BBC News. In the course of so doing he sharpened the break with his patron nation that had been heralded in the spring by his Harvard commencement address (10 June 2004). That address, however, had been little noticed and, in any event, had dealt with concepts, not specifics. Now, he became more exact.

By this time opposition to the Iraq war and anger at its effects were widespread even in the victor countries of the coalition.

Cushioned by these developments, he completed his repositioning on Iraq when he characterised the war as "illegal".

"I have indicated it was not in conformity with the UN Charter from our point of view, from the Charter point of view, it was illegal."

"I hope we do not see another Iraq-type operation for a long time – without UN approval and much broader support from the international community," he added.

Queried about his seeming conversion, his Press Spokesman maintained that this had been Annan's position all along. It was not enough to accept the salutes for this new-found clarity. History, unlike Salome's veils, had to be re-swathed.

"Question: Ok, on Iraq. Was the Secretary-General trying to send a message when he said the Iraq war was illegal, and was this the first time he said the word, 'illegal'?

Spokesman: He has, over the past more than a year, used the words 'not in conformity with the Charter' to describe his view of the Iraq war..."

Queried further, his Spokesman scaled dizzying new heights of disingenuousness:

"Spokesman: He feels it's no different from what he's been saying for more than a year, and that position is very well known to member governments.

Question: Do you think Annan's comments are a non-story?

Spokesman: We see nothing new in it."

Kofi Annan's "illegal" accusation produced an avalanche of media reports and commentary across the globe, where, in general, it was warmly welcomed and made him a hero to those who had opposed the invasion. His remarks were poorly received, however, by the coalition partners.

Asked about Annan's comments during an interview with *The Washington Times'* editorial board, Cole-in said the coalition's actions in Iraq were "entirely legal and legal in accordance with UN Security Council's resolutions of the past."

"I don't think it was a useful statement to make at this point," Powell continued. "What does it gain anyone?"

The junior victor's office disputed Annan's comments and reiterated that the British Attorney General, Lord Goldsmith, had issued advice that Britain was acting legally.

Australia's Prime Minister said there was nothing illegal about the US-led invasion.

"There had been a series of Security Council resolutions and the advice we had [was] that it was entirely legal," John Howard stated.

His Spokesman's effort, valiant as it was, begged the question: if the world had previously known that the Secretary-General was against the war and felt it to be illegal, why had his comments produced such a furore?

The pardoning of Lubbers

October, 2004

As autumn turned to winter, controversy continued to accompany the Secretary-General. There was, first, the unsurprising return of Lubbers for there had been an awkward and forced air to the forgiveness granted to him. As it turned out, it may have been "Guilty" Lubbers after all. The OIOS investigation had, in fact, resulted in a conclusion "supporting the allegations and recommending that appropriate action be taken accordingly." This was revealed when OIOS submitted its mandatory annual report on its work to the General Assembly.

The report appeared in two versions. The original version stated only that OIOS "submitted a report to the Secretary-General on the allegations." It was later reissued "for technical reasons" after the true conclusion was leaked, no doubt by an indignant member of Nair's office. The responsibility for the "technical error" was immediately placed at Nair's door, as if Nair had an interest in disguising his own findings. This episode also confirmed that the supposedly "independent" OIOS operated on a very short leash.

When the matter was raised at the Daily Press Briefing on 28 October 2004, the SG's Press Spokesman, who by now had become practised at reconciling apparent irreconcilables, did not falter:

"Question: I was wondering why the Secretary-General basically left, decided not to take any action against Ruud Lubbers when the OIOS sent a report to him, in quotes, 'supporting the allegations and recommending that appropriate action be taken accordingly.' Why is it that the United Nations put out a different, earlier version without that conclusion?

Spokesman: Well, first of all, the Secretary-General has the right to accept or reject such recommendations. And, at the time, we told you that after carefully reviewing the OIOS report, and the submission by Mr. Lubbers, he found that the allegations against Mr. Lubbers could not be sustained... Any questions that you have about the wording of the earlier draft versus the final draft should be put to Mr. Nair.

Question: On what basis can Kofi Annan say that there was no evidence of misdeeds when an entire OIOS investigation concluded that there was?

Spokesman: He did not say there was no evidence. He said he found the charges unsustainable..."

The pardoning of Lubbers was widely noted, as was the absolution of Dileep Nair, which came next.

The absolution of Nair

November, 2004

The Nair affair had begun in mid-April 2004 when the Staff Council had called for an independent investigation but no action had been taken until the burgeoning controversies reawakened interest in it. Bertini, Annan's American Undersecretary-General for Management, was then charged with undertaking the "independent" investigation called for by the Staff Council, which resulted in an announcement in mid-November that Nair, like Lubbers before him, and like Fréchette and the Iraq Steering Committee before them, was not to be blamed or, at any rate, would not be.

(As the Spokesman for the Secretary-General put it: "After a thorough review of the personnel-related allegations, the Under-Secretary-General for Management [Bertini] reported to the Secretary-General [Annan] her findings and recommendations [on Nair]. She found that no Staff Regulations or Staff Rules were violated in the appointment and promotion of staff in OIOS, and that the relevant personnel procedures were followed. She 'recommended that no further action was necessary in the matter'.")

The Staff Council had not been consulted by Bertini about the charges they themselves had made, nor indeed had anyone else since the "independent investigation" had not encompassed interviews with staff that might have knowledge of events, having consisted of an examination of official papers.

A Staff vote of No Confidence in the senior management of the UN

Riza informed the Staff Council that it was recognised that, regardless of the absolution, there was a risk of "negative perception" in Nair's personnel decisions. Unassuaged by this latest application of the practised, if, by now, shopworn tactic for handling the alleged transgressions of senior managers, (a slap on the wrist followed by a kiss on the cheek) the Council, on November 19 passed a resolution expressing "No confidence in the senior management of the Organisation". It contended that "the failure to fully investigate the allegations upholds the findings of an independent integrity survey... that there is a lack of integrity, particularly at the higher levels of the Organisation," and noted "with grave concern the trend of exoneration of senior managers in a series of violations that have serious implications and have further eroded the trust of staff in senior management".

The inconvenient son

Kofi Annan was soon required to deal with another threatening problem when it was revealed in mid-November that his son had received emoluments from the Swiss firm Cotecna (employed in 1999 to monitor the delivery to Iraq of humanitarian goods purchased under the oil-for-food programme) for a somewhat longer period than had been previously announced.

Kojo Annan's connection to Cotecna had emerged in January 1999. In response Joe Connor (American Undersecretary-General for Management at that time) was assigned to look into the connection. On the basis of his one-day review, the UN told the world in February 1999 that Kojo Annan was no longer an employee of Cotecna and, additionally, no wrongdoing had taken place.

In March 2004 the UN amplified that Kojo Annan had worked for Cotecna from December 1995 to late 1998, resigning three weeks before Cotecna was granted the contract.

That information proved to be inaccurate for it was afterwards learnt that he had actually resigned at the end of December, following, and not preceding, the granting of the contract.

That information was also found to be inaccurate after the news broke in September 2004 that Kojo Annan had continued his connection with Cotecna through a "no compete" contract at the rate of $2,500 a month until the end of 1999.

That information was also found to be inaccurate when it was revealed in November 2004 that Kojo Annan's "no compete" contract had continued until February 2004, providing him with total payments of some $150,000.

That information was soon found to be incomplete when it was learnt in early December 2004 that Kojo Annan's compensation from Cotecna went somewhat further; Cotecna had reimbursed him for health care costs through June 2004.

That information was soon found to be still incomplete when it was reported that Kojo Annan had travelled to New York in September of 1998 for a two-week stay and billed Cotecna $500 a day "for General Assembly and various meetings related to projects," and that he had also billed Cotecna for attendance at meetings in Nigeria and South Africa during his father's official visits in the same year to those countries, and that his billing to Cotecna for expenses during this period amounted to $55,000.

At a press encounter on 29 November 2004, Kofi Annan said of his son's connection with Cotecna, "I had been working on the understanding that it ceased in 1998 and I had not expected that the relationship continued." He went on to acknowledge that, "I understand the perception problem for the UN, or the perception of conflict of interests and wrongdoing."

Exploiting the defenceless

There had been warnings, and other incidents, stretching back into the early nineties, to the operations in Cambodia, Kosovo, and Sierra Leone, and East Timor, and in Liberia and Guinea, but the previous incidents had not elicited the attention that the reports of sexual exploitation in the Congo received when dropped, in November 2004, on a world becoming accustomed to regular exposures about the failings of the UN. Rape, prostitution and paedophilia were among the crimes laid at the door of UN peacekeepers in the Congo and 150 cases were soon under investigation. In Cambodia Bulgarian troops had been accused of sexual abuses, in East

Timor Jordanian troops had been accused of rape, in Bosnia and Kosovo the accusations were of being involved in prostitution and trafficking, in West Africa local UN staff had reportedly withheld food from refugees if sexual favours were not granted, but the accusations from the Congo amounted to an amalgam of all the earlier crimes, and were of an unprecedented scale.

The Secretary-General responded immediately and well, expressing his "absolute outrage" and commissioning an OIOS investigation, which in January concluded that the problem of sexual exploitation and abuse of local Congolese women and girls was "serious and ongoing" and that "interviews with Congolese women and girls confirmed that sexual contact with peacekeepers occurred with regularity, usually in exchange for food or small sums of money. Many of these contacts... involved girls under the age of eighteen, with some as young as thirteen." Annan also pointed out that the actions of "a few bad apples" should not be allowed to tarnish the reputation of UN peacekeeping.

In response strict new rules on fraternisation were implemented and programmes intensified to ensure that peacekeepers were aware of proper rules of conduct but it was too late – another image of UN wrongdoing had flashed across the world and no amount of recovery work could undo the damage. This scandal was more chilling than any that had come before for the United Nations had betrayed its responsibility to protect the helpless, it had undermined the purpose of its peacekeeping function, it had failed in its duty to those in its care.

How many more blows, one wondered, could a leader and an institution absorb before they buckled?

40
A RARE AND VALUABLE HOMAGE

A standing ovation – Beating a retreat

———◦———

"GLENDOWER I can call Spirits from the vastie Deepe.
HOTSPUR Why so can I, or so can any man:
But will they come, when you doe call for them?"

Henry IV Part One, Act Three Scene

William Shakespeare

———◦———

"One time is another time".

West Indian proverb

———◦———

A Standing Ovation

December, 2004

On the morning of Wednesday 8, December, 2004, Secretary-General Kofi Annan appeared before a meeting of the General Assembly to present the report of his Panel on Threats, Challenges and Change. He received a standing ovation.

The last occasion at which a Secretary-General had been so vociferously hailed was on 17 December 1996, the day he was appointed. The ovation that day had not been for him, though, but for his predecessor Boutros Boutros-Ghali who, a few moments before, had delivered his farewell address as Secretary-General.

Boutros-Ghali had given a serious, substantive speech about the role of the United Nations in the world, but the applause he had received was less a commentary on what he had said than for what by that time he had become – a symbol of opposition to the United States, and a victim of American hubris.

On the day of Boutros-Ghali's farewell and Kofi Annan's assumption, it was noticeable that the new Secretary-General received only polite and restrained applause when he delivered his own address. For as much as Boutros had become America's victim, Annan was seen as America's man, and the beneficiary of an inequitable dethroning. Now, eight years later, the ovation given to his statement was unrelated to the purpose of his participation, for he had recently donned an unforeseeable mantle as a symbol of opposition to the United States and as a victim of American hubris. In its November 2004 issue, *The American Spectator*, a US journal with well-established conservative credentials, displayed a photograph on its cover of Saddam Hussein shaking hands with Annan with the UN logo in the background. The cover was coloured in UN blue and the caption advised: "Kofi saddamizes Iraq: Coalition of the bribed." This had been the most savage of the attacks on Kofi Annan that preceded his General Assembly speech (succeeding as it did in conveying in one swipe intimations of the irredeemable condition of the corrupt and sodomising South) but it had not been a solitary excrescence, and the weeks that followed were unmatched during Annan's term, and perhaps, in the history of the United Nations, in the intensity of the criticisms and imputations levelled against him, and the Organisation he headed, by the American media. But dissatisfaction with Annan was not confined to the expected opposition; it extended to previous bastions of support within the United Nations itself as well as to sections of the press that had hitherto been well-disposed towards him.

Bare ruined choirs where once the sweet birds sang.

The illegal accusation combined with the Falluja protest, the Congo revelations, the oil-for food exposures, and Kojo Annan's Cotecna connections, brought the traditional UN haters on the right wing of American politics into the open. Demands for Annan's resignation appeared in many papers and, soon enough, US Congressmen followed suit, the most notable being a US Senator involved in the Iraqi investigations. In the New York State Legislature, UN opponents arranged to have put in abeyance plans to support the renovation and expansion of the Headquarters site, a project that had been under consideration for over three years. These attacks produced a counter-reaction as the African group at the UN rallied in Annan's support to be joined soon afterwards by the Europeans and many others. The attacks on him were seen as, in reality, an assault by groups and individuals of the Host Country on the institution of the United Nations which, in the undesired world of a single super-power, was a body that few did not feel obligated to protect.

The Panel's report had not elicited the applause. That was a solid, if cautious, well-written effort. It essentially consisted of re-working conventional wisdom in a large number of areas – peace and security, terrorism, non-proliferation and disarmament, poverty, development assistance, debt relief, poverty, role of the General Assembly and the Economic and Social Council etc etera, accompanied by some useful ideas for restructuring the UN Secretariat.

But it was not simply resentment of the United States that inspired the standing ovation; Kofi had remained, at the personal level, an enormously likeable man. He gained too in contrast to Boutros who, as a fellow senior official once put it to me, "I would ask to see him and it would take weeks to set up a meeting. Then when you went into his room, and sat down at his desk, he would continue to work. When he finally looked up, it was clear he was annoyed to see you there."

Boutros was unpopular with the staff. He threatened them "with stealth and sudden violence." He was unpopular with Ambassadors, consistently going over their heads to the deal with their Foreign Ministers. He avoided their receptions. He introduced a new arrangement for the presentation of credentials which demonstrated his disdain; instead of having individual ceremonies he would delay until enough new Ambassadors were waiting then accredit them en bloc. But Boutros gained greatly in esteem in the last months of his term; the more Madeleine Albright looked to oust him, the more popular he became.

Kofi Annan restored the individual ceremonies for presentation of ambassadorial credentials. He was often seen at National Day receptions. He travelled frequently, granting scores of countries the honour of an official visit from the Secretary-General, and illuminating the competence and contribution of the Ambassadors involved. Now, as they stood and cheered him in the General Assembly Hall, they could empathise with his anguish, as they had, at the end, with Boutros. What did it matter that he had been touched by staff and filial controversies? What did it matter that he had seemed overly attentive to the views of Washington, now that he appeared no longer willing to be so? Beset by the giant, he was now one of them.

Kofi Annan had come full circle. The template civil servant had seen his hold on the affection of his staff steadily slip away; America's man had tried on Boutros' boots and found out that they fit.

"A rare and valuable homage," was the description offered by the President of the Assembly, Jean Ping of Gabon, in characterising the standing ovation.

"It was a vote of confidence."

A few days after this kaleidoscopic triumph, I accidentally encountered a former colleague who was still on the Floor. We agreed to have coffee together.

"The Nobel came too early," he suggested. "After that, everyone stopped asking questions."

"I think people stopped asking questions long before that," I said.

"They'd stopped when I was still on the Floor."

"Perhaps," he replied. "But after the Nobel no one could disagree. He had become a god."

Beating a retreat

The reception by the Assembly should have provided a boost and a comforting source of strength. A diverse collective had urged him on towards the path of independence. Some were happy to publicly express their continued admiration for him; others had done so on the basis of the colour of his skin; a few, antagonised by the United States, now found in him an ally in opposition; while the rest could, in this manner, display their usually hidden resentment at American domination.

But the path of independence implied continued opposition, and the lesson of the fall of Boutros was too recent either to forget or to neglect. The future had to be divined but the gift of divination, ill-employed, is a doubtful boon. The future feared prompts the future foretold. Horrors are revealed; hobgoblins lurk; and grotesque reptiles gobble up both the wary and the bold. Thus confronted, Kofi Annan set out to retrace the steps that he had only recently begun to take.

His connection has always been to "Democratic" America and it was to these re-defeated friends (amongst whom were Richard Holbrooke and John Ruggie) that he turned for succour and guidance. If Bush had not been re-elected a month before, Annan's friend, the Pro-Consul, might have become Secretary of State and they could, together, have planned his renaissance. Now, restless in the wings, "his" Democrats met with him, but only as advisers, and not as the wished-for, Administration decision-makers.

On December 5, 2004 Richard Holbrooke convened the crisis council at his apartment in New York. The meeting was supposed to be private, even secret, and it was reported that Annan came without his personal aides.

Within days, however, information on the meeting had leaked, evidently by one or other of the weighty participants, and Ruggie and Holbrooke felt free to discuss it with the media.

"The purpose of that meeting was to say, look, – here are five Democrats, all of whom love you, and all of whom have high regard for the institution," John Ruggie said in describing the gathering. The message they gave to Annan was, he added, "You need to take this seriously and things need to... happen." Holbrooke, characteristically, put it more plainly: "After the presidential election, a bunch of people, most of whom voted for the other guy, not the winner, sat down with Kofi Annan at his request to brainstorm about how he could improve relations with the United States government because the UN – without US support – the UN goes down."

All accounts agree that Annan did not speak during the three-hour meeting at which he was given "bluntly-worded counsel" about "the lapses in his leadership"; he confined himself to taking notes. All accounts also agree on the consensus that emerged – with Bush re-elected he could not look to his Democratic friends to bolster him; he must, therefore, regain the confidence, or at least the toleration, of Republican America; rejuvenate the Secretariat through personnel changes beginning with those around him; and intensify his programme of reform.

"The intention was to keep it confidential," Holbrooke later remarked. "No one wanted to give the impression of a group of outsiders, all of them Americans, dictating what to do to a Secretary-General." And, indeed, did not some slight breeze of disquiet fan across the brows of his faithful congregation at this latest acquiescence? Did it not occur to any of those who wished Annan well that there was an irrefutably distasteful aspect to the aesthetic of five Northerners "giving a message" to one Southerner, five Americans pointing out "the lapses in his leadership" to one African, five white men providing "bluntly-worded counsel" to one black man?

41

AN AGENDA FOR RECOVERY

The art of defenestration – An autogolpe – Attending to the Host Country – A beleaguered Secretary-General – Volcker reports – Getting the relationship with the US right – The fall of Lubbers – Successive triumphs

———◁○▷———

"1. In the performance of their duties the Secretary-General and the staff shall not seek or receive instructions from any government or from any other authority external to the Organisation. They shall refrain from any action which might reflect on their position as international officials responsible only to the Organisation.
2. Each Member of the United Nations undertakes to respect the exclusively international character of the responsibilities of the Secretary-General and the staff and not to seek to influence them in the discharge of their responsibilities."

Article 100
United Nations Charter

———◁○▷———

The art of defenestration

January, 2005

Kofi Annan soon began to put into effect the programme laid out for him by his faithful American friends. The personnel changes came first. Riza, it was announced, would be leaving by mid-January, due, according to him, for three reasons: "A-G-E." But the flurry of further announced departures cast doubt on Riza's explanation. He was replaced by Mark Malloch-Brown, the British head of UNDP, and soon Elisabeth Lindenmayer, now deputy Chef de Cabinet, was led to an abrupt resignation. On her heels was Eckhard, the Press Spokesman who, in offering his resignation, indicated that he had hoped to stay until the end of the SG's term; he was told to go by June 2005. Annan had brought five people with him from the Department of Peacekeeping Operations when he went to the 38th Floor, a mix of Southerners and Westerners, and now three were to go unexpectedly. Only Lamin Sise would remain, Shashi Tharoor having been promoted out previously, but Sise was not involved in policy articulation. This group had been unwaveringly loyal but now, in this season of crisis, it was time for them to go. It was also learnt that Marta Maurás, Fréchette's head of office was also to depart, then Bertini, head of Administration and Management, Halbwachs, in charge of Budget and Finance, and Kieran Prendergast, the British head of the Department of Political Affairs. (John Ruggie had already left by this time to be succeeded by Michael Doyle, another American academic coming fresh to the UN while Andy Mack, the Australian, had also departed with Abi Williams – American, academic, fresh – taking his place.) Some were being sacrificed while some had had enough, but the style of the executions did not suggest that Annan was the orchestrator. He had always been a discreet discarder and this was a mass defenestration.

It was hardly unusual for a political leader in distress to seek to revive his fortunes and reinvigorate his administration by the injection of new blood. Indeed, such actions were commonplace and might even be worthy of applause, depending on the circumstances. Of course such actions usually required jettisoning the old stalwarts on whose shoulders, by implication if not direct accusation, the blame for past failures needed to be placed.

In this case, however, there was a striking aspect to it. Previously, the senior staff of the 38th Floor were largely personnel drawn from the West. With the departure of Iqbal Riza, the entire senior policy, political and operational apparatus on the 38th Floor had a Western face. Whatever their personal merits (and, based on their resumes, they appeared to be considerable) it was unlikely that this group would be in a position to do other than present Kofi Annan with a one-sided perspective on international developments. Already, all three of the major political departments, the key parts of the Secretariat, were headed by officials from Western governments, deputed temporarily for assignment to the UN. Thus the head of the Department of Political Affairs was an American, the head of the Department of Peacekeeping Operations a Frenchman and the head of the Department of Safety and Security (a near-equivalent in UN terms to the US's Homeland Security Department) a British national. But in his position as Secretary-General of the most influential and universal organisation in the world, comprising Member States from five regional groups, he needed to be in receipt of a broad range of views, stemming from contrasting perspectives and orientations, from those closest to him about positions to be adopted on the major political issues of the day, which he could then weigh before adopting a course of action. No such variety would now be forthcoming.

An autogolpe

The dispatch of Riza and Lindenmayer and the assumption of Malloch-Brown represented another important volte-face. Initially, there had been a natural tendency on Kofi Annan's part to advance, or in any case, trust and rely on, long-serving Secretariat insiders like himself particularly in the staffing of his personal office. That tendency simply meant valuing experience and attachment to the Organisation, and dedication to the international ideal. But it was precisely this attitude that he was made to change by the forces that he had increasingly turned to. Already, he had come to depend on Western outsiders for his policy formulation team. Now, experience in, and attachment to, the Organisation was represented to be a fault in his personal staff at a moment when readiness to contemplate radical change was the image to convey. So, much store was placed on the advice of the Westerners, most of whom were untainted by previous contact with United Nations and its multinational cast of actors, and all of whom had no previous background of working in the Secretariat. Malloch-Brown was the closest having served briefly in his youth with the Office of the High Commissioner for Refugees. He had more recently had longer-term attachments to the World Bank and UNDP, affiliated UN system organisations. But these bodies had entirely different constitutions, ethos' and governing structures to the UN. Presumably, the attraction lay in his lack of working experience in the Secretariat.

Malloch-Brown's appointment to the post of Chef de Cabinet was, in fact, in defiance of history and custom. It had always been felt that to so appoint a national from the Security Council Permanent Five would give the appearance of undue preference to a great power, favouring one of them over the others, no matter the appointee's personal qualities. Indeed, the only other national from amongst Security Council members to have been similarly appointed was Andrew Cordier, an American who held the position for fifteen years from the time of the establishment of the UN with the title of Executive Assistant. It was that experience that had led to the informal prohibition against such appointments.

In adjusting the composition of his Executive Office Kofi Annan was, perhaps unconsciously, setting aside all that had formed him as an international official and child of the United Nations. And, with the sweeping away of the old guard, the Secretary-General had discarded those who had no agenda save to serve him. He had, in effect, undertaken a novel form of *autogolpe*: he had carried out a coup against himself.

Attending to the Host Country

In step with the defenestrations, there soon began to flow a busy stream of pleasing gestures.
– As soon as he took over as Chef, Malloch-Brown hurried to

Washington to meet with Senators and Congressmen to assure them of Annan's reform intentions.

– The successor to the head of the United Nations Children's Fund (UNICEF), whose term was not up until May, was expeditiously announced; she turned out to be Ann Veneman, Bush's recently-departed former Secretary of Agriculture. Ms. Veneman's quality emerged immediately when, at her introductory press conference on 18 January, she was asked: "The UN in general and UNICEF in particular have long-standing policies on reproductive health and education for girls that are at odds, regularly, with the Bush Administration. I'd like to have a clarification of where you stand on some of those broad issues." To which Ann Veneman replied: "I don't have a position with regard... I don't believe those issues are relevant to the missions of UNICEF."

– Another particularly open gesture came with the departure of Peter Hansen, the High Commissioner for the United Nations Relief and Works Agency for Palestine Refugees in the Near East (UNRWA). Hansen had attracted the opposition of the US and Israel for standing up to them when he thought they were wrong. For this he earned enmity, in particular of the Israeli Ambassador to the UN, who called him an "Israeli hater." Hansen commented that Mr. Gillerman's description of him was "outrageous". "I don't have a record of being an Israel hater but I can't in all honesty not criticise Israel's actions that harm Palestinian refugees," he said. "My job is not to put myself at the midpoint between the Israeli view and the refugees' view. My job was to represent the refugees."

"I was willing to stay," Hansen remarked, "but there are certain facts about the views of certain groups in the US and Israel about how I have carried out my functions and those groups influenced the decision not to reappoint me," he said. And it was learnt that at a meeting in his office in January, Annan told Hansen: "I don't have the political capital with the Americans to keep you."

– The most flamboyant example at this time concerned, not surprisingly, Iraq. After the "illegal" and Falluja interventions, no further shadow stemming from the situation in Iraq could be allowed to fall. So when on 26 January, during a press briefing, Carina Perelli, the head of the UN elections advisory office, said that she had been, "asking, begging military commanders" to stop the distribution by US troops of material promoting the election, and that, "the US military have been, I would say, overenthusiastic in trying to help out with the elections," recovery efforts were urgently initiated. The press release on the briefing omitted mention of Ms. Perelli's blasphemous criticisms. A statement was issued within hours of her briefing explaining that she had "misspoke" and that "the role of the US military in Iraq is essential for the security of the elections." The next day, these reactions produced a memorable exchange at the Spokesman's Daily Press Briefing.

"Question: So is it now UN policy that even when one of your most credible and respected officials makes a statement that is seen in any way to be sensitive in the United States, that the United Nations will disown those comments even though they are straightforward and [supportable]?

Associate Spokesperson: I'd like to repeat what I just said: it is a very sensitive time before these elections, and we just don't want anything we say to be misinterpreted and become a divisive issue.

Question: Is this a message to UN staff that they should not call a spade a spade if it will upset the United States?

Associate Spokesperson: I have nothing further to say.

Question: If the United States did not complain, why did you feel obliged to come out and correct the statement on the record? How far is this Organisation willing to go to satisfy one Member State?

Associate Spokesperson: I think that I have said as much as I can on this subject.

Question: Did the United States ask the Spokesman's Office not to comment more on this issue?

Associate Spokesperson: No.

Question: Then why are you not willing to talk about and clarify your Office's statement? This is getting ridiculous. Nobody can speak anymore in this place.

Associate Spokesperson: But she did speak to you, and we are clarifying that she did not intend to criticise the US military's profile...

Question: Do you believe, in general, that the United States puts a lot of pressure on the Spokesman's Office?

Associate Spokesperson: No...

Question: I googled the word "misspoke" and discovered that it was a very famous word from the 1970s associated with the [US President Richard] Nixon era that has since come to be synonymous with "lied". Was it in that sense that the UN used the word "misspoke" regarding Ms. Perelli's comments?

Associate Spokesperson: No."

A beleaguered Secretary-General

The mood of the time was well-captured by an article in the Inter Press Service (IPS) at the beginning of February entitled, "Is beleaguered UN Chief caving in to US pressure?" written by Thalif Deen:

"A rash of recent headlines in mainstream US newspapers portray a UN Secretary-General struggling to survive: 'Kofi Annan Must Go', 'Annan's Post at the UN May be at Risk, Officials Fear' and 'Criminal Probe Eyes Kofi's Son'. The unrelenting media and political campaign against Annan has been grounded mostly on charges of mismanagement, corruption, nepotism and sexual harassment in the UN system worldwide.

Annan has also been shaken by allegations that his son, Kojo Annan, was linked to a Swiss company currently under investigation in the scandal-tarred, multimillion dollar oil-for-food programme in Iraq. But Annan's defenders say the continued muckraking against the world body has been sparked primarily by the strong stand he took against the US military attack on Iraq in March 2003, calling it "illegal". And right-wing neo-conservatives with close ties to the White House, who believe that both the United Nations and Annan made a grievous error by not supporting the US war on Iraq, are out to get the Secretary-General.

So how does Annan, whose second five-year term ends in December 2006, try to survive against such overwhelming political odds? 'He is obviously caving into US pressure,' Jim Paul, Executive Director of the New York-based Global Policy Forum, told IPS. Even recent UN reports from the Secretary-General's office, he said, were virtually drafted either by British or US nationals, one of them from the US National Security Council. 'No policy statement can be uttered by Kofi these days that is not crafted by specialists who are (at a minimum) highly sensitive to Washington's priorities,' Paul added.

Annan has refused to reappoint the head of the Palestine refugee agency (UNRWA) Peter Hansen of Denmark, a longtime critic of Israeli policies in the occupied territories of the West Bank and Gaza, primarily because of US and Israeli pressure. The long-rumoured appointment of retiring Under-Secretary-General Kieran Prendergast of Britain as the new

UN Middle East envoy has also been stymied by the United States and Israel. Annan half-admitted the pressure he is under when he told reporters recently: '(Prendergast) would have been perfect. But we don't work in a vacuum.'

Meanwhile, as part of a high level management restructuring, Annan's Chef de Cabinet (Chief of Staff) Iqbal Riza of Pakistan went into retirement last month, followed by his second-in-command Elisabeth Lindenmayer of France. Riza, who is believed to have been forced into retirement at short notice, has been succeeded by Mark Malloch-Brown of Britain, head of the UN Development Programme (UNDP). 'These are all marks of a purge,' Paul said...

Besides Malloch-Brown, the most recent senior UN appointments include David Veness of Britain as Under-Secretary-General for Safety and Security, and Ann Veneman, the outgoing US Secretary of Agriculture, as Executive Director of UNICEF to replace another US national, Carol Bellamy...."

Around this time the Press Spokesman was asked about these appointments. "The Secretary-General supports rotating nationalities for senior positions," Fred Eckhard affirmed.

Volcker reports

At the beginning of February 2005, Volcker issued his First Interim Report.

The report was striking for what it did not find. The world had been driven close to believing that the UN was either irredeemably corrupt, or irredeemably incompetent, or both, so in the light of that expectation the UN emerged scarred but intact. The critics' virulence and hyperbole did not match Volcker's findings and as such their overreaching proved beneficial. No evidence was found of gross financial malfeasance nor of widespread examples of mismanagement. Sadly, though, my friend Benon was seriously implicated in apparent misconduct.

Benon was found to have "solicited and received several million barrels of allocations of oil... from 1998 to 2001" on behalf of an international oil company in return for advocating, it was charged, "lifting holds on oil industry spare parts". It further found that he had received $160,000 in cash between 1999 to 2003, and that his explanations for the source of these funds were unconvincing.

And so, once again, in a mesh of conflicting emotions, long-standing friendship and deep affection contended for primary loyalty against apparently grave ethical lapses. But I knew, with scant hesitation, that I could not repudiate Benon. Even if the charges against him of malfeasance and dereliction of professional duty were confirmed, even though such lapses would constitute everything I had striven to guard against throughout my own UN career, I could not do so. So I called him, spoke to him with warmth and expressed my solidarity, while being careful to never express disbelief about the accusations. (And, in the years to come, after he had fled from New York, I would frequently send him warm greetings through mutual friends even after direct contact lapsed.) For to deny Benon would be to deny another large part of my past. And Benon had never denied me.

As for the rest of Benon's friends, when I came across them, the sentiment was universal: he was being falsely accused. As evidence they pointed to the amount he was said to have obtained in return for the loan of his influence, which sum they considered puny. No, if Benon was going to do it, they would say, he would only do it for something big!

I would often wonder what toll was being taken on Kofi by the weight of these hurrying events. People made much of the fact that Sergio de Mello and others of the Baghdad dead had been his personal friends, but Benon had also been his personal friend, a friend of some thirty years, and we had all grown up together in the service of the United Nations, had known each other well, and had kept hoping and striving for something better. Now we all were, or used to be, in positions where we had been charged with making a beneficial difference, charged with contributing to changing the culture of the Organisation, albeit in vastly different positions of vastly different weight. Had we then, like so many before us who had come to positions of authority and power, performed no better than the rest?

Getting the relationship with the US right

Such sentimental musings were undoubtedly quite out of place in the new Secretariat that the new Chef was striving to fashion. And lest anyone might consider that the January gestures amounted to lavish displays of fealty, the world had Malloch-Brown to provide reassurance.

"Getting the relationship repaired is key," commented the new Chef at the end of February. "I cannot think of a time in the UN's sixty-year life when the organisation has prospered and done well that it hasn't rested on a strong, effective relationship" with the United States. The United Nations is not "pandering to the United States," he corrected the gallery of the doubtful, but making "a strategic effort to identify what we have in common with Washington and work to celebrate that, to really maximise it."

A few weeks later, Malloch-Brown was to reach new fictional heights in interpreting the UN/US relationship when the appointment of John Bolton, a former State Department Assistant Secretary of State, as the new US Ambassador was announced. (Bolton had been unable to obtain the support of the US Senate and had been put in place as a result of a "Recess" appointment by President Bush). Bolton's coming was generally viewed as the equivalent of the application of the cat-o'-nine-tails considering the views he had expressed about the institution, and the concept of international cooperation, in the past ("The Secretariat building in New York has thirty-eight stories. If you lost ten stories it wouldn't make a bit of difference," and "There is no United Nations. There is an international community that occasionally can be led by the only real power left in the world – the United States – when it suits our interests and when we can get others to go along") being among the most noteworthy.

The New Yorker described the appointment as "Stiffing the UN," while *The New York Times* called it "a slap at the international community," but the no-longer-so-new Chef had his own benign interpretation. In an interview with Fox News (Sunday, 13 March, 2005), he was asked, "What do you make of the nomination of John Bolton to be the new US Ambassador, particularly given his critical comments over the years about the UN and his apparent assignment to shake things up?" To which Malloch-Brown replied, "People forget that a little bit more than ten years ago he was a very effective Assistant Secretary of State in the State Department dealing with the UN. Second, you know, a US Ambassador to the UN has to be very effective in New York, but he also has to be very effective in Washington. And, of course, that's where there's a real silver lining to John Bolton's appointment, because if he can corral the different congressional points of view and the administration's point of view into a single set of recommended reforms for the UN, which we can respond to, that's good news for us."

But the willful world might be excused if, instead of Malloch-Brown's optimistic incantations, it preferred the interpretation of events put forward by a journalist at the time of Peter Hansen's dismissal – "The reports that Mr. Hansen of the UNRWA is not being reappointed by the Secretary-General under pressure from the United States and Israel, is this how the United Nations is going to function? Dictated to by Israel and the United States?" Or, at any rate, by the United States.

The exchange at the Press Briefing about Carina Perelli's "misspeaking" introduced the enticing possibility that what had so far been drama could yet turn into farce. Annan himself contributed to this evolution when, on 15 February, asked if the assassination of former Prime Minister of Lebanon Rafic Hariri (which had just taken place) made a Syrian withdrawal from Lebanon more or less likely, he offered this assessment: "I think it depends on where one sits. Where you stand depends on where you sit." [This was later recalled by me to be a quotation from, "Yes, Minister", the satirical British TV series. Upon further investigation the saying was revealed to be the "Miles' Law", established by Rufus E. Miles, Jr. (1910–1996), an Assistant Secretary under Presidents Dwight D. Eisenhower, John F. Kennedy and Lyndon B. Johnson. Miles developed it, he explained, from "memorable encounters with reality."]

The fall of Lubbers

It was left to Lubbers, on the occasion of his second return, to confirm the descent into farce. On Friday, 18 February *The Independent* revealed that it had got hold of the full OIOS report on Lubbers. In reporting on the matter, the newspaper, in a headlined, front-page story, provided details of the famous "friendly gesture" that indicated it allegedly went much further than bottom-grabbing. Further salacious details were also provided about the accusations against Lubbers from four other female staff of UNHCR.

Lubbers was at UN Headquarters the same day the *Independent*'s revelations appeared and was offered up by the Spokesman's office to the press. Asked to explain his "friendly gesture", Lubbers chose to give a demonstration, beckoning the enquiring journalist to approach.

"Are you afraid of me?" he asked preparing to act out the gesture. "I am, slightly," was the reply as Lubbers, performing, perhaps, a modified version, tapped him on the back.

In taking the opportunity to reassert his innocence, Lubbers remarked that he would be seeing Nane Annan the next day and would "lead her out of the room the same way" [as he had led his accuser.]

Whether Lubbers did indeed accomplish this particular mission is not known (or whether the promise, or threat, of it spurred the 38th Floor into action) but by Sunday, 20 February he was gone.

Lubbers had been forced out, his position having been made untenable after the worldwide publicity that the *Independent*'s reporting attracted, and, as he himself inferred in his letter of resignation, because Kofi Annan was in some considerable measure of political difficulty.

Having issued a public statement on 20 February in response to Lubbers' resignation letter that, "The Secretary-General is convinced that it is in the best interest of UNHCR, its staff and the refugees it serves that the page be turned and a new chapter started," Annan sent a letter to the staff of UNHCR the next day contending that, "My decision to accept his resignation should not be interpreted as a finding of guilt".

It did not go unremarked that there had been no new substantive developments that mandated Lubbers' departure. The information made available by the *Independent* had been known to the Secretary-General since July of 2004 when OIOS had submitted its findings. At that time, the UN had fostered the impression that Lubbers had been cleared by the OIOS.

When in October the news leaked that the contrary was the case, the UN had fostered the impression that the mix-up of not including the "guilty" verdict in OIOS' annual report to the General Assembly had been the fault of its author, Dileep Nair.

It was supreme farce at its most perverse.

(Sex and farce seemed to have become weirdly conjoined in the UNHCR universe at this time. Lubbers again had something to do with it as he had been responsible for appointing the actress Angelina Jolie ["Lara Croft Tomb Raider: The Cradle of Life", and "Lara Croft Tomb Raider: The Angel of Darkness"] as a Goodwill Ambassador for UNHCR.

"We are very pleased that Ms. Jolie has generously agreed to give her time and energy to support UNHCR's work ..." Lubbers said in announcing her appointment. "We are proud to welcome her to the UNHCR family."

"I love sex! I never get enough; I need it more than anyone I know."

This was just one of many striking pronouncements from the "Goodwill Ambassador" who had her own ideas on how to spread goodwill. Giving her views on sexual etiquette, she advised that she didn't have a boyfriend, and didn't want one. She had lovers.

"We meet in hotel rooms and the whole thing is very precise and organised," Lara Croft told London's *Mail on Sunday.* "As long as you have safe sex and you don't confuse your family, I think it's very healthy."

As part of her health kick, no doubt, "The Cradle of Life," it was learnt, sported several scars from playing with knives (including an X on her arm, a slice on her stomach and a nick on her neck), or as she puts it, "You're young, you're drunk, you're in bed, you have knives; stuff happens."

Lara Croft's other major obsession, one also learnt, was tattoos. This posed something of a problem for the make-up "artists" during filming as she reportedly had a large collection of them including:

1. Five slash-like columns of Khmer script writing on her left shoulder blade;
2. A dragon on her left arm;
3. Roman numerals XIII on her left forearm;
4. A Tennessee Williams quote, "A prayer for the wild at heart, kept in cages," on her left inside forearm;
5. A rune-shaped design resembling a small letter H on her inside left wrist;
6. A black dragon with a blue tongue on her lower hip;
7. "Quod me nutrit me destruit," Latin for, "What nourishes me also destroys me," located on her lower stomach;
8. A large black crucifix on her lower hip;
9. Energy waves located a little below her navel;
10. Japanese Kanji for "death" on her left shoulder;
11. A dragon with tribal design on her lower back;
12. A blue box – signifying a window – on her lower back; and
13. Two black American Indian symbols on her lower back.

On UN Day in October 2003, Lara Croft was given the UN Correspondents Association's first "Citizen of the World" Award for her work with refugees. It was presented by Nane Annan. The award was in honour of Sergio Vieira de Mello. Declining to be overshadowed, in October 2004 *Esquire* magazine put the "Angel of Darkness" on its cover and anointed her "The Sexiest Woman Alive." She commented in an accompanying interview: "The tattoos, the blood, cutting myself – it's all very much who I am." She added, "If you knew me privately, you might think that I was even wilder than my reputation."

It was a funny sort of world that the celebrity-entranced United Nations had chosen to cavort in.)

Successive triumphs

Although it had not been accomplished elegantly, the end of Lubbers could be viewed positively by the Secretary-General and his advisers. If Lubbers had remained, he would have been a lingering reproach, a reminder of moral indecision and managerial squeamishness. His departure could be added to the list of positive developments arriving with the New Year to counteract the prevailing mood of malaise and disarray. The first was the opportunity provided by the tsunami.

At first the extent of the tsunami's effect was not realised but as soon as the scale of the disaster began to become apparent, Annan acted resolutely and speedily. He worked to mobilise the international community, orchestrated a worldwide appeal for funds, established effective relief coordination mechanisms and made a well-publicised tour of the affected region. He then appointed Bill Clinton as his Special Envoy for Tsunami Recovery and, subsequently, appointed Erskine Bowles, Clinton's former Chief of Staff as the Deputy Special Envoy. In recognition of the aftermath of the oil-for-food malfeasance, the UN also made sure that stringent and transparent financial monitoring arrangements were set up to give confidence to the donors.

The tsunami was eventually estimated to have taken upwards of 225,000 lives but it proved to be an ironic life raft for the UN. At a moment in its history when the UN was at its lowest ebb, an unprecedented tragedy allowed the UN to prove it could still be effective, reminded the world of the positive aspects of its work, and gave the Secretary-General the means to initiate the labour of his restoration.

The next was the Iraq elections. Here Kofi had taken an enormous risk. The country remained in turmoil and his staff was against the UN's return but Annan had agreed to the American-Iraqi request and sent in a small team of UN electoral advisers. He gambled that he needed to so act in order to retain a degree of credibility with the coalition partners, particularly the "First Two." The UN team lived in the "Green Zone," and were guarded by the invaders, and Annan had to know that more UN deaths in Baghdad would mean an inevitable rupture with his staff. But there were no deaths, and the UN team performed admirably, training thousands of Iraqis on how to conduct and monitor the elections. When they took place at the end of January and resulted in a 60% turnout on the basis of the efficient electoral arrangements put in place by the UN, Kofi Annan was able to enjoy a second successive triumph.

42
CASUALTIES OF WAR

The internment of Benon – Vindication – The shaming of Nair – George Soros and a slight hiccup

The internment of Benon

March, 2005

On the 22 March, the *New York Sun* got in the game when it reported that the UN had agreed to pay Benon Sevan's legal fees. Naturally, this created consternation since it had the smell of a cover-up about it. The first response was to prevaricate. It came in a UN press release issued on the same day with the convoluted headline, "The UN agreed to pay Benon Sevan's legal fees, but not for period subsequent to Volcker's adverse findings, and no payments yet made." Volcker himself was the first to be cited.

"The Independent Inquiry Committee agreed to permit Mr. Benon Sevan, the head of the Office of the Iraq Programme, to have legal counsel during his interviews with the IIC. As we understand it, the decision was taken on an exceptional basis due to the importance that the Committee placed on Mr. Sevan's cooperation to the conduct of the inquiry..."

Others shared the widely-distributed blame.

"In October 2004, the UN Office of Legal Affairs advised Mr. Iqbal Riza, then the Chef de Cabinet, that such a step was in the interests of the UN..." Having been set up, the former Chef is then buried: "As a result a verbal undertaking was given to Mr. Sevan [happily clarified under questioning to have been given by the unlamented Mr. Riza] that reasonable legal fees as determined by the United Nations would be paid by the Organisation." So Volcker had been responsible for initiating the process, which had been carried forward by Riza upon recommendation of the Legal Office.

This was a small masterpiece of obfuscation, managing to cast blame on a far-flung set of characters. Volcker himself refused to play this game. The next day he let it be known that the Committee's agreement to allow Mr. Sevan to be accompanied by a lawyer, "was not motivated, as suggested by the UN statement, by a desire to induce Mr. Sevan to cooperate." At no time had the Committee, "proffered an opinion on the payment of Mr. Sevan's legal costs."

Finally, on March 28, the day before Volcker's Second Interim Report was to appear, this particular bit of business was disposed of when it was announced that Benon's legal costs would not, after all, be covered by the United Nations. This was not surprising. The previous announcement was entirely unconvincing as it had been delivered in the form of mealy-mouthed accountings and ineffective distancing from events. ("As we understand it ..." was the key clause in the press release, suggesting that someone else, anyone else, was to blame for the debacle.) As with Lubbers there had been no new substantive developments affecting the matter but that was not the point, especially since the accusation was being publicly voiced that Annan had agreed to pay Benon's legal fees in order to keep him quiet. So embarrassments had to be shed regardless of previous promises and commitments. No explanation was provided nor was one required; Benon now had to be cast adrift.

Vindication

With the issuance of the Second Interim Volcker Report, Kofi Annan, with a little more than a year and a half to go, would reach the high point of the remainder of his tenure as Secretary-General. The imagined charge against him (because it was never formally made, there was no "indictment" that he had to answer, he had been subject to an inquiry, not an investigation) was that he had used his position to influence the choice of Cotecna as a

UN contractor for the oil-for-food programme in an effort to assist his son who worked for that company. In this regard the report found that, "There is no evidence that the selection of Cotecna in 1998 was subject to any affirmative or improper influence by the Secretary-General in the bidding or selection process".

Kofi Annan rightly made much of this verdict, appearing at a Press Conference to stress his vindication, and answering loudly "Hell, no" when asked whether he would resign. With this result, he could be satisfied that he had survived two vicious whispering campaigns. The first had implied that he had somehow been colluding with and protecting Benon in an unarticulated conspiracy as shown by his willingness to sanction payment of Benon's legal fees. He had confronted that by reversing himself on the payment of these fees. The second, favouritism to Cotecna, had now also been rebutted.

But the initial Volcker findings did not represent a complete victory. Swept aside by Kofi Annan, and generally ignored by the media, was a sharply critical finding regarding the role that he had played in investigating the potential for conflict of interest due to his son being employed by a firm that was seeking a UN contract. The Committee found his actions "inadequate". Additionally, on "whether the conduct of the Secretary-General in the selection and retention of Cotecna was adequate", Volcker found that "*the evidence is not reasonably sufficient* to show that the Secretary-General knew that Cotecna had submitted a bid on the humanitarian inspection contract in 1998".

Also virtually unnoticed was the resignation of two of Volcker's investigators on the grounds that Volcker had been "too soft" on Annan. But one of the three Committee members, Mark Pieth, did choose to remark, "We did not exonerate Kofi Annan. A certain mea culpa would have been appropriate".

The shaming of Nair

Following on the Lubbers revelations, another earlier obfuscation returned to bite in the person of Dileep Nair, who had been awarded the benefit of an internal investigation conducted by a senior official, which investigation's conclusion, like all of this type at this time, proved, in the end, to be untenable.

In looking into the Staff Union's allegations, Volcker concluded, in his Second Interim Report, that at least one of the accusations had merit when he found that funds had been misused and Staff Rules violated. Specifically, the report said that Nair had drawn on funds allocated to his office under the UN programme for Iraq to hire a fellow Singaporean as his personal assistant on work unrelated to the oil-for-food programme. Unsatisfied by this limited rendering the Staff Union pressed its demands for a further review, which eventually resulted in an independent investigation being commissioned. Nair was found to be guiltless of the sexual harassment and corruption charges made against him by the Staff Union but a main conclusion of this report still was "that the investigation found that, in two cases involving appointment and promotion in OIOS, it appeared that Mr. Nair had predetermined the outcome of the selection process..."

It was unfortunate that two investigations of the UN's chief investigator had found him wanting. It was humiliating that yet again independent inquiries had found the UN's initial internal investigation to be flawed, giving the appearance of a cover-up. But, by this time, Dileep Nair had completed his term of office, so it turned out, due to the timing of the final verdicts, to be only a minor embarrassment for the United Nations. As for Nair, he had already left the UN, and the castigations affected him not at all except as they touched on his reputation.

George Soros and a slight hiccup

June, 2005

The advent of summer brought with it a slight hiccup to the recovery agenda when its operational leader, the new Chef, was revealed on 17 June, by the now relentless *New York Sun*, to be a tenant on the Westchester County, New York estate, of the billionaire financier George Soros.

The revelation posed two public relations problems for Malloch- Brown, whose reputed public relations skills had played a role in his elevation. First, the annual rent of US $120,000 would absorb much of his net annual salary. Second, Soros was a proud supporter of the Democratic Party, the coffers of whose affiliated organisations he was known to have frequently helped to replenish. Thus, located in one story were the two problems that Kofi Annan currently faced in dealing with the Republican Administration and Republican legislators – intimations of another financial scandal and excessive closeness to the Democratic opposition.

A UNDP Spokesman first clarified that Malloch-Brown was taking care of the rent from his savings. Then at a UN Press Conference on 20 June at which he addressed the controversy, Malloch-Brown, after insisting that he was paying a full commercial rent and had never hidden his relationship with George Soros, set about endearing himself to the UN Press Corps and, especially, two reporters who had the temerity to raise questions about the matter.

"*Chef de Cabinet:* So my challenge to you, James, and to Benny, is who gave you this story? What was their motive? What is it that now gives free rein to any amount of bile, unproven but still publishable, with no questioning of the motives of those who provided it? Perhaps when you're ready to answer that question, I'll be ready to answer a few more.

Question: I think I could answer that right now, actually. And then maybe I could get a follow-up in return for that. Of course, a lot of people [inaudible] don't like you and some of those perhaps have given us those stories. That's perfectly understandable, and we can surely sort out their motives. *Their motives are perfectly transparent. They don't like you.* My question then is – are there any other properties with which you have any financial relationship with George Soros?

Chef de Cabinet: No, I have no financial involvement with George Soros, of any kind. I pay a full commercial rent for the one property of his I live in. The direction of your questions, and the fact that, even when the allegation is proven untrue, a full commercial rent is confirmed, you and your friends keep at it, makes me put to you that you may want to question your own motives.....

Question: Don't you think it's slightly odd that the person who said they wanted to be squeaky clean has a financial relationship, albeit a normal, commercial financial relationship, with someone who does business with the UN and the agency you're the head of? Wouldn't you feel that rather odd if somebody else in another rank had a commercial relationship that the Organisation does business with?

Chef de Cabinet: No, I wouldn't, James, not if it was on proper, full, commercial lines and had never been a secret and never been hidden. It is of particular genius from you and your friends that something which is open knowledge to everybody is suddenly produced as some great, guilty secret. Get back to the plenty of real stories that are around here.... [and] stop dragging down everyone you touch, particularly yourself, by the way you're behaving...."

Malloch-Brown had come to the briefing ready for a row. He could simply have issued a press statement outlining the facts of the case. However, the case was a little labyrinthan as the veiled reference by a questioner to Soros "[doing] business with the UN and the agency [you have] been head of" snidely suggested. Yes, he was a friend of Soros. Yes, he had known George Soros at least since the early nineties when he was a member of the Soros Advisory Committee on Bosnia in 1993–94. And yes, George Soros' Open Society Institute had engaged in joint activities with UNDP when the Chef was in charge including, beginning in late 2003, the somewhat unusual project to supply funds to supplement the salary of the new Georgian President Mikheil Saakashvili and other public officials, especially law enforcement officials. Even though UNDP had funded salary-supplement programmes to Third World governments before, this was a pioneering endeavour as UNDP's remit was to help Third World countries, which Georgia, by definition, was not. (In the wake of the cold war and with strategically-placed Eastern European countries needing assistance, the Western donor countries to UNDP had managed to force an enlargement of UNDP's mandate.) Moreover, this was a particularly unusual and risky activity, plunging the UN deep into a bloody, internecine, political convulsion, particularly considered against the background of Soros' Open Society Institute having supported Saakashvili and other opposition NGO groups *before* the "Rose Revolution", thereby contributing to enabling a change of regime.

It was evident, therefore, that Malloch-Brown had a close, long-standing personal and working relationship with Soros. The real question was whether he was beholden to him but to pursue that question involved making imputations, and even accusations, which, unless supported by evidence, risked the receipt of a legal writ for defamation and slander. So while it was certainly not unreasonable to question the nature of the private-cum-professional relationship with George Soros, and although overall the thing looked to be a bit odd, and it did seem rather curious that someone should commit what amounted to much of his entire salary to rent, who dared to challenge the assertion that he had saved a lot and, in any event, he did have a wife who, it was reported, was gainfully employed.

(In February 2006, Malloch-Brown agreed to be interviewed by Claudia Rosett, well known as an unrelenting critic of the Organisation in general and Kofi Annan in particular, presumably in the expectation that he could disarm her. In this he was mistaken. According to Rosett, Malloch-Brown became upset at her continuing questioning about his housing arrangements, aborted the interview with the announcement that, "I am doing God's work", and departed in haste.)

43
THE LONG VALEDICTION

The admonitions of Mr. Volcker – At odds with the Third World – In Larger Freedom – A Staff vote of No Confidence in the Secretary-General – The departure of Louise – The Fraudulent Eight

———◦——

"You do look, my son, in a moved sort,
As if you were dismay'd: be cheerful, sir.
Our revels now are ended. These our actors,
As I foretold you, were all spirits and
Are melted into air, into thin air ....."

The Tempest

William Shakespeare

———◦——

September, 2005–December, 2006

Another reputation was shattered when Carina Perelli, the Director of the United Nations Electoral Division, last seen speaking truth to power about the misconduct on the part of the US military as a result of their interference in the supposedly neutral running of the Iraqi elections, was herself summarily dismissed for misconduct. She had been accused of "harassment, including sexual harassment, and abuse of authority".

The admonitions of Mr. Volcker

A later edition of Volcker seemed to provide incontrovertible evidence that Benon had indeed transgressed, and had done so in collusion with a relative of Boutros-Ghali, which provided more manna for outrage and scandal. Benon fled the country, cast into exile to his native Cyprus, where he was safe from extradition, a step ahead of an indictment by the American authorities. But it was a cruel exile as he was unable to leave his safe haven for fear of prosecution by the US Justice Department.

The semi-discarded Iqbal Riza (following his removal from the post of Chef de Cabinet he had been granted a Special Adviser job by Kofi Annan at a dollar a year) was revealed to be a "shredder", responsible for authorising the destruction of thousands of pages of his "Chron files" [chronological records], a complete collection of three years of daily correspondence emanating from the Secretary-General's office during the material years of controversy, which destruction continued for months notwithstanding a Secretary-General's directive commanding the preservation of all relevant papers. The Chef had argued that the destroyed files simply contained duplicates of papers to be found in other records in the Secretariat, and in any case the continued destruction was inadvertent, but the Committee did not agree with him and issued an adverse finding. It did not go unremarked that Riza had approved the shredding of these back-up files the day after the Security Council approved the establishment of the Volcker Committee, nor that ten days earlier Riza had himself instructed department heads to preserve files related to the Programme. Riza appealed for a reconsideration of the finding, alluding to the severe damage to his reputation, but Volcker was not to be moved.

In his final reports Volcker concluded that the UN's Oil-for-Peace Programme had been mismanaged by the Secretariat. Illegal kickback schemes, price surcharges and oil smuggling had been taking place on the UN's watch. Worse, the Secretariat seemed to know a great deal about these illegalities but either chose to do nothing about them or made only infrequent, ineffective passes at the problem. Benon was found to be a main culprit, diligently concealing the facts when they came to his attention, perhaps, it may be speculated, because he did not wish to offend those providing him with oil allocations.

The Secretary-General and his Deputy did not emerge well from the inquiry. Kofi Annan was found inter alia to have had "an inadequate response to, and investigation of, Iraqi abuses and corruption of the Programme... a lack of adequately ensuring that the sanctions objective of the Programme received adequate attention... "and" a failure to provide adequate oversight" of Benon. In summary, the Volcker Committee reported that "the cumulative management performance of the Secretary-General fell short of the standards that the United Nations Organisation should strive to maintain".

Louise had been charged with supervising Benon and thus the Iraqi Programme. The Committee found that she knew this yet "her oversight of Mr. Sevan was not adequate. The Deputy Secretary-General offered very little direction to Mr. Sevan, particularly on matters concerning the sanctions violations." The last time Louise had been publicly exposed she had offered to resign only to have Kofi refuse the offer. The pantomime is not repeated on this occasion.

As for the Chef, the Report assesses, "Mr. Riza frequently met with the Secretary-General and Mr. Sevan to discuss important matters concerning the Programme. With far greater frequency than the Deputy Secretary-General, Mr. Riza also participated in meetings with Iraqi officials relating to the Programme... Mr. Riza played a greater role than he was willing to state," Volcker concluded.

As embarrassing, in a way, as the actual conclusions were the vigorous attempts (as described in the Report) by the Secretary-General, the Deputy Secretary-General, and the Chef de Cabinet to deflect responsibility for the evidenced mismanagement. Kofi Annan let it be known that Benon reported to the Security Council, which managed the Programme, notwithstanding the fact that he, Annan, had set it up and appointed Benon: in any event, he maintained, he had delegated his oversight responsibilities to his Deputy. Louise did not seem to realise that she was supposed to supervise Benon: in any event, she contended, Benon had long-standing ties and working relationships with Annan and Riza and consequently dealt primarily with them. The Chef sought to portray himself as a mere paper-pusher but the Committee noted that also meant that he saw all the papers and could, therefore, have intervened as he felt necessary and as his job description required.

"The 38th Floor", the Committee chided, "evince(d) a reluctance to accept responsibility for the significant management failures that occurred within the OIP during the life of the Programme."

In an appearance before the Security Council on Thursday, September, 2005, Volcker offered these remarks: "Our assignment has been to look for mis- or mal-administration in the oil-for-food-programme, and for evidence of corruption within the UN Organisation and by contractors. Unhappily we found both," Volcker told the Council. "We have found no corruption by the Secretary-General," he went on, "but his behaviour has not been exonerated by any stretch of the imagination". Saddam's graveyard, ever welcoming and occupying a vast terrain, which had already accepted for burial the reputations (in many cases) and the careers (in others), of a long list of American and British political victims, as well as those of Richard Butler, Rolf Ekéus, Denis Halliday and Hans von Sponeck, now contentedly took in Kofi Annan, Louise Fréchette, Iqbal Riza and Benon Sevan, and still had room for many more.

At odds with the Third World

The disregard that the 38th Floor had consistently shown in their internal deliberations towards developing countries, and the urge to accrete authority at the expense of Member States, especially those from the South, witnessed by me during my time there (and commented upon earlier in this text), had, in fact, not gone unobserved by those who were expected to recognise and applaud the rationality of the ambition. I had often wondered why developing countries had raised no public objection to the creeping incursions (confining themselves largely to angry but subdued mutterings) and had concluded that his position as an African and a Third World leader had kept the uneasy quiescent. That silence was now to be broken.

In the autumn of 2005 dissatisfaction on the part of the South was made evident as a result of the perceived attentiveness by the Secretary-General to the wishes of Washington as well as the actions of Mark Malloch-Brown, the Chef de Cabinet, who had been put in place to perform lifeguarding exertions.

"The Group of 77 (and China) is constrained to seek clarification as to whether it is now the practice of senior officials of the Secretariat to report directly to national parliaments on actions taken by the membership of the United Nations," the Chairman of the Group of 77, Ambassador Stafford Neil of Jamaica, said in a letter to Annan.

Malloch-Brown had first got himself into trouble due to a briefing he had provided to the House International Relations Committee of the US Congress, seeking US support for the proposed reform agenda of the United Nations in four main areas – development, security, human rights and management restructuring. "To help achieve this," Malloch-Brown told US Congressmen, "we rely on our friends not only in the Administration but also here in Congress. *You, after all, have the power of the purse, and that ensures you an attentive audience wherever you go,*" he helpfully pointed out.

Malloch-Brown had given the impression that he was appealing to the US Congress, over the heads of the other Member States, to support Annan's approaches to reform and had called on them to employ their financial suzerainty over the UN to help achieve these goals.

Subsequently, Malloch-Brown had exercised no restraint in commenting on the attitudes to reform by some groups of Member States.

"We have a hell of a structural problem", he complained. "The Security Council and Member States generally interfere in the management of this Organisation. They've not given the Secretary-General the authority or the resources or the means to run a modern Organisation that can be held properly accountable to its membership". He also accused Member States of interfering in the work of the Secretariat: "We instead have a highly politicised interference in the day-to-day decision-making by ambassadors and their minions." Explaining the division of powers between legislative and executive bodies in the United States and Britain, Malloch-Brown said: "And in the UN context, the Congress or legislature has run wild and has trampled all over the freedom of management to manage, so that every single post, every single mini bit of the budget has to be approved by a vast governmental committee of 191 members. And we've got to push back against that."

Malloch-Brown's comments at least had the ring of authenticity about them. He was boldly and openly advancing the philosophy of governance that the 38th Floor had been seeking to implement since the early days of Kofi Annan's tenure. In a zero-sum game, the Secretariat wanted more than its present allocation.

Neil also took exception to this.

"I have been requested by Member States of the Group of 77 and China to write to you to express their concern regarding the content of public statements being made by senior officials of the Secretariat which the Group considers inappropriate and reflect negatively on the Organisation."

"It is in violation of the UN Charter," he continued, "which requires the staff of the Secretariat to be politically neutral and to refrain from any action inconsistent with their status as international civil servants responsible only to the Organisation."

Kofi Annan and his collaborators were not the first to seek to augment the authority of the 38th Floor at the expense of Member States but they were probably the most insistent. He could interpret his position as Chief Administrative Officer of the Organisation modestly or expansively but if he chose the latter path he could only tread as far as the Member States of the United Nations would allow him to go. During the course of his Secretary-Generalship, the notion had been developed that he was, properly, the "Prime Minister" of our unique community: this ambition amounted to no more than a *folie de grandeur.* It cast the Secretariat as the executive authority in the United Nations when the carefully-balanced Articles of the Charter had dispersed such authority among various entities. At root the Secretary-General was an international civil servant, the most prominent one to be sure, who could employ the persuasive possibilities of his position in order to influence events, but he was still required to be invariably civil and to never neglect the obligation of service. He was the Chief "Administrative" Officer not the Chief "Executive" one.

On Monday, 21 November, Secretary-General Kofi Annan appeared before a closed-door meeting of the Group of 77, numbering 132 Member States, the preponderance of the membership of the United Nations, to which he had been summoned.

"We are not going to usurp your powers," he told them. "There has been a lot of misunderstandings and misapprehensions". He explained that he had no plans to marginalise the role of the General Assembly, to take away its decision-making powers, or even "impose decisions on Member States". Contrary to speculation, he assured delegates, "this is not a grab for power".

The Secretary-General then addressed the visit of his main adviser to Washington: "When Mark Malloch-Brown went to Washington DC, he went to offer information, not to testify under oath."

Annan also referred to a statement made by the new Under-Secretary-General for Management, Christopher Burnham, whose appointment was determined by the Bush Administration, and who had been quoted as saying that his "loyalties" were with George W. "We have discussed this, and he apologised to me. This matter is closed," Annan said.

(Burnham and his background had become something of an embarrassment. His previous position had been as Acting Under Secretary of State for Management in the US State Department.

When his appointment was announced by Louise in May it was done with some fanfare and with satisfaction: his provenance, apparently, automatically guaranteed his competence. She had said that the selection of Burnham would reassure Washington "that we're very serious about getting the most competent people to manage our Organisation.")

With regard to accusations that the reform of the United Nations was primarily American-driven, Annan said that his proposed reforms will "have the interests of all members not just one country". He also said that in the reform exercise the future of all programmes and mandates will depend on Member States. "You will decide what should be cut and what should be rejected. It's your prerogative," he said.

The Secretariat will have characterised the Secretary-General's explanations as simple clarifications, provided due to "misunderstandings and misapprehensions" of his actions. To many, however, he appeared to have announced a major retreat after years of proceeding in a contrary direction.

In Larger Freedom

Two major initiatives were launched by the Secretary-General in furtherance of his attempt to redirect the dialogue, support his recovery, and construct a favourable, lasting, legacy. The first had been his "Panel to save the World" and his later presentation of proposals for action based on the Panel's recommendations. He called this Report, "In Larger Freedom", a phrase drawn from the Charter. In it he proposed an expansion of the Security Council, a strengthening of the UN's commitment to development, a formal acknowledgement of the doctrine of "Responsibility to Protect", the establishment of a Peacebuilding Commission (intended to be alert to possible signs of conditions leading to wars and internal disputes and thence intervene opportunely) and the reordering of the Human Rights Commission into an arm of the General Assembly with augmented authority.

Consideration of the report had being underway for some six months before John Bolton arrived on the scene, and delegations were making appreciable progress towards agreed conclusions. The new American Ambassador proclaimed his disregard of the process, and, simultaneously, demonstrated the approach to negotiations that he meant to adopt, by immediately tabling 350 amendments to the text under consideration.

In the end, and after a year of tortuous negotiation, the General Assembly accepted in principle, and then later fleshed out in practice, three of Annan's major proposals but only after Bolton had withdrawn the bulk of his proposals. These were on "Responsibility to Protect", the Peacebuilding Commission, and the Human Rights Commission, which were undoubted achievements. Even though no gains were registered on Security Council reform, overall his last, grand reform effort was a decided success, thus burnishing the record he would leave behind him as Secretary-General.

A Staff Vote of No Confidence in the Secretary-General

The second was wide-scale review of administrative and management procedures that Louise was charged with conducting. "Investing in the United Nations" was the title bestowed on this particular adventure, launched in March 2006, which called for a widespread restructuring of the Secretariat involving lay-offs, buy-outs and outsourcing of services and jobs.

The Staff Union immediately characterised the report as a Washington-inspired prescription designed to remodel the administration of the Secretariat along American corporate lines. Many delegations took the same view.

Previously, his prestige had fostered a welcoming reception for many of his proposals to the General Assembly, even compliance; and as an African, if not Africa's man, the combination of African and Western support, as well as staff support derived from him having been a staff member who had risen through the ranks, had been a force that was hard to gainsay. That era was over, as was confirmed when Fréchette's report resulted in the Staff Council, for the first time in the history of the United Nations, adopting a motion of, "No Confidence in the Secretary-General and his senior management team".

"Investing in the United Nations" quickly foundered, assaulted by the staff and butchered by Third World governments.

The departure of Louise

It had now become a timely moment for Louise to go. The embarrassments of Lubbers, Nair, Benon, Riza and Carina Perelli had been disposed of. They had all gone, all humiliated, most dismissed, with one sidelined with a kiss. She was the only one (besides, of course, Annan himself), who had been publicly scarred and publicly scourged, to have survived. Twice she had been identified in independent public inquiries as a main offender, only twice to be reprieved by the Secretary-General.

Annan lauds her for her efforts in gracious words. He congratulates her on her new responsibilities, praises her as a pioneer and an inspiration to women and points to her legacy of "reform and renewal". We are told that she "had informed the Secretary-General of her intention to leave the UN early next year to take up a new post as a Distinguished Fellow at the Centre for International Governance Innovation in Waterloo, Canada..." thus indicating that she hadn't been pushed. She would "remain at the United Nations until April 2006, in order to complete her role in coordinating the preparation for the Secretary-General's proposals for implementing comprehensive UN management reform..." thus suggesting that not only was the timing of the departure her own, but that the SG had confidence enough in her to have her supervise the work on what would be his final reform report.

But the public effort at projecting a voluntary and blameless departure does not entirely convince, despite Annan's kindly-chosen language. And the media reaction is uniform – "a Canadian who was criticised for tolerating corruption in the oil-for-food-programme"; "criticised for lack of programme oversight"; "came in for strong criticism from the Volcker panel for being negligent in curbing corruption in the $64 billion Iraqi oil-for-food programme she oversaw"; "who was criticised by former US Federal Reserve Chairman Paul Volcker for failing to properly manage the scandal-plagued Iraq oil-for-food programme"; "also came under fire after the August 2003 truck bomb attack on UN headquarters in Baghdad that killed twenty-two people. An investigation into the attack faulted a steering group headed by Fréchette that was responsible for UN policy and procedures in Iraq"; "reprimanded... for failure to anticipate the threat and take appropriate action"; "headed the steering committee that sent the UN to Iraq..." It was yet another sad ending to a once-exalted United Nations career.

[Louise was not shy in defending herself. In an interview with the Canadian Centre for International Governance Innovation (CIGI) dated 31 March, 2006, she explained why things may have gone wrong:

"There was no power attached to the post," Fréchette said, "Through the eight years that I spent in the role of Deputy Secretary-General, I've never had formal authority for anything."]

The announcement of Louise's departure was made at a Press Briefing on 16 December 2005.

The following assurance was also provided at the time:

"*Question:* Is Mark Malloch-Brown going to be Deputy Secretary-General?

Spokesman: No. As I told you, as appropriate, the Secretary-General may augment his staff on the 38th Floor to cover some of the functions that were done by the Deputy Secretary-General. As Chef de Cabinet, Mr. Malloch-Brown has quite enough on his plate."

On 6 March 2006 it was announced that Louise Fréchette would be succeeded by Mark Malloch-Brown as Deputy Secretary-General.

The determined Mr. Bolton

Married to the sadnesses of the Volcker admonitions, and the debilitating struggle to obtain approval for his various reform initiatives, Kofi Annan had to endure, in the latter part of his term, the sustained opposition of John Bolton. Arriving in New York with a long-standing, preset view of the role of the Organisation (indicated by his comments at an event called "The Global Structures Convocation" on February 3, 1994, in New York, when he said, "The United States makes the UN work when it wants it to work, and that is exactly the way it should be, because the only question, the only question for the United States is what is in our national interest. And if you don't like that, I'm sorry, but that is the fact"), he expeditiously displayed a readiness to confront Kofi Annan.

An early clash came over remarks made by Louise Arbour, UN High Commissioner for Human Rights, on December 7, 2005, Human Rights Day. Arbour had implied that the US-led war on terror undermined the global ban on torture. She avoided directly naming the United States in her statement and press conference commemorating Human Rights Day. But she criticised two practices that applied to the United States: holding prisoners in secret detention centres and rendering suspects to third countries without independent oversight. Bolton wasted no time: he counter-attacked immediately.

"Today is Human Rights Day. It would be appropriate, I think, for the UN's High Commissioner for Human Rights to talk about the serious human rights problems that exist in the world today," Bolton told reporters. "It is disappointing that she has chosen to talk about press commentary about alleged American conduct…" He added: "I think it is inappropriate and illegitimate for an international civil servant to second-guess the conduct that we're engaged in in the war on terror, with nothing more as evidence than what she reads in the newspapers."

Annan dug in his heels. It was a clear indication that, after all the condemnations that had been levelled against him by US politicians and media alike, he was no longer prepared to sit in silence in the face of American criticism. "The Secretary-General has no disagreement with the statement she made yesterday and he sees no reason to object to any of it," Annan's Press Spokesman stated. "The Secretary-General, in fact, intends to take this matter up with Ambassador Bolton as soon as possible," the Spokesman added.

The Fraudulent Eight

The new year began badly when Bolton was provided, it seemed, with further evidence to support his contention of the institutional rottenness of the UN, after an internal Secretariat investigation by the revived OIOS concluded that there was rampant waste and price inflation as well as suspicion that UN officials colluded with vendors in awarding contracts for a variety of peacekeeping programmes.

"We have no idea yet as to the scope of this, but I believe that we have significant evidence of fraud and corruption," the Under-Secretary-General for Management, Christopher Burnham, commented.

Eight officials involved in procurement including Andrew Toh, the Singaporean head of the office, were suspended, with pay, and sent home. The fraudulent sums involved were said to amount to some $60 million.

Soon, thereafter, a special tribunal, the UN Procurement Task Force, was set up under the leadership of a former FBI official to secure the evidence against the "Fraudulent Eight" by unearthing the missing millions that the supposed malefactors were presumed to have squirrelled away, so that the verdict which had, in all essentials, already been pronounced, could be judicially confirmed.

Bolton made the most of it.

"It is very disturbing. It shows the sad record of mismanagement that we are trying to deal with through the reform process," he said.

A few weeks later, at a Columbia Law School symposium held by the Federalist Society, a conservative law organisation, Bolton went as far as he could possibly go.

"We find an organisation that is deeply troubled by bad management, by sex and corruption and by a growing lack of confidence in its ability to carry out missions that are given to them," Bolton concluded.

In the end, little eventually came of this great "scandal". One was indeed found guilty but six of the eight were quietly reinstated, and subsequently publicly exonerated with some even receiving compensation. In winning a case for compensation against the Administration (two years' salary) in which he charged damage to his reputation and absence of due process, one staff member also obtained the judgment that, "The Organisation's actions [create the impression that they] were a rushed response for purposes of preserving its relations with Member States, rather than for the purpose of initiating an impartial inquiry founded on the Organisation's regulations and accompanying due process principles".

In another follow-up case, the Administration sought to officially reprimand another of the reprieved following the issuance of its own exoneration but lost again, and was ordered to make four months' salary compensation for further reputational damage.

And in yet another case the Administration intervened to stop a case going forward in order to avoid the embarrassment of another public defeat by quietly granting compensation to one of the uncharged, but disgraced, eight.

But the times required burnt offerings...

So poor, poor Mr. Toh (who, in commenting on the situation, said, "Despite the absence of any allegations against me, let alone any accusations of illicit payments, I was compelled by Deputy Secretary-General Mark Malloch-Brown in November

2006 to disclose details of my financial records under threat of disciplinary action... Worse, he also demanded the disclosure of the accounts of my wife and refused to answer my query on what rules exist for the UN to seek disclosure of personal details of a spouse. I disclosed details of my accounts... under duress"), who could not be found to have engaged in any fraud whatsoever with the findings revealing that he had received no improper benefits, or a transfer of funds, from any vendor or other source, and who was exonerated by two internal investigative bodies one of whom recommended that he be compensated for the reputational damage, but whose record of exemplary service as a public servant provided no protection against the needs of the moment, was found to have "mismanaged" and to have neglected to reveal the existence of a bank account opened in the name of his daughter which, unfortunately for the investigators, was discovered to have no purloined funds in it, fell, nevertheless, to the roll of the tumbrils and, after twenty-one months of suspension and banishment, was sentenced to a demotion.

[But more burnt offerings were required... So four years after the great scandal first burst forth, and following Annan's departure, the Task Force snatched a delayed, if satisfying, triumph when it was responsible for securing not a scolding, or a reprimand, or even a withholding of salary, or suspension or demotion, any of which punishments would have more suitably fitted the situation, but the summary dismissal from the UN of two of the "Fraudulent Eight", though not for fraud, or taking bribes, or favouritism, or indeed any illicit actions connected to the original charges against them, but for accepting hospitality on one or two occasions from a contractor who took them to dinner and a nightclub, where, among other infractions they "lap-danced", and were thence ruinously discarded for it.

Of course accepting hospitality from people you were doing business with, from people who wanted favours from you, who were seeking to have their nationals placed in preferred positions, or seeking changes in policy to their benefit, and were prepared to offer far more elaborate, and expensive, hospitality than that afforded the "lap-dancers", was not unknown at the United Nations. Indeed, Secretaries-General, and their Deputies, and their Chefs de Cabinet, not to speak of an entire platoon, nay army, of officials of far more exalted status than the dismissed two, were regularly in receipt, in their honour, of lunches, dinners and even more elaborate entertainments, not to speak of suites or hotel rooms put at their disposal when they travelled abroad, and planes made available to ferry them about. But none of these were summarily dismissed....]

44
ENDING

Final flurries – Kumbaya

―――◄○►―――

"We can never, even by the strictest examination,
get completely behind the secret springs of action..."

Fundamental Principles of the Metaphysic of Morals

Immanuel Kant

―――◄○►―――

Final flurries

By 6 June 2006, Mark Malloch-Brown, by now elevated to succeed
Louise as Deputy Secretary-General, who had welcomed Bolton's
appointment with the comment inter alia that, "People forget a
little bit more than ten years ago he was a very effective Assistant
Secretary of State in the State Department dealing with the UN...",
decided to take on those for whom he had earlier expressed
admiration. In a speech on that day he remarked that, "The
prevailing practice of seeking to use the UN almost by stealth
as a diplomatic tool while failing to stand up for it against its
domestic critics is simply not sustainable. You will lose the UN one
way or another. [That] the US is constructively engaged with the
UN is not well known or understood, in part because much of the
public discourse that reaches the US heartland has been largely
abandoned to its loudest detractors such as Rush Limbaugh and
Fox News."

Bolton called Malloch-Brown's remarks "a very, very, grave
mistake."

"Even though the target of the speech was the United States, the victim, I fear, will be the United Nations," Bolton told reporters after speaking with Annan. He accused Malloch-Brown of employing "a condescending, patronising tone about the American people" and said, "My hope is he looks at the potential adverse effects that these intemperate remarks would have on the organisation and repudiate it." Bolton was reported to have told Annan on the phone: "I've known you since 1989 and I'm telling you this is the worst mistake by a senior UN official that I have seen in that entire time."

Annan confirmed his continuing intransigence through his Spokesman. "The Secretary-General stands by the statements made by his Deputy. So there is no question of any action to be taken against the Deputy Secretary-General," he said.

(Still, lest one may have thought that Malloch-Brown had changed tack completely, he later said that his talk was a "sincere and constructive critique of US policy toward the UN by a friend and admirer.")

On October 6, 2006 Bolton made a particularly pointed attack on the Secretary-General when he asked for a full disclosure of his financial situation before he completed his term of office. The implication that could fairly be derived from this request was that Annan had some financial secrets to hide.

The response was rapid. Annan's Spokesman said Annan would not be coerced by any nation to disclose his personal financial information. "The UN is an intergovernmental organisation," the Spokesman continued, "It is not a national government. [Financial] Disclosure forms are an internal control mechanism, they were filled out by about 1,000 staff members under the understanding that they would remain confidential."

Kumbaya

On 5 December 2006 President George W. Bush held a private, farewell dinner for Kofi Annan.

By now both adversaries were on their way out (as was this

author, resigning my post towards the end of the year.) Annan's term was to conclude at the end of the month and Bolton had given up trying to be confirmed as Permanent Representative by a persistently hostile Senate Committee on Foreign Relations, and would himself depart at the same time. ("I'm not happy about it," Bush said in a one-minute appearance with Bolton before cameras in the Oval Office. "I think he deserved to be confirmed. And the reason why I think he deserved to be confirmed is because I know he did a fabulous job for the country.")

After the dinner Bolton delighted in remarking that, "Nobody sang 'Kumbaya.'"

On being apprised by the press of Bolton's comment, Annan asked: "But does he know how to sing it?"

Four days later, Kofi Annan unburdened himself. In an address delivered at the Harry Truman Presidential Library in Independence, Missouri, he said: "No nation can make itself secure by seeking supremacy over all the others". And there was more.

"When [America] appears to abandon its own ideals and objectives, its friends abroad are naturally troubled and confused".

He ended with an appeal: "You Americans did so much, in the last century to build an effective multilateral system with the United Nations at its heart... And in order to function, the system still cries out for farsighted American leadership in the Truman tradition." And, by evident implication, not in the Bush one.

Kofi Annan will have hoped that his views would have historical resonance as did Dwight Eisenhower's when, in his farewell address, he warned against the "military-industrial complex". No lover of the United Nations could do other than wish for a similar outcome.

In my end is my beginning.....
The houses are all gone under the sea.
The dancers are all gone under the hill.

THE END

POSTSCRIPT

3 p.m, 28 October 2017, British Airways Executive Lounge, Heathrow Airport, London.

Honey, there's Kofi – and Nane too!

Hello, hello, it's been a long time. (Kisses)

What are you doing here, SG?

I'm on my way to an Elders Meeting.

And I'm going with him. I spend all my time in airport lounges.

And what about you?

Our daughter – "The Princess" – got married last week in London. We stayed on for a week afterwards and are now returning to Berlin.

What are you doing in Berlin?

L was appointed Ambassador there a little over a year ago.

And where is the Princess?

Oh, they are still on honeymoon. They spent a week in the Maldives and are now on their way to Sri Lanka.

You must give me her email address and telephone number.

(We sit down, me next to Kofi, L next to Nane. We chat desultorily. And then...)

What do you hear about things at the UN?

My friends have begun to become a bit disillusioned with Guterres. Everyone welcomed his appointment. But that business when he went to Washington and hung around in the Chief of Staff's office hoping that Trump would look in was really demeaning and embarrassing. People feel that he should only have gone if he had an appointment. And then he proposes a budget which really panders to Washington's wishes.

You have to be careful. I remember when they tried to get me involved in a group on Syria. I declined. A Secretary-General has to retain his independence.

We have to leave now to catch our flight. Lovely to see you and give my congratulations to the Princess.

(*Farewells and kisses*.)

(The next day he calls A on Facetime in Sri Lanka. We had not warned her that he might get in touch.

"Uncle Kofi!", she proclaims in astonishment

He had asked to speak to her husband and they had all had a warm chat.

Afterwards she phones to tell us about it. She was bubbling with joy.

Well, he was always a very nice man.)

INDEX

9/11 180, 204, 258
38th Floor 143–4, 254
tensions with Member States 338, 340

"A" (Miles Stoby's daughter) see Stoby,
    Aisha,
"A" and "T" 33–4, 50, 78–9
"*A luta continua*" 135
Abul Naga, Fayza 86
Abulhasan, Mohammad Abdullah
    125–6
Accountability Panel see SIAP (Security
    in Iraq Accountability Panel)
Afghanistan 117, 204
Africa 29–30, 94, 106, 155, 161
    see also individual countries
Africa Month 62–3
African Union 242
Age, The 155–7
Agence France-Presse 185
Ahtisaari, Martti 66, 197
Ahtisaari Panel and Report 196–200,
    245
AIDS 39–40, 62, 138
Ajali, Boubakar 73–4, 115
Akram, Munir 232
Albright, Madeleine 62, 70, 95, 103,
    122–3, 244
Kofi Annan, support for 106, 207, 286
Algeria 257
Ali, Muhammad 137
Alkatiri, Mari 156, 188
Allawi, Ayad 265
All-Japan Council of Patriotic
    Organisations 209
Al-Quds 188
America see US
American Spectator, The 305
Amores-Mantas, Lilia 100
Annabi, Hédi 44
Annan, Kofi

see also Stoby, Miles: Kofi Annan,
    relationship with; Stoby, Miles: Kofi
    Annan, views on
Africa Month 63
AIDS 164
appointment as UN Secretary-
    General 42, 286–7, 305
attributes 186, 306, 307
Burundi 36–7
criticism of 101, 107, 109–10
Cyprus 258–9, 264–5
Darfur 284
Earth Day 83
as the embodiment of the UN 15
General Assembly speech, 2004 304,
    306, 307
Indonesia 145
international travel 37–8, 91, 108
Iraq
    Interim Government 266
    Lakhdar Brahimi, appointment of
        235–6
    opposition to US and UK 205–7,
        296–8
    response to the war 72, 170–2
    Richard Butler, appointment of
        107–8
    post-war 172–4, 194, 195, 202–5
    elections 223–5, 326
    staff safety in Baghdad 196–7,
        197–8, 228, 245–6, 247–50,
        262–4
Israel/Palestine conflict 189–90,
    191–2
leadership crisis 305–6
    personnel changes 310–13, 317–
        18, 344–5
    vindication 328–9
leaving the UN 352–3
Lebanon 110, 321
legacy 284–5, 342–3

Messengers of Peace 136, 137
Millennium Forum 96
Millennium Summit 51–2, 126, 129
  pre-Summit dinner 123–4
  national sovereignty speech 20–1
NGOs 139–40
Nobel Prize 168, 294–5, 307
re-election as Secretary-General
  160–2
Rwanda 42, 43–4, 241–2, 244, 250–2
Ryoichi Sasakawa 209, 210
Sierra Leone 91, 93–5, 133–5
Smoking War 219, 221
surveillance of 230, 232–3, 234
Theo-Ben Gurirab, meeting with
  80–2
tsunami, 26 December 2004 325–6
UN, vision for 124, 164–5
UN achievements 293–5
UN corruption scandals
  Dileep Nair 300
  oil-for-food programme 239,
    276–7, 278, 302, 328–9, 337–8
  peacekeepers accused of sexual
    exploitation 303
  Ruud Lubbers 274–5, 299, 323,
    325
UN reform 60, 101, 340–2
  "Investing in the United Nations"
    report 343–4
  "In Larger Freedom" report 342–3
  Senior Adviser on UN Reform
    166–7
US, relationship with 59–60, 142,
  147, 164–5
  criticism of US 347, 352, 353
    over Iraq 185–6, 205–7, 280–3,
    296–8, 317
  Democratic supporters, crisis
    meeting with 308–9
  International Criminal Court
    283–4
  loss of US support 305, 306
Zimbabwe 98–9
Annan, Kojo 238–9, 301–2, 317, 329

Annan, Nane 25, 26, 42, 83, 220, 322,
  324, 354
Arab views of the UN 190–2
Arbour, Louise 346–7
Arias, Inocencio 232
al-Assad, Hafez 103
Assebe, Wagaye 192–3
Australia 23–4, 153
  East Timor 23–4, 155–7, 187–8

Baghdad bombing see bombing of UN
  Headquarters in Baghdad
Barak, Ehud 110
BBC News 229, 296–7
Bédié, Henri Konan 102–3
Bellamy, Carol 318
Bernal, Jose Antonio 189
Bertini, Catherine 41, 274, 275, 300,
  311
"Better World for All, A" 108–9
Blackwill, Robert 252–3, 264
Blair, Tony 126–7
Blix, Hans 62, 171
Bloomberg, Michael 221
Bolton, John 320–1, 343, 346–7, 347–8,
  351–2, 353
bombing of UN Headquarters in
  Baghdad 168–70, 180, 196 see also
  Ahtisaari Panel and Report; SIAP
  (Security in Iraq Accountability
  Panel)
Bone, James 121
Bosnia 269, 303
Bosnian–Serbian war 31–3, 47
Bouteflika, Abdelaziz 21, 124
Boutros-Ghali, Boutros
  leaving the UN 305
  re-election campaign 42, 106, 146,
    286–7
  as Secretary-General 31, 44, 233–4,
    243, 306–7
Boutros-Ghali, Mrs (Lilly Kahil) 215
Bowles, Erskine 325
Brahimi, Lakhdar
  Iraq elections 235–6, 237, 239

Iraq Interim Government 261–2, 265–7
    return to Iraq 252–3, 264
Brahimi report 132, 146, 155
Bremer, L. Paul 174, 228, 239, 252–3, 265, 266–7
Bristol–Meyers 39
Britain *see* UK
Brundtland, Gro Harlem 212
budget of the UN 56, 59, 60, 151–4
bugging *see* surveillance of the UN
Burghardt, Jutta 70, 72
Burnham, Christopher 341–2, 347
Burundi 29–30, 36–7, 40, 62
Bush, George (Senior) 72
Bush, George W. 175, 283
    election as President 142, 146
    Iraq 170, 261
    Kofi Annan, relationship with 280–1, 352–3
    meeting with Hunte and Stoby 181–4
Butler, Richard 64, 72, 106, 107–8, 231, 338
Butts, Calvin O. 39–40

Cain, Kenneth 269
Cambodia 302
Canada 148
Card, Andy 181
Caribbean 153, 167, 292
CARICOM (Caribbean Community to the UN) 292
Carlsson, Ingvar 42
Carroll, Lewis 202
Castro, Fidel 127–8
celebrity involvement with the UN 14, 25–6, 39, 83–5, 136–9, 323–5
Charter of the UN 310, 340
Chávez, Hugo 124
Chef de Cabinet post 313
China 38, 162, 166, 208, 231
Chirac, Jacques 22, 86, 128
Christopher, Warren 286
CIA 65, 230, 265

"Citizen of the World" Award 324
Clinton, Bill 41, 79, 83, 143, 147, 283
    Millennium Summit 125, 126, 127–8
    "My Life" 286–7
    Rwanda 243–4
    Special Envoy for Tsunami Recovery 325
Clinton, Hillary 39, 79, 83
Clough, Arthur Hugh 49, 113, 131, 159, 175, 291
CNN (Cable News Network) 136
Cole-in *see* Powell, Colin
Congo 242, 302–3
Connecticut 88
Connor, Joe 301
Cook, Robin 98
Cooper, Gary *see* Kansteiner, Walter
Coppola, Francis Ford 151
Cordier, Andrew 313
Corell, Hans 59, 120
Côte d'Ivoire 102–3
Cotecna 239, 301–2, 328–9
CPA (Coalition Provisional Authority) 191, 195
Croatia 103
Croft, Lara *see* Jolie, Angelina
Crossette, Barbara 47
Crown Princess Victoria of Sweden 99–100
Cunningham, James B. 217
Cuomo, Andrew 83
Cyprus 97, 142, 256–9, 264–5

Dadzie, Kenneth K.S. 216
Dag Hammarskjöld Library 155
Dahlgren, Hans 106
Dallaire, Roméo 243, 244–5
Darfur 251, 284
D'Aubuisson, Roberto 209
de Saram, John 106
Deen, Thalif 317–18
Deloitte Consulting LLP 271
Democratic Party 141–2, 147, 207, 308–9, 331

Denktash, Rauf 258
Department of General Assembly
   Affairs 163
Department of Public Information 155,
   180, 211
DESA (Department of Economic and
   Social Affairs) 109
Designated Official *see* Lopes da Silva,
   Ramiro
"Dialogue among Civilizations" 122–3
diamond trade 94, 97
Dinkins, David 39
Disney 25, 26
Doctors without Borders 59
Douglas, Michael 139
Downer, Alexander 188
Doyle, Michael 311
Dubya *see* Bush, George W.
Duke Ellington Orchestra 27
al-Dulaimi, Saadoun 267
Dutch role in Bosnian–Serbian war 31–3
Duvall, Robert 151
Dylan, Bob 56

Earth Day 83–5
East Timor 18–19, 23–4, 155–7, 187–8,
   302–3
Eckhard, Fred 29, 91, 99, 311, 318
ECOSOC (UN Economic and Social
   Council) 108
Egypt 78, 86–7, 106, 146
Eisenhower, Dwight 353
Ekéus, Rolf 52–3, 61–2, 64, 72, 231, 338
Eldon, Stewart 41–2, 70
"Emergency Sex and Other Desperate
   Measures" 269–70
Eminent Persons Panel *see* Panel of
   Eminent Persons ("Panel to Save the
   World")
Esquire 324–5
European Ambassadors' lunch 76–7
European Union 86, 258–9, 264
Evans, Gareth 212

"F" (relative of Miles Stoby) 25, 26
Falun Gong 38
al Farah, Reham 169, 170
fascism 209
al-Fateh Revolution 103
Fawzi, Ahmad 261, 265, 266, 267
Feisal, Sayyid 126
Financial Times 270
Finland 66, 74, 114–16, 123
Five Eyes (FVEY) intelligence alliance
   23–4
Florida Times-Union 111
Fonda, Jane 50
Fox News 321, 351
France 86, 107, 133, 152, 206, 251
"Fraudulent Eight" 347–50
Fréchette, Louise 76, 108, 216, 254–5
   leaving the UN 344–6
   Miles Stoby, relationship with 60–1,
      114, 200–1
   Millennium Summit involvement 128,
      129, 130
      planning 20, 28, 60–1, 68, 102, 114
   North/South tensions 145–6, 148
   oil-for-food scandal 337–8
   Rwanda 250, 252
   Sierra Leone 92, 134
   staff security in Iraq 195, 198–200,
      245–6
   UN reform 343–4
   US, views on 146–7, 342
Frontline 244
Frost, Robert 5
Fund for Population Activities 41

Gaddafi, Muammar 103
gas reserves 23, 155–6, 157, 187–8
Gastaut, Therese 28
Gaza 189, 192
General Assembly 13, 151, 343
   Kofi Annan's speech, 2004 304, 307
   Millennium Summit 73, 74, 114, 115
   reform of 214–15, 217–18
Georgia 333

Gergen, David 143
Germany 77, 206
Gillerman, Dan 314
Global People's Parliament 96
globalisation 96, 124
Glover, Danny 138
Goh, Chok Tong 124
Goldsmith, Peter 298
Goodwill Ambassadors 136–9, 323–5
Gordimer, Nadine 137
Gore, Al 62, 63, 79, 83, 141, 142
Goulding, Marrack 229, 231
Gratchev, Victor 107
Gray, Linda 138, 139
Great Smoking War 219–22
Greater Sunrise gas field 157, 187–8
Greece 257–8, 259, 265
Greek Cypriots 256–7, 258, 259, 264–5
Greenstock, Jeremy 76
Group of 77 (and China) 338–42
Guardian, The 92, 187–8
Gulf War 72, 171
Gurirab, Theo-Ben 21, 65–7, 73, 74, 116, 126
    Kofi Annan, meeting with 80–2
Gusmão, Xanana 187
Guterres, António 354
Guyana 11, 52, 66, 256–7

Halliday, Denis 72, 338
Halliwell, Geri 137, 138
Hammarskjöld, Dag 15, 137, 256
Hannay, David 212
Hansen, Peter 314, 317, 321
Hariri, Rafic 321
Harlem All Stars 83
Harold (Theo-Ben Gurirab's Chef de Cabinet) see Urib, Harold
Harvard Commencement address 280, 296
Hayes, Isaac 39
Hayworth, Patrick 29–30, 93, 99
Heaney, Seamus 137
Heller, Joseph 194

Helms, Jesse 56–9, 60, 63, 151, 153–4, 177
Hezbollah 110
Hitler, Adolf 54, 71
HIV 39–40, 62, 138
Hoge, Warren 223
Holbrooke, Richard
    Africa Month 62–3
    Brahimi report 132
    criticism of UN 59, 105, 180
    Kofi Annan, views on 235, 278, 286
    crisis meeting 308–9
    leaving the UN 154–5
    Security Council 56, 58, 71
    UN appointment 47
    UN budget 151, 152–4
Holkeri, Harri 91, 116
Holland 31–3, 268
Holmes, Kim 177
Hooper, Rick 169
Howard, John 155–6, 298
Huffington, Arianna 85
Human Rights Day 346–7
humanitarian organisations in Iraq 194–5
Hunte, Julian 166–7, 176–7, 181–3, 289
    General Assembly reform 214, 250
    Security Council reform 226–8, 254–5
al-Hussein, Noor 39
Hussein, Saddam 52–3, 72, 170, 238, 305
Hyland, Tom 155

IAEA (International Atomic Energy Agency) 171
Iceland 77
ICRC (International Committee of the Red Cross) 191, 197
Iglesias, Enrique 212
Ilona (Professor of Public Health from Yale) 88, 89
IMF (International Monetary Fund) 108
Independent, The 212, 322
India 133–4, 148

Indonesia 18–19, 23–4, 145, 156, 188
Integrity Survey of UN staff 270–2, 276
intelligence services 230–1
    see also surveillance of the UN
Inter Press Service 317–18
International Court of Justice 156, 188
International Criminal Court 283–4
"Investing in the United Nations" report
    343–4
Iran 122–3, 125
Iraq see also oil-for-food programme
    disarmament 52–3, 61–2
    Hans von Sponeck 70–2
    humanitarian organisations in 194–5
    Kofi Annan's response to war 170–2,
        205–7, 280–3
    legitimacy and legality of war 202,
        281–3, 296–8
    post-war governance 265–7
    public opinion of the UN 191–2, 197
    Rolf Ekéus 52–3
    "Saddam's graveyard" 72, 279, 338
    sanctions and no-fly zones 50–1, 53,
        65, 172
    unilateral actions of US and UK 29,
        53, 106–7
    UN's post-war involvement 172–4,
        194–6, 202–7, 281
      bombing of UN Headquarters 168–
        70, 180, 196
    elections 223–5, 237, 239, 281,
        315–16, 326
    Lakhdar Brahimi 235–6, 252–3,
        261–2
    staff safety 190–1, 195–7, 228, 245–
        6, 262–4
    see also Ahtisaari Panel and
        Report; SIAP (Security in Iraq
        Accountability Panel)
    violence in 189, 228, 236–7, 253
Iraqi National Accord 265
Iraq–Kuwait war 72, 171
Israel 79, 86–7, 317–18
    Middle East conflict 188–90, 191–2,
        314

Shebaa Farms 110, 111
Italy 77
Izvestiya 219

"J" (a New York socialite involved with
    Earth Day) 83, 84, 85
Jackson, Jesse 39–40
Jain, Bawa 114, 121
Japan 37, 208, 209
Japan Motorboat Racing Association
    209, 210
Jetley, Vijay 91, 94, 132, 133
Jian, Chen 165–6
Jiang, Zemin 38
Jin, Yongjian 115
John (Assistant Secretary-General) see
    Ruggie, John
Johnson, Magic 39, 40
Jolie, Angelina 323–5
Jolliffe, Jill 155
Jones, Elizabeth 177

Kabbah, Ahmad Tejan 93, 94
Kagame, Paul 242, 251
Kahil, Lilly 215
Kansteiner, Walter 176–7, 186
Kay, David 52
Kaye, Danny 136
Kerry, John 33
KGB 230
Khan, Riz 136–7
Khane, Moncef 64, 91, 100
Khatami, Mohammad 122–3, 125
Khrushchev, Nikita 137, 256
King, Betty 46, 118
Kissinger, Henry 160
Kmonícek, Hynek 220
Knudson, Rolf 100
Kok, Wim 33
Kosovo 20, 59, 303
Kouchner, Bernard 59
"Kumbaya" 352–3
Kurdish Liberation Army 53
Kuroyanagi, Tetsuko 138
Kuwait 125–6, 152

Kyprianou, Spyros 257

"L" (Miles Stoby's wife) *see* al-
    Mughairy, Lyutha
Lake, Tony 286
Lantos, Tom 278
Lavrov, Sergei 219, 220–1, 222, 232
leaking of Security Council reform
    document 226–8
Lebanon 110–11, 122, 321
Levitte, Jean-David 85–6
Liberia 97
Libya 103
Limbaugh, Rush 351
Lindenmayer, Elisabeth 311, 318
Lockhart, Joe 128
Lone, Salim 168, 170, 190–1
Lopes da Cruz, Francisco 19
Lopes da Silva, Ramiro 199–200, 245–6,
    248–9
Lubbers, Ruud 268, 273–6, 298–9,
    322–3, 325
Luers, William 279

Mack, Andy 79, 311
Mail on Sunday 324
Makarios III, Archbishop of Cyprus 256,
    257
Malloch-Brown, Mark
    as Chef de Cabinet 311, 312–13,
        314, 318, 320–1
    UN reform 339–40
    as Deputy Secretary-General 345–6,
        348–9, 351–2
    George Soros controversy 330–4
    UNDP 99, 109
Malta 258
Mandela, Nelson 30, 40, 62
Martin, Ivanhoe 268
Martin Luther King Day 223, 224
Marx, Groucho 236
Maurás, Marta 311
media *see* press
Megawati *see* Sukarnoputri, Megawati
Melian Dialogue 225

Mello, Sergio Vieira de 168, 169, 174,
    195–6, 319, 324
Messengers of Peace 136–9
MI6 265
Middle East conflict 188–90, 191–2
Miles, Rufus E. 322
Millennium Declaration 129–30, 164
Millennium Forum 35–6, 96, 102, 110,
    114
Millennium Report 79–80, 86, 96, 129
Millennium Summit
    co-presidency 66, 67, 74, 114–16,
        123
    the event 125–9
    funding 33
    invitations to 51–2, 68, 75, 102–3
    Miles Stoby's role 12, 73–4, 114,
        128–9, 130
    planning 28, 41, 50–1, 65–8
    pre-Summit dinner 123–4
    Roundtables 128–9
    San Marino 120–1
    Secret Service protection 117–18
    Security Council Summit 76–7
    success of 129–30
Milosevic, Slobodan 20
Mishima, Yukio 212
Miyet, Bernard 132–3
Moon, Sun Myung 209
Mortimer, Edward 58, 79, 92, 99, 132,
    278
Moussa, Amre 212
Mugabe, Robert 98–9
al-Mughairy, Lyutha, "L" (Miles Stoby's
    wife) 25, 26, 27, 79, 287, 354
Earth Day 83, 85
Murdoch, Rupert 54, 121
Mussolini, Benito 209
Myat, Tun 199–200, 245–6, 248–9

Nader, Ralph 141
Naipaul, V.S. 17, 288
Nair, Dileep 272–3, 299, 300–1, 323,
    329–30
Namibia 66, 74, 80, 81, 114–16, 123

Natabara 84, 85
national anthems 85
national sovereignty, questioning of
　20–1
NATO (North Atlantic Treaty
　Organisation) 20, 31, 133, 258, 259
Negroponte, John 181, 215, 217
Neil, Stafford 339, 340
Netherlands 31–3, 276
New York Sun 327, 331
New York Times 47, 93, 223, 239, 243,
　282, 321
New Yorker 171, 241, 321
NGOs (non-governmental
　organisations) 40, 96, 102, 109,
　139–40, 195
Nigeria 134
Nippon Foundation 208, 210, 211
Nixon, Richard 316
No Authority 83, 85
"No confidence in the Secretary-
　General" motion 344
Nobel Peace Prize 168, 294–5, 307
Non-Aligned Movement 155, 180
Noor (al-Hussein), Queen of Jordan 39
Noriega, Roger 177
North/South tensions 13–14, 41, 48, 86,
　124
　Group of 77 (and China) 338–42
　NGOs 139–40
　Northern bias 108–9, 136, 148,
　　164–5
nuclear disarmament 86
nuclear weapons 211
Nujoma, Sam 123
Nyerere, Julius 30

OAU (Organisation of African Unity) 21,
　42, 62
OECD (Organisation for Economic
　Cooperation and Development) 108,
　109
oil reserves 23, 155–6
oil-for-food programme 172
　scandal 238–9, 239–40, 317

Benon Sevan 276–7, 327–8
　Paul Volcker investigation 278, 318–
　　20, 328–9, 336–8
　press 239–40, 253, 260–1, 277–9
OIOS (Office of Internal Oversight
　Services) 239
　see also UN corruption scandals
Dileep Nair 272–3, 330
"Fraudulent Eight" 347
Integrity Survey 270–2, 276
Ruud Lubbers 274, 275–6, 298–9,
　322–3
sexual harassment allegations 268
Osment, Haley Joel 26

"P-3" (US, UK, France) 133, 134
"P-5" (China, France, Russia, UK, US)
　203–4, 215
Palestine 188–90, 191–2, 314
Panel of Eminent Persons ("Panel to
　Save the World") 186, 212–13, 342
Panyarachun, Anand 212
Patachi, Adnan 266
Paul, Jim 317, 318
　peacekeeping
　budget 151
　corruption and sexual exploitation
　　scandal 269–70, 302–3
　role of the UN 132–5, 146, 180
Perelli, Carina 315–16, 321, 335
Pérez de Cuéllar, Javier 15, 51, 171,
　212
Pew Research Centre 189
Picco, Gianni 122–3, 125
Pieth, Mark 329
Ping, Jean 307
PLO (Palestine Liberation Organisation)
　190
political impartiality of the UN 141–2,
　146–7
Postlewait, Heidi 269
Powell, Colin 161, 175, 178–9, 181, 262, 298
Prendergast, Kieran 311, 318
Presidential elections (US) 141–2,
　146–7

press
  Dileep Nair 273
  "Emergency Sex" publication 269–
    70
  George Soros/Mark Malloch-Brown
    controversy 331–2, 333–4
  Integrity Survey of UN staff 272
  Iraq war 282–3, 297–8
  Kofi Annan 305
  Louise Fréchette 345
  oil-for-food programme 239–40,
    253, 260–1, 277–9
  Religious Leaders Summit 121
  Ruud Lubbers 274–5, 299, 322
  Rwanda 44
"Princess" see Stoby, Aisha
"Pro-Consul" see Holbrooke, Richard
public opinion of the UN 57, 189–92, 197

Rabbani, Burhanuddin 117
Rabin, Leah 33
Ramos-Horta, José 19
realpolitik 13, 23, 173
reform programme see UN reform
Reilly, William K. 208–9
Religious Leaders Summit 53, 114,
  118–20, 121
Republican Party 146–7, 207, 331
Rice, Condoleezza 161, 181, 182, 266
Richardson, Bill 83
Ricupero, Rubens 41
Ritter, Scott 52, 107
Riza, Iqbal 29, 101, 103–4, 111, 147
  Benon Sevan's legal fees 327–8
  Crown Princess of Sweden 99–100
  leaving the UN 311, 318
  Millennium Summit 68, 74, 129
  oil-for-food scandal 336, 337–8
  Rwanda 42, 43, 44, 244, 250
  Sierra Leone 92–3
Ronaldo, Cristiano 138
Rosett, Claudia 333–4
Rubin, James 70
RUF (Revolutionary United Front) 90,
  91, 95, 105

Ruggie, John 20, 41, 59, 100, 146, 147,
  278
  Kofi Annan, crisis meeting with
    308–9
  Millennium Report 79, 130
Russia 38, 59, 107, 206, 231, 259
  see also Soviet Union
Russian Tea Room 78
Rwanda 20, 42–5, 241–5, 250–2, 269

Saakashvili, Mikheil 333
Sabah, Sheikh 126
Sadik, Nafis 41
Safire, William 239
Salim, Salim 62, 212
San Marino 120–1
Sankoh, Foday 95, 97
Sarandon, Susan 137–8
Sartre, Jean-Paul 291
Sasakawa, Ryoichi 207–12
Sasakawa, Yohei 208
Sasakawa Environmental Prize 208,
  210, 211
Sawers, John 174
Scowcroft, Brent 212
Second World War 208, 211
Secret Service, US 117–18
secret services 230–1 see also
  surveillance of the UN
Secretariat, Northern support for 148
Secretariat reform 343–4
Secretary-General, role of 310, 340–1
Security Coordinator see Myat, Tun
Security Council
  Cyprus 257, 259
  International Criminal Court 283–4
  Iraq 61–2, 70–1, 106–7
    war 171, 172, 202, 282–3
  Jesse Helms attending meeting of
    56–9
  peacekeeping and humanitarian
    crises 24, 31–2, 93, 110, 252
  reform of 178, 226–8, 254–5, 342–3
  Volcker Report 338
Senate Foreign Relations Committee 105

Serbia *see* Bosnian–Serbian war
Sevan, Benon
  Baghdad bombing 169–70
  friendship with Miles Stoby 71–2,
    215–16, 319
  oil-for-food scandal 238, 276–7,
    279, 318–19, 336, 337–8
  legal fees 327–8, 329
sex slaves 181–2, 183–4
sexual exploitation allegations against
  UN peacekeepers 302–3
sexual harassment allegations 268,
  272–3, 273–6, 322–3, 330, 335
al-Shahristani, Hussain 265–6
Shakespeare, William 296, 304, 335
Shawcross, William 92
Shebaa Farms 110–11
Short, Clare 230, 232
SIAP (Security in Iraq Accountability
  Panel) 245–6, 262–4
UN staff reaction 247–50
Sierra Leone 90–5, 97, 105, 132, 133–4
Sise, Lamin 29, 68, 92, 93, 132, 311
al-Sistani, Ayatollah Ali 224, 237
Smith, Ian 98
Smoking War 219–22
Soderberg, Nancy 111
Sorensen, Gillian 27, 136, 139, 147
Soros, George 330–4
Southern nations *see* North/South
  tensions; Third World nations
Soviet Union 14, 208
  see also Russia
Special Adviser on Genocide 251
spies *see* surveillance of the UN
Sponeck, Hans von 29, 65, 232, 338
leaving the UN 70–2
Srebrenica 31–3, 42, 47
St Lucia 178, 181
Staff Council 300–1, 344
Staff Union 247–50, 330, 343
Star-Spangled Banner 85
Stassinopoulos, Agapi 85
state sovereignty, questioning of 20–1
Steele, Jonathan 187

Stephanopoulos, George 143, 144
Stoby, Aisha, "A" (Miles Stoby's
  daughter) 25, 26, 83, 354–5
Stoby, Miles
  birthday 86
  Benon Sevan, relationship with 71–2,
    215–16, 276–7, 319
  Kofi Annan, relationship with 11–12,
    22, 42–3, 148–50, 162, 166, 241,
    259–60, 287–9, 292–3, 319, 354–5
  Kofi Annan, views on 101–2, 160,
    163–5, 186, 206–7, 293–5
  disillusionment 288–90
  Lakhdar Brahimi, relationship with
    236
  Louise Fréchette, relationship with
    60–1, 114, 129, 130, 134, 200–1
  memoir writing 11, 13, 14, 15
  Millennium Summit, role in 12, 73–4,
    114, 128–9, 130
  national sovereignty, views on 20–1,
    22
  NGOs, views on 139–40
  peacekeeping, views on 134–5
  personal reflections 69, 75–6, 77, 87,
    288–9
  Richard Butler, relationship with
    107–8
  Rolf Ekéus, relationship with 52
  UN, views on 13–15, 48, 101–2, 146,
    192–3, 288
  UN Association Connecticut, speech
    88–90
  UN career 11–12, 48, 142–4, 148–50,
    162–3
  CARICOM 292
  Cyprus 256–7
  Department of General Assembly
    Affairs 163, 165–6
  General Assembly reform 214–15,
    217–18
  Guyana Deputy Permanent
    Representative 52
  leaving the UN 289–90, 352–3
  Security Council reform 226–8

Strong, Maurice 102
Sudan 284
Suharto 188
Sukarno 145
Sukarnoputri, Megawati 145
surveillance of the UN 41, 64–5, 228–34
Sweden 42, 99–100
Switzerland 38
Syria 103–4, 110–11, 189, 192

"T" and "A" 33–4, 50, 78–9
"T" (Miles Stoby's Algerian friend) 64–5
Taliban 117, 204
Tanzania 137–8
Taylor, Charles 97
terrorism 181–2, 183–4
Thant, U 15
Tharoor, Shashi 13, 59, 100, 109, 278–9, 311
  Sierra Leone 92, 93, 134–5
Third World nations 21–2, 133
    Group of 77 (and China) 338–42
    NGOs, relationship with 139–40
    relationship with Western nations
      14, 48, 109, 124
    views of UN staff 145–6, 163
Thomson, Andrew 269
Thucydides 225
Time 278
Time–Warner 50
Toh, Andrew 347, 348–9
Tokyo Trial 208
Töpfer, Klaus 207, 209, 210, 211
Truman, Harry S. 353
Trump, Donald 75, 354
tsunami, 26 December 2004 325–6
Tudjman, Franjo 103
Turkey 53, 256–9
Turkish Cypriots 256–7, 258, 259, 265
Turner, Ted 12, 50, 163
    "The Mouth from the South" 53–5
    Religious Leaders Summit 118–19,
      121

UK (United Kingdom)
    Iraq 29, 53, 106–7, 202, 298
    Sierra Leone 94–5, 105, 133, 134
    surveillance of the UN 228–30, 232–3
    UN corruption scandals, reaction to
      278, 279
    US, relationship with 229
    Zimbabwe 99
UN budget 151–4
UN Charter 310, 340
UN Chronicle 190–1
UN Correspondents Association 324
UN corruption scandals 317
    see also oil-for-food programme
    Dileep Nair 272–3, 300–1, 329–30
    "Fraudulent Eight" 347–50
    George Soros/Mark Malloch-Brown
      controversy 330–4
    Integrity Survey 270–2, 276
    peacekeepers 269–70, 302–3
    Ruud Lubbers 268, 273–6, 298–9,
      322–3, 325
UN Day 27, 197, 324
UN Electoral Division 335
UN Headquarters bombing see
    bombing of UN Headquarters in
    Baghdad
UN Office of Legal Affairs 327–8
UN Organisational Integrity Survey
    270–2, 276
UN Peace Medal 212
UN peacekeepers accused of sexual
    exploitation and corruption 269–70,
    302–3
UN political impartiality 141–2, 146–7
UN Procurement Task Force 347, 349
UN, public opinion of 57, 189–92, 197
UN reform
    General Assembly 214–15, 217–18
    "Investing in the United Nations"
      report 343–4
    "In Larger Freedom" report 342–3
    Miles Stoby's role 162–3
    North/South tensions 339–42
    Secretariat 343–4
    Security Council 226–8, 254–5

US role 178, 183, 339–42
UN relationship with US 190, 255
  see also Annan, Kofi: US,
    relationship with George Bush
    administration 182–3, 314, 315–
    16, 320–1
  human rights 346–7
  UN criticism of US 305, 351–2
  UN reform 339–42
UN staff
  personnel changes during crisis of
    Kofi Annan's leadership 310–13,
    317–18
  privileges for 215–16
  Smoking War 219–22
  safety in Iraq 195–7, 197–200, 203–
    4, 228
  see also Ahtisaari Panel and Report;
    SIAP
  (Security in Iraq Accountability Panel)
  selection of 165–6, 192–3, 330
  vote of no confidence in senior
    management 300–1, 344
  Western dominance among 311–12,
    313
UNCTAD (UN Conference on Trade and
  Development) 41, 109
UNDP (United Nations Development
  Programme) 99, 109, 231, 313, 333
UNEP (UN Environmental Programme)
  207, 208, 211
UNESCO (UN Educational, Scientific
  and Cultural Organisation) 122
UNFIP (UN Fund for International
  Partnerships) 116
UNHCR (UN High Commissioner for
  Refugees) 322–3
UNICEF (UN International Children's
  Emergency Fund) 136, 137, 195,
  314, 318
Unification Church 209
UNMOVIC (UN Monitoring, Verification
  and Inspection Commission) 52, 64
UNRWA (UN Relief and Works Agency)
  314, 317

UNSCOM (UN Special Commission) 52,
  72, 107
Urib, Harold 74, 80, 115
US (United States)
  see also Annan, Kofi: US,
    relationship with; UN relationship
    with US
  Congress 339
  Cyprus 264
  human rights 346–7
  influence at the UN 136, 147–8, 255,
    286–7
  International Criminal Court 283–4
  Iran 122–3, 125
  Iraq
    Hans von Sponeck 29
    Interim Government 266–7
    opposition of Kofi Annan 280–3
    opposition to the war 185–6
    post-war 204–5, 205–7, 223–5, 237
    elections 315–6
    unilateral action with UK 53,
     106–7
    war, legitimacy of 202
  Israel 86–7
  peacekeeping role 133
  Presidential elections 141–2, 146–7
  public opinion of UN 57
  Secret Service protection 117–18
  Sierra Leone 93, 134
  surveillance of the UN 228–30
  Syria 104
  UK, relationship with 229
  UN budget contributions 56, 59, 60,
    151–4
  UN corruption scandals, reaction to
    278, 279
  UN reform 60, 183, 217–18, 339–42
Ustinov, Peter 137

Veneman, Ann 314, 318
Veness, David 318
veto 254–5
Victoria, Crown Princess of Sweden
  99–100

Videla, Jorge Rafael 209
Volcker, Paul 278, 279
    Benon Sevan's legal fees 327–8
    Final Report 336–8
    First Interim Report 318–20
    Second Interim Report 328–9, 330
vote of no confidence in UN senior
    management 300–1

Wahid, Abdurrahman 145
Waldheim, Kurt 15, 77, 87
    Millennium Summit invitation 51–2,
        68, 75
Wall Street Journal 238, 239, 279
Wallenberg, Raoul 42
Walt Disney 25, 26
Washington Post 243, 278
Washington Times, The 298
weapons of mass destruction 171
Western dominance among UN staff
    311–12, 313
Western nations, dominance of 14, 41,
    164–5, 338–42
    see also North/South tensions; Third
    World nations
Whitlam, Gough 23
Whitman, Walt 168
WHO (World Health Organisation) 211
Wilde, Oscar 86
Williams, Abi 311
Wishing Star, The 25–6
Wolfensohn, James 62
women, under representation of 119–
    20, 136, 178
Woodward, Bob 143
World Aids Day 39–40
World Anti-Communist League 209
World Bank 108, 139, 313
World Food Programme 37, 41
World Trade Centre 180
WTO (World Trade Organisation) 40,
    41, 139
WWF (World Wildlife Fund) 209

Yakuza 209, 210

al-Yawar, Ghazi 266
Yeltsin, Boris 38
"Yes Minister" 321
Younes, Nadia 126, 127, 169
Yugoslavia 257

Zimbabwe 98–9